Aristophanes

The Birds of Aristophanes

With Notes, and a Metrical Table

Aristophanes

The Birds of Aristophanes
With Notes, and a Metrical Table

ISBN/EAN: 9783337022051

Printed in Europe, USA, Canada, Australia, Japan

Cover: Foto ©Thomas Meinert / pixelio.de

More available books at **www.hansebooks.com**

THE BIRDS

OF

ARISTOPHANES.

WITH NOTES, AND A METRICAL TABLE,

BY

C. C. FELTON, LL.D.,

PRESIDENT OF HARVARD UNIVERSITY, LATE ELIOT PROFESSOR OF GREEK LITERATURE.

THIRD EDITION, REVISED.

PREFACE.

THE Birds of Aristophanes has always been regarded as one of his most delightful pieces. Like the Clouds, it is comparatively free from the objectionable license of thought and language, which deforms several of his plays to such a degree that they cannot be used in schools or colleges. It is true there are some passages in this play also too freely executed: but it has been decided, on mature reflection, to let them stand, so as to offer the drama entire, on the principles which guided my decision in editing the Clouds.

The text of this edition is reprinted from the Poetae Scenici of Dindorf. In the preparation of the notes, I have used Commentaries of Christian Daniel Beck, together with the notes and Scholia edited by Invernizius; the notes of Bothe, to whose valuable edition I am under great obligations; and the brief, but excellent, annotations of Blaydes. Credit is always given for what has been taken from the labors of these distinguished scholars.

In addition to the critical apparatus just mentioned, I have endeavored to explain from other sources a branch of the subject to which less attention has heretofore been given; — I mean the natural history of the birds, which are very entertaining figures among the persons of the play. I have carefully examined Aristotle's History of Animals, from which I have drawn illustrative descriptions. But it is well known that a considerable portion of the birds of Aristophanes are not mentioned in Aristotle's work, and some of them are thought to be unknown. Several branches of the natural history of Greece has been almost entirely neglected since the researches of the philosopher of Stagira; and here is an opportunity for a naturalist, who is at the same time a good classical scholar, to make valuable contributions both to science and philology. Sibthorp's magnificent work, the "Flora Hellenica," is ample on the Botany of Greece; but comparatively little has been done in the departments of ornithology and ichthyology.

I suspected that the poet's selection of birds was not made at random, but that, in every instance, they were chosen with a special meaning, and to effect a particular purpose, in point of art. In considering the play from this point of view, I have been much indebted to my friend and colleague, Professor Agassiz, of whose profound and comprehensive knowledge of ornithology I have been permitted to avail myself in attempting to determine the species of some of the birds not hitherto identified; and I have come to the conclusion, that, in all cases, the character and habits of the birds are exactly and curiously adapted to the parts they perform in the comedy, showing Aristophanes to have been a careful observer of nature, as well as a consummate poet. I have also used with profit a little work, entitled "Beitraege zur Ornithologie Griechenlands, von Heinrich Graf von der Mühle," or, *Contributions to the Ornithology of Greece, by Henry Count von der Mühle;* a work of interest and importance, though written without any reference to the classical bearings of the subject.

Great care has been taken to illustrate the political allusions, and the application of judicial expressions, in the course of the piece. For this purpose the excellent writings of Hermann, Smith, and Boeckh have been freely cited. St.

John's admirable work on the Manners and Customs of the Hellenes has also been consulted.

It is probably impossible, at present, to feel the full force of the wit and gayety of Aristophanes, much of which turned upon temporary and local relations. Still, a careful study of contemporary history, political and judicial institutions, popular prejudices and delusions, and the influence of oracles and other means of working upon ignorant or even cultivated credulity, will make all the material points of the comedy of Aristophanes sufficiently clear.

The satire of the Birds is more playful, comprehensive, and genial than that of any other of the poet's comedies. The spirit of parody and burlesque, which is a general trait of the Aristophanic drama, here displays itself most freely and amusingly. Even the solemn genius of Pindar does not escape entirely the poet's whimsical perversions. The dithyrambic poets in general are unsparingly ridiculed; the philosophers and men of science are not allowed to pass untouched; while profligates and impostors of every class and description are here, as well as in the Clouds, held up to scorn and contempt.

Much discussion has been held upon the question as to the specific object the poet aimed at in his plan. Some have endeavored to show that the main drift of the piece is to expose the folly of the Athenians in their dreams of universal empire, at the time of the Sicilian Expedition; and these critics have fancied they could identify, not only the political parties in the Peloponnesian War, but individual characters in the history of the times. This is pressing matters of fact too far in judging of a poetical work. No doubt Aristophanes sought to lay the foundation of all his pieces in the actual life, public and private, of his age. But his genius could not so completely bind itself to the prosaic realities around him. His Pegasus trod the firm earth, but never bowed his neck to the yoke. Some of the leading ideas were unquestionably suggested by the popular madness which the versatile and profligate genius of Alcibiades had done so much to kindle among the Athenians of his time; but the groundwork only of the play was laid in political passions and historical events. That established, the poet gave free scope to his brilliant fancy, boundless wit, and unsurpassed powers of invention, and produced a poem, not only fitted to amuse and delight his countrymen, but to interest the lovers of literature in future ages, by the richest union of sportive satire and creative imagination that the comic theatre of Athens ever witnessed.

The following Argument is somewhat condensed from the works of the poet Gray. It is prefixed to the spirited translation of the Rev. Henry Francis Cary.

This new edition has been carefully revised, not only by myself, but by my friend Professor Goodwin, who has added valuable notes and illustrations. His excellent work on the Greek Moods and Tenses has been constantly used, as the student will find by numerous references, indicated by the letter G., scattered through the commentary.

C. C. FELTON.

CAMBRIDGE, *March* 1, 1861.

IN preparing the third edition for the press, many corrections have been made in the Greek text, chiefly of typographical errors in accents and punctuation. Besides a great number of similar changes in the notes, corrections more or less affecting the sense (and in some cases additions) have been made in the notes on the following verses: 63, 133, 448 – 450, 453, 476, 489, 507, 694, 760 – 761, 853 – 860, 1107, 1210, 1215 – 1216, 1228 – 1229, 1605, 1620, 1721.

W. W. GOODWIN.

CAMBRIDGE, *March* 10, 1868.

ARGUMENT.*

"EUELPIDES and Pisthetaerus, two ancient Athenians, thoroughly weary of the folly, injustice, and litigious temper of their countrymen, determine to leave Attica for good and all; and having heard much of the fame of Epops, king of the birds, who was once a man under the name of Tereus, and had married an Athenian lady, they pack up a few necessary utensils, and set out for the court of that prince, under the conduct of a jay and a raven, birds of great distinction in augury, without whose direction the Greeks never undertook anything of consequence. Their errand is to inquire of the birds, who are the greatest travellers of any nation, where they may meet with a quiet, easy settlement, far from all prosecutions, lawsuits, and sycophant informers, to pass the remainder of their lives in peace and liberty.

"The scene is a wild, unfrequented country, which terminates in mountains; there the old men are seen, (accompanied by two slaves, who carry their little baggage,) fatigued and fretting at the carelessness of their guides, who, though they cost them a matter of a groat in the market, are good for nothing but to bite them by the fingers and lead them out of the way. They travel

---

* Works of Gray, edited by Mathias, Vol. II. pp. 151 - 160.

on, however, till they come to the foot of the rocks, which stop up their passage, and put them to their wits' end. Here the raven croaks, and the jay chatters and looks up into the air, as much as to say that this is the place: upon which they knock with a stone and with their heels (as though it were against a door) against the side of the mountain.

"Trochilus, a bird that waits upon Epops, appears above; he is frightened at the sight of two men, and they are much more so at the length of his beak and the fierceness of his aspect. He takes them for fowlers; and they insist upon it, that they are not men, but birds. In their confusion, their guides, whom they held in a string, escape and fly away. Epops, during this, is asleep within, after having dined upon a dish of beetles and berries: their noise awakens him, and he comes out of the grove.

"At the strangeness of his figure, they are divided between fear and laughing. They tell him their errand, and he gives them the choice of several cities fit for their purpose, one particularly on the coast of the Red Sea, all which they refuse, for many comical reasons. He tells them the happiness of living among the birds; they are much pleased with the liberty and simplicity of it; and Pisthetaerus, a shrewd old fellow, proposes a scheme to improve it, and make them a far more powerful and considerable nation. Epops is struck with the project, and calls up his consort, the nightingale, to summon all his people together with her voice. They sing a fine ode.

"The birds come flying down, at first one by one, and perch here and there about the scene; and at last the Chorus, in a whole body, come hopping and fluttering and twittering in. At the sight of the two men they are in great tumult, and think that their king has betrayed

ARGUMENT.

them to the enemy. They determine to tear the two old men to pieces, draw themselves up in battle array, and are giving the word to fall on. Euelpides and Pisthetaerus, in all the terrors of death, after upbraiding each the other for bringing him into such distress, and trying in vain to escape, assume courage from mere despair, seize upon the kitchen furniture which they had brought with them, and, armed with pipkins for helmets, and with spits for lances, they present a resolute front to the enemy's phalanx. On the point of battle, Epops interposes, pleads hard for his two guests, who are, he says, his wife's relations, and people of wonderful abilities, and well affected to their commonwealth. His eloquence has its effect: the birds grow less violent, they enter into a truce with the old men, and both sides lay down their arms. Pisthetaerus, upon the authority of Aesop's fables, proves to them the great antiquity of their nation; that they were born before the creation of the earth, and before the gods, and once reigned over all countries, as he shows from several testimonies and monuments of different nations; that the cock wears his tiara erect, like the Persian king, and that all mankind start out of their beds at his command; that when the kite makes his first appearance in the spring, every one prostrates himself on the ground before it; that the Egyptians and Phoenicians set about their harvest as soon as the cuckoo is heard; that all kings bear an eagle on their sceptre, and many of the gods carry a bird on their head; that many great men swear by the goose, &c., &c. When he has revived in them the memory of their ancient empire, he laments their present despicable condition, and the affronts put upon them by mankind. They are convinced of what he says, applaud his oration, and desire his advice. He proposes that they shall unite, and build a city in the mid-air, whereby all commerce will effectually be stopped between heaven and earth: the gods will no longer be able to visit at ease their Semeles and Alcmenas below, nor feast on the fume of sacrifices daily sent up to them, nor men enjoy the benefit of the seasons, nor the fruits of the earth, without permission from those winged deities of the middle region. He shows how mankind will lose nothing by this change of government; that the birds may be worshipped at a far ess expense, nothing more than a few berries or a handful of corn; that they will need no sumptuous temples; that, by their great knowledge of futurity, they will direct their good votaries in all their expeditions, so as they can never fail of success; that the ravens, famed for the length of their lives, may make a present of a century or two to their worshippers; and, besides, the birds will ever be within call, when invoked, and not sit pouting in the clouds, and keeping their state so many miles off. The scheme is highly admired, and the two old men are to be made free of the city, and each of them is to be adorned with a pair of wings at the public charge. Epops invites them to his nest-royal, and entertains them nobly. The nightingale in the mean time joins the Chorus without, and the parabasis begins.

"They sing their own nobility and ancient grandeur, their prophetic skill, the benefits they do mankind already, and all the good which they design them; they descant upon the power of music, in which they are such great masters, and intermix many strokes of satire; they show the advantages of flying, and apply it to several whimsical cases; and they invite all such as would be free from the heavy tyranny of human laws to live among them, where it is no sin to beat one's father, &c., &c.

"The old men, now become birds, and magnificently fledged, after laughing awhile at the new and awkward figure they make, consult about the name which they shall give to their rising city, and fix upon that of Nephelococcygia, or Cuckoocloudland; and while one goes to superintend the workmen, the other prepares to sacrifice for the prosperity of the city, which is growing apace.

" They begin a solemn prayer to all the birds of Olympus, putting the swan in the place of Apollo, the cock in that of Mars, and the ostrich in that of the great mother Cybele, &c.

" A miserable poet having already heard of the new settlement, comes with some lyric poetry, which he has composed on this great occasion. Pisthetaerus knows his errand from his looks, and makes them give him an old coat; but, not contented with that, he begs to have the waistcoat to it, in the elevated style of Pindar: they comply, and get rid of him.

" The sacrifice is again interrupted by a begging prophet, who brings a cargo of oracles, partly relating to the prosperity of the city of Nephelococcygia, and partly to a new pair of shoes, of which he is in extreme want. Pisthetaerus loses patience, and cuffs him and his religious trumpery off the stage.

" Meto, the famous geometrician, comes next, and offers a plan which he has drawn for the new buildings, with much importance and impertinence: he meets with as had a reception as the prophet.

" An ambassador, or licensed spy, from Athens arrives, and a legislator, with a body of new laws. They are used with abundance of indignity, and go off, threatening everybody with a prosecution. The sacred rites being so often interrupted, they are forced to remove their altar, and finish them behind the scenes.

" The Chorus rejoice in their own increasing power; and (as about the time of the Dionysia it was usual to make proclamation against the enemies of the republic) they set a price upon the head of a famous poulterer, who has exercised infinite cruelties upon their friends and brethren; then they turn themselves to the judges and spectators, and promise, if this drama obtain the victory, how propitious they will be to them.

"Pisthetaerus returns, and reports, that the sacrifice appears auspicious to their undertaking: a messenger then enters, with an account how quick the works advance, and whimsically describes the employments allotted to the several birds, in different parts of the building.

"Another messenger arrives in a violent hurry, to tell how somebody from heaven has deceived the vigilance of the jackdaws, who were upon guard, and passed through the gates down into the lower air; but that a whole squadron of light-winged forces were in pursuit of this insolent person, and hoped to fetch him back again. The birds are in great perturbation, and all in a flutter about it.

"This proves to be Iris, who in her return is stopped short, and seized by order of Pisthetaerus. He examines her, Where is her passport? Whether she had leave from the watch? What is her business? Who is she? — in short, he treats her with great authority. She tells her name, and that she was sent by Jove with orders to mankind, that they should keep holiday, and perform a grand sacrifice; she wonders at their sauciness and madness, and threatens them with all her father's thunder. The governor of Nephelococcygia returns it with higher menaces, and with language very indecent indeed for a goddess and a maid to hear.

"The herald, who had been despatched to the lower world, returns with an account that all Athens was gone bird-mad; that it was grown a fashion to imitate them in their names and manners; and that shortly they might expect to see a whole convoy arrive, in order to settle among them. The Chorus run to fetch a vast cargo of feathers and wings to equip their new citizens, when they come.

"The first who appears is a profligate young fellow, who hopes to enjoy a liberty which he could not enjoy so well at home, the liberty of beating his father. Pisthetaerus allows it, indeed, to be the custom of his people; but at the same time informs him of an ancient law preserved among the storks, that they shall maintain their parents in their old age. This is not at all agreeable to the youth: however, in consideration of his affection for the Nephelococcygians, Pisthetaerus furnishes him with a feather for his helmet, and a cock's spur for a weapon, and advises him, as he seems to be of a military turn, to go into the army in Thrace.

"The next is Cinesias, the dithyrambic writer, who is delighted with the thought of living among the clouds, amidst those airy regions whence all his poetical flights are derived; but Pisthetaerus will have no such animal among his birds; he drives him back to Athens with great contempt.

"He then drives away also (but not without a severe whipping) an informer, who for the better despatch of business comes to beg a pair of wings to carry him round the islands and cities subject to Athens, whose inhabitants he is used to swear against for an honest livelihood, as did, he says, his fathers before him. The birds, in the ensuing chorus, relate their travels, and describe the strange things and strange men they have seen in them.

"A person in disguise, with all the appearance of caution and fear, comes to inquire for Pisthetaerus, to whom he discovers himself to be Prometheus, and tells him (but first he makes them hold a large umbrella over his head for fear Jupiter should spy him) that the gods are all in a starving, miserable condition; and, what is worse, that barbarian gods (who live no one knows where, in a part of heaven far beyond the gods of Greece) threaten to make war upon them, unless they will open the ports, and renew the intercourse between mankind and them, as of old. He advises Pisthetaerus to make the most of this intelligence, and to reject all offers boldly which Jupiter may make him, unless he will consent to restore to the birds their ancient power, and give him in marriage his favorite attendant, Basilea. This said, he slips back again to heaven, as he came. The Chorus continue an account of their travels.

"An embassy arrives from heaven, consisting of Hercules, Neptune, and a certain Triballian god. As they approach the city walls, Neptune is dressing and scolding at the outlandish divinity, and teaching him how to carry himself a little decently. They find Pisthetaerus busy in giving orders about a dish of wild fowl, (i. e. of birds which had been guilty of high misdemeanors, and condemned to die by the public,) which are dressing for his dinner. Hercules, who before was for bringing off the head of this audacious mortal without further conference, finds himself insensibly relent, as he snuffs the savory steam. He salutes Pisthetaerus, who receives them very coldly, and is more attentive to his kitchen than to their compliment. Neptune opens his commission; owns that his nation (the gods) are not the better for this war, and on reasonable terms would be glad of a peace. Pisthetaerus, according to the advice of Prometheus, proposes (as if to try them) the first condition, namely, that of Jupiter's restoring to the birds their ancient power; and, if this should be agreed to, he says that he hopes to entertain my lords the ambassadors at dinner. Hercules, pleased with this last compliment, so agreeable to his appetite, comes readily into all he asks; but is severely reproved by Neptune for his gluttony. Pisthetaerus argues the point, and shows how much it would be for the mutual interest of both nations; and Neptune is hungry enough to be glad of some reasonable pretence to give the thing up. The Triballian god is asked his opinion for form: he mutters somewhat, which nobody understands, and so it passes for his consent. Here they are going in to dinner, and all is well; when Pisthetaerus bethinks himself of the match with Basilea. This makes Neptune fly out again: he will not hear of it; he will return home instantly; but Hercules cannot think of leaving a good meal so; he is ready to acquiesce in any conditions. His colleague attempts to show him that he is giving up his patrimony for a dinner; and what will become of him after Jupiter's death, if the birds are to have everything during his lifetime. Pisthetaerus clearly proves to Hercules that this is a mere imposition; that by the laws of Solon a bastard has no inheritance; that if Jove died without legitimate issue, his brothers would succeed to his estate, and that he speaks only out of interest. Now the Triballian god is again to determine the matter; they interpret his jargon as favorable to them; so Neptune is forced to give up the point, and Pisthetaerus goes with him and the barbarian to heaven to fetch his bride, while Hercules stays behind to take care that the roast meat is not spoiled.

"A messenger returns with the news of the approach of Pisthetaerus and his bride; and accordingly they appear in the air in a splendid machine, he with Jove's thunderbolt in his hand, and by his side Basilea, magnificently adorned: the birds break out in loud songs of exultation, and conclude the drama with their hymeneal."

ARGUMENT.

The play was performed in the Archonship of Chabrias, B. C. 414. Ameipsias was first, with the Revellers; Aristophanes second, with the Birds; Phrynichus third, with the Monotropos, or Recluse. (See the first ὑπόθεσις, page 3.)

ΑΡΙΣΤΟΦΑΝΟΥΣ ΟΡΝΙΘΕΣ

ΤΑ ΤΟΥ ΔΡΑΜΑΤΟΣ ΠΡΟΣΩΠΑ.

ΕΥΕΛΠΙΔΗΣ.
ΠΕΙΣΘΕΤΑΙΡΟΣ.
ΤΡΟΧΙΛΟΣ, θεράπων Ἔποπος.
ΕΠΟΨ
ΧΟΡΟΣ ΟΡΝΙΘΩΝ.
ΦΟΙΝΙΚΟΠΤΕΡΟΣ.
ΚΗΡΥΚΕΣ.
ΙΕΡΕΥΣ.
ΠΟΙΗΤΗΣ.
ΧΡΗΣΜΟΛΟΓΟΣ.
ΜΕΤΩΝ γεωμέτρης.
ΕΠΙΣΚΟΠΟΣ

ΨΗΦΙΣΜΑΤΟΠΩΛΗΣ.
ΑΓΓΕΛΟΙ.
ΙΡΙΣ.
ΠΑΤΡΑΛΟΙΑΣ.
ΚΙΝΗΣΙΑΣ διθυραμβοποιός.
ΣΥΚΟΦΑΝΤΗΣ.
ΠΡΟΜΗΘΕΥΣ.
ΠΟΣΕΙΔΩΝ.
ΤΡΙΒΑΛΛΟΣ.
ΗΡΑΚΛΗΣ.
ΟΙΚΕΤΗΣ Πεισθεταίρου.

ΥΠΟΘΕΣΙΣ.

Δύο εἰσὶν Ἀθήνηθεν ἐκκεχωρηκότες πρεσβῦται διὰ τὰς δίκας. Πορεύονται δὲ πρὸς τὸν Τηρέα ἔποπα γενόμενον, πευσόμενοι παρ' αἰτοῦ ποία ἐστὶ πόλις εἰς κατοικισμὸν βελτίστη. Χρῶνται δὲ τῆς ὁδοῦ καθηγεμόσιν ὀρνέοις, ὁ μὲν κορώνῃ, ὁ δὲ κολοιῷ. Ὀνομάζονται δὲ ὁ μὲν Πεισθέταιρος, ὁ δὲ Εὐελπίδης, ὃς καὶ πρότερος ἄρχεται. Ἡ σκηνὴ ἐν Ἀθήναις. Τὸ δρᾶμα τοῦτο τῶν ἄγαν δυνατῶς πεποιημένων. Ἐδιδάχθη ἐπὶ Χαβρίου διὰ Καλλιστράτου ἐν ἄστει, ὃς ἦν δεύτερος τοῖς Ὄρνισι, πρῶτος Ἀμειψίας Κωμασταῖς, τρίτος Φρύνιχος Μονοτρόπῳ. Ἔστι δὲ λέ. Φοβερὰ δὲ τότε τοῖς Ἀθηναίοις τὰ πράγματα. Τό τε γὰρ ναυτικὸν ἀπώλετο περὶ Σικελίαν, Λάμαχος οὐκ ἔτι ἦν, Νικίας ἐτεθνήκει, Δεκέλειαν ἦσαν τειχίσαντες Λακεδαιμόνιοι, Ἆγις ὁ Λακεδαιμονίων στρατηγὸς περιεκάθητο τὴν Ἀττικήν, Ἀλκιβιάδης τὰ Λακεδαιμονίων ἐφρόνει καὶ ἐκκλησιάζων συνεβούλευε τὰ χρηστὰ Λακεδαιμονίοις. Ταῦτα αἱ Ἀθηναίων συμφοραί, διὰ ταῦτα αἱ Ἀθηναίων φυγαί. Καὶ ὅμως οὐκ ἀπείχοντο τοῦ κακοπραγμονεῖν καὶ συκοφαντεῖν.

ΑΛΛΩΣ.

Τῆς τῶν Ἀθηναίων πολιτείας τὸ μέγιστον ἦν κλέος αὐτόχθοσι γενέσθαι, καὶ αὕτη φιλοτιμία πρώτη τὸ μηδέπω μηδεμιᾶς πόλεως φανείσης αὐτὴν πρῶτον ἀναβλαστῆσαι. Ἀλλὰ τῷ χρόνῳ ὑπὸ προεστώτων πονηρῶν καὶ πολιτῶν δυσχερῶν ἀνετέτραπτο, καὶ διωρθοῦτο πάλιν. Ἐπὶ οὖν τοῦ Δεκελεικοῦ πολέμου, πονηρῶν τινῶν τὰ πράγματα ἐγχειρισθέντων, ἐπισφαλὴς γέγονεν ἡ παρ' αὐτῶν κατάστασις. Καὶ ἐν μὲν ἄλλοις δράμασι διὰ τῆς κωμῳδικῆς ἀδείας ἤλεγχεν Ἀριστοφάνης τοὺς κακῶς πολιτευομένους, φανερῶς μὲν οὐδαμῶς, οὐ γὰρ ἐπὶ τούτῳ ἦν λεληθότως δέ, ὅσον ἀνῆκεν ἀπὸ κωμῳδίας προσκρούειν. Ἐν δὲ τυ.s Ὄρνισι καὶ μέγα τι διανενόηται. Ὡς γὰρ ἀδιόρθωτον ἤδη νόσον τῆς πολιτείας νοσούσης καὶ διεφθαρμένης ὑπὸ τῶν προεστώτων, ἄλλην τινὰ πολιτείαν αἰνίττεται, ὡσανεὶ συγκεχυμένων τῶν καθεστώτων· οὐ μόνον δὲ τοῦτο, ἀλλὰ καὶ τὸ σχῆμα ὅλον καὶ τὴν φύσιν, εἰ δέοι, συμβουλεύει μετατίθεσθαι πρὸς τὸ ἠρεμαίως βιοῦν. Καὶ ἡ μὲν ἀπότασις αὕτη. Τὰ δὲ κατὰ θεῶν βλάσφημα ἐπιτηδείως ᾠκονόμηται. Καινῶν γάρ φησι τὴν πόλιν προσδεῖσθαι θεῶν, ἀφροντιστούντων τῆς κατοικίας Ἀθηνῶν τῶν ὄντων καὶ παντελῶς ἠλλοτριωκότων αὐτοὺς τῆς χώρας. Ἀλλ' ὁ μὲν καθόλου στίχος τοιοῦτος. Ἕκαστον δὲ τῶν κατὰ μέρος οὐκ εἰκῇ, ἀλλ' ἄντικρυς Ἀθηναίων καὶ τῶν παρ' αὐτοῖς ἐγχειριζομένων τὰ κοινὰ ἐλέγχει τὴν φαύλην διάθεσιν, ἐπιθυμίαν ἐγκατασπείρων τοῖς ἀκούουσιν ἀπαλλαγῆναι τῆς ἐνεστώσης μοχθηρᾶς πολιτείας. Ὑποτίθεται γὰρ περὶ τὸν ἀέρα πόλιν, τῆς γῆς ἀπαλλάσσων· ἀλλὰ καὶ βουλὰς καὶ συνόδους ὀρνίθων, ταῖς Ἀθηναίων δυσχεραίνων. Ἀλλὰ καὶ ὅσα παίζει, ἐπίσκοπον, ἢ ψηφισματογράφον, ἢ τοὺς λοιποὺς εἰσάγων, οὐχ ἁπλῶς, ἀλλὰ γυμνοῖ τὰς πάντων προαιρέσεις, ὡς αἰσχροκερδείας ἕνεκεν χρηματίζονται. Εἶθ' ὕστερον καὶ τὸ θεῖον εἰς ἀπρονοησίαν κωμῳδεῖ. Τὰ δὲ ὀνόματα τῶν γερόντων πεποίηται, ὡς εἰ πεποιθοίη ἕτερος τῷ ἑτέρῳ καὶ ἐλπίζοι ἔσεσθαι ἐν βελτίοσι. Τινὲς δέ φασι τὸν ποιητὴν τὰς ἐν ταῖς τραγῳδίαις τερατολογίας ἐν μὲν ἄλλοις διελέγχειν, ἐν δὲ τοῖς νῦν τὴν τῆς Γιγαντομαχίας συμπλοκὴν ἕωλον ἀποφαίνων, ὄρνισιν ἔδωκε διαφέρεσθαι πρὸς θεοὺς περὶ τῆς ἀρχῆς.

Ἐπὶ Χαβρίου τὸ δρᾶμα καθῆκεν εἰς ἄστυ διὰ Καλλιστράτου· εἰς δὲ Λήναια τὸν Ἀμφιάραον ἐδίδαξε διὰ Φιλωνίδου. Λάβοι δ' ἄν τις τοὺς χρόνους ἐκ τῶν πέρυσι γενομένων ἐπὶ Ἀριστομνήστου τοῦ πρὸ Χαβρίου. Ἀθηναῖοι γὰρ πέμπουσι τὴν Σαλαμινίαν, τὸν Ἀλκιβιάδην μεταστελλόμενοι ἐπὶ κρίσει τῆς τῶν μυστηρίων ἐκμιμήσεως. Ὁ δὲ ἄχρι μὲν Θουρίου εἴπετο τοῖς μεθήκουσιν, ἐκεῖθεν δὲ δρασμὸν ποιησάμενος εἰς Πελοπόννησον ἐπεραιώθη. Τῆς δὲ μετακλήσεως μέμνηται καὶ Ἀριστοφάνης, ἀποκρύπτων μὲν τὸ ὄνομα, τὸ δὲ πρᾶγμα δηλῶν ἐν οἷς γέ φησι

Μηδαμῶς
Ἡμῖν παρὰ θάλατταν, ἵν' ἀνακύψεται
Κλητῆρ' ἄγουσ' ἔωθεν ἡ Σαλαμινία.

ΑΡΙΣΤΟΦΑΝΟΥΣ ΓΡΑΜΜΑΤΙΚΟΥ.

Διὰ τὰς δίκας φεύγουσιν Ἀθήνας δύο τινές·
Οἱ πρὸς τὸν ἔποπα, τὸν λεγόμενον Τηρέα,
Ἐλθόντες ἠρώτων ἀπράγμονα πόλιν
Εἷς δ' ὄρνις ἔποπι συμπαρὼν μετὰ πλειόνων
Πτηνῶν διδάσκει, τί δύνατ' ὀρνίθων γένος,
Καὶ πῶς, ἐάν περ κατὰ μέσον τὸν ἀέρα
Πόλιν κτίσωσι, τῶν θεῶν τὰ πράγματα
Αὐτοὶ παραλήψοντ'. Ἐκ δὲ τοῦδε φάρμακον
Πτέρυγάς τ' ἐποίουν· ἠξίωσαν δ' οἱ θεοί,
Ἐπίθεσιν οὐ μικρὰν ὁρῶντες γενομένην.

ΟΡΝΙΘΕΣ.

ΕΥΕΛΠΙΔΗΣ.
Ὀρθὴν κελεύεις, ᾗ τὸ δένδρον φαίνεται;

ΠΕΙΣΘΕΤΑΙΡΟΣ.
Διαρραγείης· ἥδε δ' αὖ κρώζει πάλιν.

ΕΥΕΛΠΙΔΗΣ.
Τί, ὦ πονήρ', ἄνω κάτω πλανύττομεν;
Ἀπολούμεθ' ἄλλως τὴν ὁδὸν προφορουμένω.

ΠΕΙΣΘΕΤΑΙΡΟΣ.
Τὸ δ' ἐμὲ κορώνῃ πειθόμενον τὸν ἄθλιον
Ὁδοῦ περιελθεῖν στάδια πλεῖν ἢ χίλια.

ΕΥΕΛΠΙΔΗΣ.
Τὸ δ' ἐμὲ κολοιῷ πειθόμενον τὸν δύσμορον
Ἀποσποδῆσαι τοὺς ὄνυχας τῶν δακτύλωι.

ΠΕΙΣΘΕΤΑΙΡΟΣ.
Ἀλλ' οὐδ' ὅπου γῆς ἐσμὲν οἶδ' ἔγωγ' ἔτι.

ΕΥΕΛΠΙΔΗΣ.
Εντευθενὶ τὴν πατρίδ' ἂν ἐξεύροις σύ που;

ΠΕΙΣΘΕΤΑΙΡΟΣ.
Οὐδ᾽ ἂν μὰ Δία γ᾽ ἐντεῦθεν Ἐξηκεστίδης.

ΕΥΕΛΠΙΔΗΣ.
Οἴμοι.

ΠΕΙΣΘΕΤΑΙΡΟΣ.
Σὺ μὲν, ὦ τᾶν, τὴν ὁδὸν ταύτην ἴθι.

ΕΥΕΛΠΙΔΗΣ.
Ἦ δεινὰ νὼ δέδρακεν οὐκ τῶν ὀρνέων,
Ὁ πινακοπώλης Φιλοκράτης μελαγχολῶν,
Ὃς τώδ᾽ ἔφασκε νῷν φράσειν τὸν Τηρέα, 15
Τὸν ἔποφ᾽, ὃς ὄρνις ἐγένετ᾽ ἐκ τῶν ὀρνέων·
Κἀπέδοτο τὸν μὲν Θαρρελείδου τουτονὶ
Κολοιὸν ὀβολοῦ, τηνδεδὶ τριωβόλου.
Τὼ δ᾽ οὐκ ἄρ᾽ ᾔστην οὐδὲν ἄλλο πλὴν δάκνειν.
Καὶ νῦν τί κέχηνας; ἔσθ᾽ ὅποι κατὰ τῶν πετρῶν 20
Ἡμᾶς ἔτ᾽ ἄξεις; οὐ γάρ ἐστ᾽ ἐνταῦθά τις
Ὁδός.

ΠΕΙΣΘΕΤΑΙΡΟΣ.
Οὐδὲ μὰ Δί᾽ ἐνταῦθά γ᾽ ἀτραπὸς οὐδαμοῦ.

ΕΥΕΛΠΙΔΗΣ.
Ἡ δ᾽ ἡ κορώνη τῆς ὁδοῦ τι λέγει πέρι;

ΠΕΙΣΘΕΤΑΙΡΟΣ.
Οὐ ταὐτὰ κρώζει μὰ Δία νῦν τε καὶ τότε.

ΕΥΕΛΠΙΔΗΣ.
Τί δὴ λέγει περὶ τῆς ὁδοῦ;

ΠΕΙΣΘΕΤΑΙΡΟΣ.
Τί δ᾽ ἄλλο γ᾽ ἢ 25
Βρύκουσ᾽ ἀπέδεσθαί φησί μου τοὺς δακτύλους;

ΟΡΝΙΘΕΣ.

ΕΥΕΛΠΙΔΗΣ.

Οὐ δεινὸν οὖν δῆτ' ἐστὶν ἡμᾶς δεομένους
Ἐς κόρακας ἐλθεῖν καὶ παρεσκευασμένους,
Ἔπειτα μὴ 'ξευρεῖν δύνασθαι τὴν ὁδόν ;
Ἡμεῖς γὰρ, ὦνδρες οἱ παρόντες ἐν λόγῳ, 30
Νόσον νοσοῦμεν τὴν ἐναντίαν Σακᾷ·
Ὁ μὲν γὰρ ὢν οὐκ ἀστὸς εἰσβιάζεται,
Ἡμεῖς δὲ φυλῇ καὶ γένει τιμώμενοι,
Ἀστοὶ μετ' ἀστῶν, οὐ σοβοῦντος οὐδενὸς
Ἀνεπτομεσθ' ἐκ τῆς πατρίδος ἀμφοῖν ποδοῖν, 35
Αὐτὴν μεν οὐ μισοῦντ' ἐκείνην τὴν πόλιν
Τὸ μὴ οὐ μεγάλην εἶναι φύσει κεὐδαίμονα
Καὶ πᾶσι κοινὴν ἐναποτῖσαι χρήματα.
Οἱ μὲν γὰρ οὖν τέττιγες ἕνα μῆν' ἢ δύο
Ἐπὶ τῶν κραδῶν ᾄδουσ', Ἀθηναῖοι δ' ἀεὶ 40
Ἐπὶ τῶν δικῶν ᾄδουσι πάντα τὸν βίον.
Διὰ ταῦτα τόνδε τὸν βάδον βαδίζομεν,
Κανοῦν δ' ἔχοντε καὶ χύτραν καὶ μυρρίνας
Πλανώμεθα ζητοῦντε τόπον ἀπράγμονα,
Ὅπου καθιδρυθέντε διαγενοίμεθ' ἄν. 45
Ὁ δὲ στόλος νῷν ἐστι παρὰ τὸν Τηρέα
Τὸν ἔποπα, παρ' ἐκείνου πυθέσθαι δεομένῳ,
Εἴ που τοιαύτην εἶδε πόλιν ᾗ 'πέπτατο.

ΠΕΙΣΘΕΤΑΙΡΟΣ.

Οὗτος.

ΕΥΕΛΠΙΔΗΣ.

Τί ἔστιν ;

ΠΕΙΣΘΕΤΑΙΡΟΣ.
                 Ἡ κορώνη μοι πάλαι
Ἄνω τι φράζει.

          ΕΥΕΛΠΙΔΗΣ.
                 Χὠ κολοιὸς οὑτοσὶ   50
Ἄνω κέχηνεν ὡσπερεὶ δεικνύς τί μοι·
Κοὐκ ἔσθ᾽ ὅπως οὐκ ἔστιν ἐνταῦθ᾽ ὄρνεα.
Εἰσόμεθα δ᾽ αὐτίκ᾽, ἢν ποιήσωμεν ψόφον.

          ΠΕΙΣΘΕΤΑΙΡΟΣ.
Ἀλλ᾽ οἶσθ᾽ ὃ δρᾶσον; τῷ σκέλει θένε τὴν πέτραν.

          ΕΥΕΛΠΙΔΗΣ.
Σὺ δὲ τῇ κεφαλῇ γ᾽, ἵν᾽ ᾖ διπλάσιος ὁ ψόφος.   55

          ΠΕΙΣΘΕΤΑΙΡΟΣ.
Σὺ δ᾽ οὖν λίθῳ κόψον λαβών.

          ΕΥΕΛΠΙΔΗΣ.
                    Πάνυ γ᾽, εἰ δοκεῖ.
Παῖ παῖ.

          ΠΕΙΣΘΕΤΑΙΡΟΣ.
          Τί λέγεις, οὗτος; τὸν ἔποπα παῖ καλεῖς;
Οὐκ ἀντὶ τοῦ παιδός σ᾽ ἐχρῆν ἐποποῖ καλεῖν;

          ΕΥΕΛΠΙΔΗΣ.
Ἐποποῖ. Ποιήσεις τοί με κόπτειν αὖθις αὖ;
Ἐποποῖ.

          ΤΡΟΧΙΛΟΣ.
          Τίνες οὗτοι; τίς ὁ βοῶν τὸν δεσπότην;   60

          ΕΥΕΛΠΙΔΗΣ.
Ἄπολλον ἀποτρόπαιε, τοῦ χασμήματος.

ΤΡΟΧΙΛΟΣ.
Οἴμοι τάλας, ὀρνιθοθήρα τουτωί.

ΕΥΕΛΠΙΔΗΣ.
Οὕτως τι δεινὸν οὐδὲ κάλλιον λέγειν;

ΤΡΟΧΙΛΟΣ.
Ἀπολεῖσθον.

ΕΥΕΛΠΙΔΗΣ.
Ἀλλ' οὐκ ἐσμὲν ἀνθρώπω.

ΤΡΟΧΙΛΟΣ.
Τί δαί;

ΕΥΕΛΠΙΔΗΣ.
Ὑποδεδιὼς ἔγωγε, Λιβυκὸν ὄρνεον.

ΤΡΟΧΙΛΟΣ.
Οὐδὲν λέγεις.

ΕΥΕΛΠΙΔΗΣ.
Καὶ μὴν ἐροῦ τὰ πρὸς ποδῶν.

ΤΡΟΧΙΛΟΣ.
Ὁδὶ δὲ δὴ τίς ἐστὶν ὄρνις; οὐκ ἐρεῖς;

ΠΕΙΣΘΕΤΑΙΡΟΣ.
Ἐπικεχοδὼς ἔγωγε Φασιανικός.

ΕΥΕΛΠΙΔΗΣ.
Ἀτὰρ σὺ τί θηρίον ποτ' εἶ πρὸς τῶν θεῶν;

ΤΡΟΧΙΛΟΣ.
Ὄρνις ἔγωγε δοῦλος.

ΕΥΕΛΠΙΔΗΣ.
Ἡττήθης τινὸς
Ἀλεκτρυόνος;

ΤΡΟΧΙΛΟΣ.
   Οὐκ, ἀλλ᾽ ὅτε περ ὁ δεσπότης
Ἔποψ ἐγένετο, τότε γενέσθαι μ᾽ ηὔξατο
Ὄρνιν, ἵν᾽ ἀκόλουθον διάκονόν τ᾽ ἔχῃ.

ΕΥΕΛΠΙΔΗΣ.
Δεῖται γὰρ ὄρνις καὶ διακόνου τινός;

ΤΡΟΧΙΛΟΣ.
Οὗτός γ᾽, ἅτ᾽, οἶμαι, πρότερον ἄνθρωπός ποτ᾽ ὤν,   75
Τοτὲ μὲν ἐρᾷ φαγεῖν ἀφύας Φαληρικάς·
Τρέχω 'π' ἀφύας ἐγὼ λαβὼν τὸ τρυβλίον.
Ἔτνους δ᾽ ἐπιθυμεῖ, δεῖ τορύνης καὶ χύτρας·
Τρέχω 'πὶ τορύνην.

ΕΥΕΛΠΙΔΗΣ.
       Τροχίλος ὄρνις οὑτοσί.
Οἶσθ᾽ οὖν ὃ δρᾶσον, ὦ τροχίλε; τὸν δεσπότην   80
Ἡμῖν κάλεσον.

ΤΡΟΧΙΛΟΣ.
     Ἀλλ᾽ ἀρτίως νὴ τὸν Δία
Εὕδει καταφαγὼν μύρτα καὶ σέρφους τινάς.

ΕΥΕΛΠΙΔΗΣ.
Ὅμως ἐπέγειρον αὐτόν.

ΤΡΟΧΙΛΟΣ.
       Οἶδα μὲν σαφῶς
Ὅτι ἀχθέσεται, σφῷν δ᾽ αὐτὸν οὕνεκ᾽ ἐπεγερῶ.

ΠΕΙΣΘΕΤΑΙΡΟΣ.
Κακῶς σύ γ᾽ ἀπόλοι᾽, ὥς μ᾽ ἀπέκτεινας δέει.   85

ΟΡΝΙΘΕΣ.

ΕΥΕΛΠΙΔΗΣ.
Οἴμοι κακοδαίμων, χὠ κολοιός μ' οἴχεται
Ὑπὸ τοῦ δέους.

ΠΕΙΣΘΕΤΑΙΡΟΣ.
Ὦ δειλότατον σὺ θηρίον.
Δείσας ἀφῆκας τὸν κολοιόν;

ΕΥΕΛΠΙΔΗΣ.
Εἰπέ μοι,
Σὺ δὲ τὴν κορώνην οὐκ ἀφῆκας καταπεσών;

ΠΕΙΣΘΕΤΑΙΡΟΣ.
Μὰ Δί' οὐκ ἔγωγε.

ΕΥΕΛΠΙΔΗΣ.
Ποῦ γάρ ἐστιν;

ΠΕΙΣΘΕΤΑΙΡΟΣ.
Ἀπέπτατο. 90

ΕΥΕΛΠΙΔΗΣ.
Οὐκ ἄρ' ἀφῆκας· ὠγάθ', ὡς ἀνδρεῖος εἶ.

ΕΠΟΨ.
Ἄνοιγε τὴν ὕλην, ἵν' ἐξέλθω ποτέ.

ΕΥΕΛΠΙΔΗΣ.
Ὦ Ἡράκλεις, τουτὶ τί ποτ' ἐστὶ θηρίον;
Τίς ἡ πτέρωσις; Τίς ὁ τρόπος τῆς τριλοφίας;

ΕΠΟΨ.
Τίνες εἰσί μ' οἱ ζητοῦντες;

ΕΥΕΛΠΙΔΗΣ.
Οἱ δώδεκα θεοὶ 95
Εἴξασιν ἐπιτρῖψαι σε.

ΕΠΟΨ.
Μῶν με σκώπτετον
Ὁρῶντε τὴν πτέρωσιν; ἦ γὰρ, ὦ ξένοι,
Ἄνθρωπος.

ΕΥΕΛΠΙΔΗΣ.
Οὐ σοῦ καταγελῶμεν.

ΕΠΟΨ.
Ἀλλὰ τοῦ ;

ΠΕΙΣΘΕΤΑΙΡΟΣ.
Τὸ ῥάμφος ἡμῖν σου γέλοιον φαίνεται.

ΕΠΟΨ.
Τοιαῦτα μέντοι Σοφοκλέης λυμαίνεται
Ἐν ταῖς τραγῳδίαισιν ἐμὲ τὸν Τηρέα.

ΕΥΕΛΠΙΔΗΣ.
Τηρεὺς γὰρ εἶ σύ; πότερον ὄρνις ἢ ταῶς ;

ΕΠΟΨ.
Ὄρνις ἔγωγε.

ΕΥΕΛΠΙΔΗΣ.
Κᾆτά σοι ποῦ τὰ πτερά ;

ΕΠΟΨ.
Ἐξερρύηκε.

ΕΥΕΛΠΙΔΗΣ.
Πότερον ὑπὸ νόσου τινος ;

ΕΠΟΨ.
Οὔκ, ἀλλὰ τὸν χειμῶνα πάντα τὤρνεα
Πτερορρυεῖ τε καὖθις ἕτερα φύομεν.
Ἀλλ᾽ εἴπατόν μοι, σφὼ τίν᾽ ἐστόν ;

ΟΡΝΙΘΕΣ.

ΕΥΕΛΠΙΔΗΣ.
Νώ; βροτώ.

ΕΠΟΨ.
Ποδαπὼ τὸ γένος δ';

ΕΥΕΛΠΙΔΗΣ.
Ὅθεν αἱ τριήρεις αἱ καλαι.

ΕΠΟΨ.
Μῶν ἡλιαστά;

ΕΥΕΛΠΙΔΗΣ.
Μἀλλὰ θατέρου τροπου,
Ἀπηλιαστά.

ΕΠΟΨ.
Σπείρεται γὰρ τοῦτ' ἐκεῖ 110
Τὸ σπέρμ;

ΕΥΕΛΠΙΔΗΣ.
Ὀλίγον ζητῶν ἂν ἐξ ἀγροῦ λάβοις.

ΕΠΟΨ.
Πράγους δὲ δὴ τοῦ δεομένω δεῦρ' ἤλθετον;

ΕΥΕΛΠΙΛΗΣ.
Σοὶ ξυγγενέσθαι βουλομένω.

ΕΠΟΨ.
Τίνος πέρι;

ΕΥΕΛΠΙΔΗΣ.
Ὅτι πρῶτα μὲν ἦσθ' ἄνθρωπος, ὥσπερ νώ, ποτέ,
Κἀργύριον ὠφείλησας, ὥσπερ νώ, ποτέ, 115
Κοὐκ ἀποδιδοὺς ἔχαιρες, ὥσπερ νώ, ποτέ·
Εἶτ' αὖθις ὀρνίθων μεταλλάξας φύσιν,

2

Καὶ γῆν ἐπεπέτου καὶ θάλατταν ἐν κύκλῳ,
Καὶ πάνθ' ὅσαπερ ἄνθρωπος ὅσα τ' ὄρνις φρονεῖς·
Ταῦτ' οὖν ἱκέται νὼ πρὸς σὲ δεῦρ' ἀφίγμεθα,   120
Εἴ τινα πόλιν φράσειας ἡμῖν εὔερον,
Ὥσπερ σισύραν ἐγκατακλινῆναι μαλθακήν.

ΕΠΟΨ.
Ἔπειτα μείζω τῶν Κραναῶν ζητεῖς πόλιν;

ΕΥΕΛΠΙΔΗΣ.
Μείζω μὲν οὐδέν, προσφορωτέραν δὲ νῷν.

ΕΠΟΨ.
Ἀριστοκρατεῖσθαι δῆλος εἶ ζητῶν.

ΕΥΕΛΠΙΔΗΣ.
                              Ἐγώ;   125
Ἥκιστα· καὶ τὸν Σκελλίου βδελύττομαι.

ΕΠΟΨ.
Ποίαν τιν οὖν ἥδιστ' ἂν οἰκοῖτ' ἂν πόλιν;

ΕΥΕΛΠΙΔΗΣ.
Ὅπου τὰ μέγιστα πράγματ' εἴη τοιαδί·
Ἐπὶ τὴν θύραν μου πρῴ τις ἐλθὼν τῶν φίλων
Λέγοι ταδί· πρὸς τοῦ Διὸς τοὐλυμπίου,   130
Ὅπως παρέσει μοι καὶ σὺ καὶ τὰ παιδία
Λουσάμενα πρῴ· μέλλω γὰρ ἑστιᾶν γάμους·
Καὶ μηδαμῶς ἄλλως ποιήσῃς· εἰ δὲ μή,
Μή μοι τότε γ' ἔλθῃς, ὅταν ἐγὼ πράττω κακῶς.

ΕΠΟΨ.
Νὴ Δία ταλαιπώρων γε πραγμάτων ἐρᾷς.   135
Τί δαὶ σύ;

ΟΡΝΙΘΕΣ.

ΠΕΙΣΘΕΤΑΙΡΟΣ.
Τοιούτων ἐρῶ κἀγώ.

ΕΠΟΨ.
Τίνων;

ΠΕΙΣΘΕΤΑΙΡΟΣ.
"Οπου ξυναντῶν μοι ταδί τις μέμψεται
"Ωσπερ ἀδικηθεὶς παιδὸς ὡραίου πατήρ·
Καλῶς γέ μου τὸν υἱὸν, ὦ Στιλβωνίδη,
Εὑρὼν ἀπιόντ' ἀπὸ γυμνασίου λελουμένον 140
Οὐκ ἔκυσας, οὐ προσεῖπας, οὐ προσηγάγου,
Οὐκ ὠρχιπέδησας, ὢν ἐμοὶ πατρικὸς φίλος.

ΕΠΟΨ.
Ὦ δειλακρίων σὺ τῶν κακῶν οἵων ἐρᾷς.
Ἀτὰρ ἔστι γ' ὁποίαν λέγετον εὐδαίμων πόλις
Παρὰ τὴν ἐρυθρὰν θάλατταν.

ΕΥΕΛΠΙΔΗΣ.
Οἴμοι, μηδαμῶς 145
Ἡμῖν γε παρὰ θάλατταν, ἵν' ἀνακύψεται
Κλητῆρ' ἄγουσ' ἕωθεν ἡ Σαλαμινία.
Ἑλληνικὴν δὲ πόλιν ἔχεις ἡμῖν φράσαι;

ΕΠΟΨ.
Τί οὐ τὸν Ἠλεῖον Λέπρεον οἰκίζετον
Ἐλθόνθ';

ΕΥΕΛΠΙΔΗΣ.
Ὁτιὴ νὴ τοὺς θεοὺς, ὃς οὐκ ἰδὼν 150
Βδελύττομαι τὸν Λέπρεον ἀπὸ Μελανθίου.

ΕΠΟΨ.
Ἀλλ' εἰσὶν ἕτεροι τῆς Λοκρίδος Ὀπούντιοι,
Ἵνα χρὴ κατοικεῖν.

ΕΥΕΛΠΙΔΗΣ.
                Ἀλλ' ἔγωγ' Ὀπούντιος
Οὐκ ἂν γενοίμην ἐπὶ ταλάντῳ χρυσίου.
Οὗτος δὲ δὴ τίς ἔσθ' ὁ μετ' ὀρνίθων βίος ; 155
Σὺ γὰρ οἶσθ' ἀκριβῶς.

ΕΠΟΨ.
            Οὐκ ἄχαρις ἐς τὴν τριβήν·
Οὗ πρῶτα μὲν δεῖ ζῆν ἄνευ βαλαντίου.

ΕΥΕΛΠΙΔΗΣ.
Πολλήν γ' ἀφεῖλες τοῦ βίου κιβδηλίαν.

ΕΠΟΨ.
Νεμόμεσθα δ' ἐν κήποις τὰ λευκὰ σήσαμα
Καὶ μύρτα καὶ μήκωνα καὶ σισύμβρια. 160

ΕΥΕΛΠΙΔΗΣ.
Ὑμεῖς μὲν ἄρα ζῆτε νυμφίων βίον.

ΠΕΙΣΘΕΤΑΙΡΟΣ.
Φεῦ φεῦ·
Ἦ μέγ' ἐνορῶ βούλευμ' ἐν ὀρνίθων γένει,
Καὶ δύναμιν ἣ γένοιτ' ἄν, εἰ πίθοισθέ μοι.

ΕΠΟΨ.
Τί σοι πιθώμεσθ' ;

ΠΕΙΣΘΕΤΑΙΡΟΣ.
            Ὅ τι πίθησθε ; πρῶτα μὲν 165
Μὴ περιπέτεσθε πανταχῇ κεχηνότες·

ΟΡΝΙΘΕΣ.

Ὡς τοῦτ' ἄτιμον τοὔργον ἐστίν. Αὐτίκα
Ἐκεῖ παρ' ἡμῖν τοὺς πετομένους ἢν ἔρῃ,
Τίς ὄρνις οὗτος ; ὁ Τελέας ἐρεῖ ταδί ·
Ἄνθρωπος ὄρνις ἀστάθμητος πετόμενος, 170
Ἀτέκμαρτος, οὐδὲν οὐδέποτ' ἐν ταὐτῷ μένων.

ΕΠΟΨ.
Νὴ τὸν Διόνυσον, εὖ γε μωμᾷ ταυταγί.
Τί ἂν οὖν ποιοῖμεν ;

ΠΕΙΣΘΕΤΑΙΡΟΣ.
    Οἰκίσατε μίαν πόλιν.

ΕΠΟΨ.
Ποιαν δ᾽ ἂν οἰκίσαιμεν ὄρνιθες πόλιν ;

ΠΕΙΣΘΕΤΑΙΡΟΣ.
Ἄληθες, ὦ σκαιότατον εἰρηκὼς ἔπος, 175
Βλέψον κάτω.

ΕΠΟΨ.
   Καὶ δὴ βλέπω.

ΠΕΙΣΘΕΤΑΙΡΟΣ.
      Βλέπε νῦν ἄνω.

ΕΠΟΨ.
Βλέπω.

ΠΕΙΣΘΕΤΑΙΡΟΣ.
   Περίαγε τὸν τράχηλον.

ΕΠΟΨ.
      Νὴ Δία,
Ἀπολαύσομαί τι δ᾽, εἰ διαστραφήσομαι.

ΠΕΙΣΘΕΤΑΙΡΟΣ.

Εἶδές τι;

ΕΠΟΨ.

Τὰς νεφέλας γε καὶ τὸν οὐρανόν.

ΠΕΙΣΘΕΤΑΙΡΟΣ.

Οὐχ οὗτος οὖν δήπου 'στὶν ὀρνίθων πόλος; 180

ΕΠΟΨ.

Πόλος; τίνα τρόπον;

ΠΕΙΣΘΕΤΑΙΡΟΣ.

Ὥσπερ εἴποι τις τόπος.
Ὁτιὴ δὲ πολεῖται τοῦτο καὶ διέρχεται
Ἅπαντα, διὰ τοῦτό γε καλεῖται νῦν πόλος·
Ἢν δ' οἰκίσητε τοῦτο καὶ φράξηθ' ἅπαξ,
Ἐκ τοῦ πόλου τούτου κεκλήσεται πόλις. 185
Ὥστ' ἄρξετ' ἀνθρώπων μὲν ὥσπερ παρνόπων,
Τοὺς δ' αὖ θεοὺς ἀπολεῖτε λιμῷ Μηλίῳ.

ΕΠΟΨ.

Πῶς;

ΠΕΙΣΘΕΤΑΙΡΟΣ.

Ἐν μέσῳ δήπουθεν ἀήρ ἐστι γῆς.
Εἶθ' ὥσπερ ἡμεῖς, ἢν ἰέναι βουλώμεθα
Πυθῶδε, Βοιωτοὺς δίοδον αἰτούμεθα, 190
Οὕτως, ὅταν θύσωσιν ἄνθρωποι θεοῖς,
Ἢν μὴ φόρον φέρωσιν ὑμῖν οἱ θεοὶ,
Διὰ τῆς πόλεως τῆς ἀλλοτρίας καὶ τοῦ χάους
Τῶν μηρίων τὴν κνῖσαν οὐ διαφρήσετε.

ΟΡΝΙΘΕΣ.

ΕΠΟΨ.

Ἰοὺ ἰού·
Μὰ γῆν, μὰ παγίδας, μὰ νεφέλας, μὰ δίκτυα,
Μὴ 'γὼ νόημα κομψότερον ἤκουσά πω·
"Ωστ' ἂν κατοικίζοιμι μετὰ σοῦ τὴν πόλιν,
Εἰ ξυνδοκοίη τοῖσιν ἄλλοις ὀρνέοις.

ΠΕΙΣΘΕΤΑΙΡΟΣ.
Τίς ἂν οὖν τὸ πρᾶγμ' αὐτοῖς διηγήσαιτο;

ΕΠΟΨ.
Σύ.
Ἐγὼ γὰρ αὐτοὺς βαρβάρους ὄντας πρὸ τοῦ
Ἐδίδαξα τὴν φωνήν, ξυνὼν πολὺν χρόνον.

ΠΕΙΣΘΕΤΑΙΡΟΣ.
Πῶς δῆτ' ἂν αὐτοὺς ξυγκαλέσειας;

ΕΠΟΨ.
Ῥᾳδίως.
Δευρὶ γὰρ ἐμβὰς αὐτίκα μάλ' ἐς τὴν λόχμην,
Ἔπειτ' ἀνεγείρας τὴν ἐμὴν ἀηδόνα,
Καλοῦμεν αὐτούς· οἱ δὲ νῷν τοῦ φθέγματος
Ἐάνπερ ἐπακούσωσι, θεύσονται δρόμῳ.

ΠΕΙΣΘΕΤΑΙΡΟΣ.
Ὦ φίλτατ' ὀρνίθων σύ, μή νυν ἔσταθι·
Ἀλλ' ἀντιβολῶ σ', ἄγ' ὡς τάχιστ' ἐς τὴν λόχμην
Ἔσβαινε κἀνέγειρε τὴν ἀηδόνα.

ΕΠΟΨ.
Ἄγε σύννομέ μοι, παῦσαι μὲν ὕπνου,
Λῦσον δὲ νόμους ἱερῶν ὕμνων,

Οὓς διὰ θείου στόματος θρηνεῖς
Τὸν ἐμὸν καὶ σὸν πολύδακρυν Ἴτυν,
Ἐλελιζομένη διεροῖς μέλεσιν 215
Γένυος ξουθῆς·
Καθαρὰ χωρεῖ διὰ φυλλοκόμου
Μίλακος ἠχὼ πρὸς Διὸς ἕδρας,
Ἵν' ὁ χρυσοκόμας Φοῖβος ἀκούων
Τοῖς σοῖς ἐλέγοις ἀντιψάλλων 220
Ἐλεφαντόδετον φόρμιγγα, θεῶν
Ἵστησι χορούς·
Διὰ δ' ἀθανάτων στομάτων χωρεῖ
Ξύμφωνος ὁμοῦ
Θεία μακάρων ὀλολυγή. 225
(Αὐλεῖ.)

ΠΕΙΣΘΕΤΑΙΡΟΣ.
Ὦ Ζεῦ βασιλεῦ, τοῦ φθέγματος τοὐρνιθίου·
Οἷον κατεμελίτωσε τὴν λόχμην ὅλην.

ΕΥΕΛΠΙΔΗΣ.
Οὗτος.

ΠΕΙΣΘΕΤΑΙΡΟΣ.
Τί ἔστιν;

ΕΥΕΛΠΙΔΗΣ.
Οὐ σιωπήσει;

ΠΕΙΣΘΕΤΑΙΡΟΣ.
Τί δαί;

ΕΥΕΛΠΙΔΗΣ.
Οὖποψ μελῳδεῖν αὖ παρασκευάζεται. 230

ΕΠΟΨ.

Εποποποποποποποποῖ,
Ἰὼ ἰὼ, ἰτὼ ἰτὼ ἰτὼ ἰτὼ
Ἴτω τις ὧδε τῶν ἐμῶν ὁμοπτέρων·
Ὅσοι τ' εὐσπόρους ἀγροίκων γύας
Νέμεσθε, φῦλα μυρία κριθοτράγων   235
Σπερμολόγων τε γένη
Ταχὺ πετόμενα, μαλθακὴν ἱέντα γῆρυν·
Ὅσα τ' ἐν ἄλοκι θαμὰ
Βῶλον ἀμφιτιττυβίζεθ' ὧδε λεπτὸν
Ἡδομένᾳ φωνᾷ·   240
Τιὸ τιὸ τιὸ τιὸ τιὸ τιὸ τιό·
Ὅσα θ' ὑμῶν κατὰ κήπους ἐπὶ κισσοῦ
Κλάδεσι νομὸν ἔχει,
Τά τε κατ' ὄρεα, τά τε κοτινοτράγα, τά τε κομαρο-
  φάγα,
Ἀνύσατε πετόμενα πρὸς ἐμὰν ἀοιδάν·   245
Τριοτὸ τριοτὸ τοτοβρίξ·
Οἵ θ' ἑλείας παρ' αὐλῶνας ὀξυστόμους
Ἐμπίδας κάπτεθ', ὅσα τ' εὐδρόσους γῆς τόπους
Ἔχετε λειμῶνά τ' ἐρόεντα Μαραθῶνος,
Ὄρνις τε πτεροποίκιλος   250
Ἀτταγᾶς ἀτταγᾶς·
Ὧν τ' ἐπὶ πόντιον οἶδμα θαλάσσης
Φῦλα μετ' ἀλκυόνεσσι ποτᾶται,
Δεῦρ' ἴτε πευσόμενοι τὰ νεώτερα,
Πάντα γὰρ ἐνθάδε φῦλ' ἀθροίζομεν   255

Οἰωνῶν ταναοδείρων.
Ἥκει γάρ τις δριμὺς πρέσβυς,
Καινὸς γνώμην,
Καινῶν ἔργων τ' ἐγχειρητής.
Ἀλλ' ἴτ' ἐς λόγους ἅπαντα,   260
Δεῦρο δεῦρο δεῦρο δεῦρο.
Τοροτοροτοροτοροτίξ.
Κικκαβαῦ κικκαβαῦ.
Τοροτοροτοροτορολιλιλίξ.

ΠΕΙΣΘΕΤΑΙΡΟΣ.
Ὁρᾷς τιν' ὄρνιν;

ΕΥΕΛΠΙΔΗΣ.
Μὰ τὸν Ἀπόλλω 'γὼ μὲν οὔ·   265
Καίτοι κέχηνά γ' εἰς τὸν οὐρανὸν βλέπων.
Ἄλλως ἄρ' οὔποψ, ὡς ἔοικ', ἐς τὴν λόχμην
Ἐμβὰς ἐπῶζε, χαραδριὸν μιμούμενος.

ΦΟΙΝΙΚΟΠΤΕΡΟΣ.
Τοροτὶξ τοροτίξ.

ΠΕΙΣΘΕΤΑΙΡΟΣ.
Ὠγάθ', ἀλλὰ χοὑτοσὶ καὶ δή τις ὄρνις ἔρχεται.   270

ΕΥΕΛΠΙΔΗΣ.
Νὴ Δί' ὄρνις δῆτα. Τίς ποτ' ἐστίν; Οὐ δήπου ταῶς;

ΠΕΙΣΘΕΤΑΙΡΟΣ.
Οὗτος αὐτὸς νῷν φράσει· τίς ἐστιν ὄρνις οὑτοσί;

ΕΠΟΨ.
Οὗτος οὐ τῶν ἠθάδων τῶνδ' ὧν ὁρᾶθ' ὑμεῖς ἀεί,
Ἀλλὰ λιμναῖος.

ΠΕΙΣΘΕΤΑΙΡΟΣ.

Βαβαί, καλός γε καὶ φοινικιους.

ΕΠΟΨ.

Εἰκό'ως· καὶ γὰρ ὄνομ' αὐτῷ γ' ἐστὶ φοινικόπτερος. 275

ΕΥΕΛΠΙΔΗΣ.

Οὖτος, ὦ σέ τοι.

ΠΕΙΣΘΕΤΑΙΡΟΣ.

Τί βωστρεῖς;

ΕΥΕΛΠΙΔΗΣ.

Ἕτερος ὄρνις ούτοσί.

ΠΕΙΣΘΕΤΑΙΡΟΣ.

Νὴ Δί' ἕτερος δῆτα χοῦτος ἔξεδρον χώραν ἔχων.
Τίς ποτ' ἔσθ' ὁ μουσόμαντις ἄτοπος ὄρνις ὀριβάτης;

ΕΠΟΨ.

Ὄνομα τούτῳ Μῆδός ἐστι.

ΠΕΙΣΘΕΤΑΙΡΟΣ.

Μῆδος; Ὦναξ Ἡράκλεις·
Εἶτα πῶς ἄνευ καμήλου Μῆδος ὢν εἰσέπτατο; 230

ΕΥΕΛΠΙΔΗΣ.

Ἕτερος αὖ λόφον κατειληφώς τις ὄρνις ούτοσί.

ΠΕΙΣΘΕΤΑΙΡΟΣ.

Τί τὸ τέρας τουτί ποτ' ἐστίν; Οὐ σὺ μόνος ἄρ' ἦσθ'
ἔποψ,
Ἀλλὰ χοῦτος ἕτερος;

ΕΠΟΨ.

Ἀλλ' οὗτος μέν ἐστι Φιλοκλέους
Ἐξ ἔποπος, ἐγὼ δὲ τούτου πάππος, ὥσπερ εἰ λέγοις

ΑΡΙΣΤΟΦΑΝΟΥΣ

Ἱππόνικος Καλλίου κἀξ Ἱππονίκου Καλλίας.   285

ΠΕΙΣΘΕΤΑΙΡΟΣ.
Καλλίας ἄρ' οὗτος οὕρνις ἐστίν· ὡς πτερορρυεῖ.

ΕΠΟΨ.
Ἅτε γὰρ ὢν γενναῖος ὑπὸ τῶν συκοφαντῶν τίλλεται,
Αἵ τε θήλειαι προσεκτίλλουσιν αὐτοῦ τὰ πτερά.

ΠΕΙΣΘΕΤΑΙΡΟΣ.
Ὦ Πόσειδον, ἕτερος αὖ τις βαπτὸς ὄρνις οὑτοσί.
Τίς ὀνομάζεταί ποθ' οὗτος;

ΕΠΟΨ.
                    Οὑτοσὶ κατωφαγᾶς.   290

ΠΕΙΣΘΕΤΑΙΡΟΣ.
Ἔστι γὰρ κατωφαγᾶς τις ἄλλος ἢ Κλεώνυμος;

ΕΥΕΛΠΙΔΗΣ.
Πῶς ἂν οὖν Κλεώνυμός γ' ὢν οὐκ ἀπέβαλε τὸν λόφον,

ΠΕΙΣΘΕΤΑΙΡΟΣ.
Ἀλλὰ μέντοι τίς ποθ' ἡ λόφωσις ἡ τῶν ὀρνέων;
Ἦ 'πὶ τὸν δίαυλον ἦλθον;

ΕΠΟΨ.
            Ὥσπερ οἱ Κᾶρες μὲν οὖν
Ἐπὶ λόφων οἰκοῦσιν, ὠγάθ', ἀσφαλείας οὕνεκα.   295

ΠΕΙΣΘΕΤΑΙΡΟΣ.
Ὦ Πόσειδον, οὐχ ὁρᾷς ὅσον συνείλεκται κακὸν
Ὀρνέων;

ΕΥΕΛΠΙΔΗΣ.
        Ὦναξ Ἄπολλον, τοῦ νέφους.   Ἰοὺ ἰού·
Οὐδ' ἰδεῖν ἔτ' ἔσθ' ὑπ' αὐτῶν πετομένων τὴν εἴσοδον.

ΠΕΙΣΘΕΤΑΙΡΟΣ.
Ούτοσὶ πέρδιξ, ἐκεινοσὶ δὲ νὴ Δί᾽ ἀτταγάς,
Οὑτοσὶ δὲ πηνέλοψ, ἐκεινοσὶ δέ γ᾽ ἀλκυών. 300

ΕΥΕΛΠΙΔΗΣ.
Τίς γάρ ἐσθ᾽ ουπισθεν αὐτῆς ;

ΠΕΙΣΘΕΤΑΙΡΟΣ.
"Οστις ἐστί ; Κειρύλος.

ΕΥΕΛΠΙΔΗΣ.
Κειρύλος γάρ ἐστιν ὄρνις ;

ΠΕΙΣΘΕΤΑΙΡΟΣ.
Οὐ γάρ ἐστι Σποργίλος ;
Χαὐτηί γε γλαῦξ.

ΕΥΕΛΠΙΔΗΣ.
Τί φής ; Τίς γλαῦκ᾽ Ἀθήναζ᾽ ἤγαγε ;

ΠΕΙΣΘΕΤΑΙΡΟΣ.
Κίττα, τρυγών, κορυδός, ἐλεᾶς, ὑποθυμίς, περιστερά,
Νέρτος, ἱέραξ, φάττα, κόκκυξ, ἐρυθρόπους, κεβλήπυ-
ρις, 305
Πορφυρίς, κερχνῄς, κολυμβίς, ἀμπελίς, φήνη, δρύοψ.

ΕΥΕΛΠΙΔΗΣ.
Ἰοὺ ἰοὺ τῶν ὀρνέων,
Ἰοὺ ἰοὺ τῶν κοψίχων·
Οἷα πιππίζουσι καὶ τρέχουσι διακεκραγότες.
Ἆρ᾽ ἀπειλοῦσίν γε νῷν ; Οἴμοι, κεχήνασίν γέ τοι 310
Καὶ βλέπουσιν εἰς σὲ κἀμέ.

ΠΕΙΣΘΕΤΑΙΡΟΣ.
Τοῦτο μὲν κἀμοὶ δοκεῖ.

ΧΟΡΟΣ.
Ποποποποποποῦ μ᾽ ἄρ᾽ ὃς ἐκάλεσε ; τίνα τόπυν ἄρα
νέμεται ;

ΕΠΟΨ.
Οὑτοσὶ πάλαι πάρειμι κοὐκ ἀποστατῶ φίλων.

ΧΟΡΟΣ.
Τιτιτιτιτιτιτιτιτίνα λόγον ἄρα ποτὲ πρὸς ἐμὲ φίλον
ἔχων ;

ΕΠΟΨ.
Κοινόν, ἀσφαλῆ, δίκαιον, ἡδύν, ὠφελήσιμον.   315
Ἄνδρε γὰρ λεπτὼ λογιστὰ δεῦρ᾽ ἀφῖχθον ὡς ἐμέ.

ΧΟΡΟΣ.
Ποῦ ; Πᾶ ; Πῶς φῄς ;

ΕΠΟΨ.
Φήμ᾽ ἀπ᾽ ἀνθρώπων ἀφῖχθαι δεῦρο πρεσβύτα δύο·
Ἥκετον δ᾽ ἔχοντε πρέμνον πράγματος πελωρίου.

ΧΟΡΟΣ.
Ὦ μέγιστον ἐξαμαρτὼν ἐξ ὅτου 'τράφην ἐγώ,   320
Πῶς λέγεις ;

ΕΠΟΨ.
Μήπω φοβηθῇς τὸν λόγον.

ΧΟΡΟΣ.
Τί μ᾽ εἰργάσω ;

ΕΠΟΨ.
Ἄνδρ᾽ ἐδεξάμην ἐραστὰ τῆσδε τῆς ξυνουσιας.

ΧΟΡΟΣ.
Καὶ δέδρακας τοῦτο τοὔργον ;

ΕΠΟΨ.

Καὶ δεδρακώς γ᾽ ἥδομαι.

ΧΟΡΟΣ

Κἄστὸν ἤδη ποι παρ᾽ ἡμῖν;

ΕΠΟΨ.

Εἰ παρ᾽ ὑμῖν εἴμ᾽ ἐγώ.

ΧΟΡΟΣ.

Στροφή.

Ἔα ἔα, 325
Προδεδόμεθ᾽ ἀνόσιά τ᾽ ἐπάθομεν·
Ὃς γὰρ φίλος ἦν, ὁμότροφά θ᾽ ἡμῖν
Ἐνέμετο πεδία παρ᾽ ἡμῖν
Παρέβη μὲν θεσμοὺς ἀρχαίους,
Παρέβη δ᾽ ὅρκους ὀρνίθων· 330
Ἐς δὲ δόλον ἐκάλεσε, παρέβαλέ τ᾽ ἐμὲ παρὰ
Γένος ἀνόσιον, ὅπερ ἐξότ᾽ ἐγένετ᾽ ἐπ᾽ ἐμοὶ
Πολέμιον ἐτράφη.

Ἀλλὰ πρὸς τοῦτον μὲν ἡμῖν ἐστιν ὕστερος λόγος·
Τω δὲ πρεσβύτα δοκεῖ μοι τώδε δοῦναι τὴν δίκην 335
Διαφορηθῆναί θ᾽ ὑφ᾽ ἡμῶν.

ΠΕΙΣΘΕΤΑΙΡΟΣ.

Ὡς ἀπωλόμεσθ᾽ ἄρα.

ΕΥΕΛΠΙΔΗΣ.

Αἴτιος μέντοι σὺ νῷν εἶ τῶν κακῶν τούτων μόνυς.
Ἐπὶ τί γάρ μ᾽ ἐκεῖθεν ἦγες;

ΠΕΙΣΘΕΤΑΙΡΟΣ.

Ἵν᾽ ἀκολουθοίης ἐμοί.

ΕΥΕΛΠΙΔΗΣ.
Ἵνα μὲν οὖν κλάοιμι μεγάλα.

ΠΕΙΣΘΕΤΑΙΡΟΣ.
Τοῦτο μὲν ληρεῖς ἔχων
Κάρτα· πῶς κλαυσεῖ γάρ, ἢν ἅπαξ γε τὠφθαλμὼ
'κκοπῇς ;   340

ΧΟΡΟΣ.
'Αντιστροφή.
Ἰὼ ἰώ,
Ἔπαγ', ἔπιθ', ἐπίφερε πολέμιον
Ὁρμὰν φονίαν, πτέρυγά τε παντᾶ
Περίβαλε περί τε κύκλωσαι·
Ὡς δεῖ τῷδ' οἰμώζειν ἄμφω   345
Καὶ δοῦναι ῥύγχει φορβάν.
Οὔτε γὰρ ὄρος σκιερὸν οὔτε νέφος αἰθέριον
Οὔτε πολιὸν πέλαγος ἔστιν ὅ τι δέξεται
Τώδ' ἀποφυγόντε με.

Ἀλλὰ μὴ μέλλωμεν ἤδη τῷδε τίλλειν καὶ δάκνειν. 350
Ποῦ 'σθ' ὁ ταξίαρχος ; Ἐπαγέτω τὸ δεξιὸν κέρας.

ΕΥΕΛΠΙΔΗΣ.
Τοῦτ' ἐκεῖνο· ποῖ φύγω δύστηνος ;

ΠΕΙΣΘΕΤΑΙΡΟΣ.
Οὗτος, οὐ μενεῖς ;

ΕΥΕΛΠΙΔΗΣ.
Ἵν' ὑπὸ τούτων διαφορηθῶ ;

ΠΕΙΣΘΕΤΑΙΡΟΣ.
Πῶς γὰρ ἂν τούτους δοκεῖς
Ἐκφυγεῖν ;

ΕΥΕΛΠΙΔΗΣ.
Οὐκ οἶδ' ὅπως ἄν.

ΠΕΙΣΘΕΤΑΙΡΟΣ.
Ἀλλ' ἐγώ τοί σοι λέγω
Ὅτι μένοντε δεῖ μάχεσθαι λαμβάνειν τε τῶν χυτρῶν. 355

ΕΥΕΛΠΙΔΗΣ.
Τί δὲ χύτρα νώ γ' ὠφελήσει;

ΠΕΙΣΘΕΤΑΙΡΟΣ.
Γλαῦξ μὲν οὐ πρόσεισι νῷν.

ΕΥΕΛΠΙΔΗΣ.
Τοῖς δὲ γαμψώνυξι τοισδί;

ΠΕΙΣΘΕΤΑΙΡΟΣ.
Τὸν ὀβελίσκον ἁρπάσας
Εἶτα κατάπηξον πρὸς αὑτόν.

ΕΥΕΛΠΙΔΗΣ.
Τοῖσι δ' ὀφθαλμοῖσι τί;

ΠΕΙΣΘΕΤΑΙΡΟΣ.
Ὀξύβαφον ἐντευθενὶ πρόσθου λαβὼν ἢ τρυβλίον.

ΕΥΕΛΠΙΔΗΣ.
Ὦ σοφώτατ', εὖ γ' ἀνεῦρες αὐτὸ καὶ στρατηγικῶς· 360
Ὑπερακοντίζεις σύ γ' ἤδη Νικίαν ταῖς μηχαναῖς.

ΧΟΡΟΣ.
Ἐλελελεῦ, χώρει, κάθες τὸ ῥύγχος· οὐ μένειν ἐχρῆν.
Ἕλκε, τίλλε, παῖε, δεῖρε, κόπτε πρώτην τὴν χύτραν.

ΕΠΟΨ.
Εἰπέ μοι τί μέλλετ', ὦ πάντων κάκιστα θηρίων,
Ἀπολέσαι, παθόντες οὐδέν, ἄνδρε καὶ διασπάσαι 365

Γῆς ἐμῆς γυναικὸς ὄντε ξυγγενῆ καὶ φυλέτα ;

ΧΟΡΟΣ.

Φεισόμεσθα γὰρ τί τῶνδε μᾶλλον ἡμεῖς ἢ λύκων ;
Ἢ τίνας τισαίμεθ' ἄλλους τῶνδ' ἂν ἐχθίους ἔτι ;

ΕΠΟΨ.

Εἰ δὲ τὴν φύσιν μὲν ἐχθροὶ, τὸν δὲ νοῦν εἰσιν φίλοι,
Καὶ διδάξοντές τι δεῦρ' ἥκουσιν ὑμᾶς χρήσιμον ; 370

ΧΟΡΟΣ.

Πῶς δ' ἂν οἷδ' ἡμᾶς τι χρήσιμον διδάξειάν ποτε,
Ἢ φράσειαν, ὄντες ἐχθροὶ τοῖσι πάπποις τοῖς ἐμοῖς ;

ΕΠΟΨ.

Ἀλλ' ἀπ' ἐχθρῶν δῆτα πολλὰ μανθάνουσιν οἱ σοφοί.
Ἡ γὰρ εὐλάβεια σώζει πάντα. Παρὰ μὲν οὖν φίλου
Οὐ μάθοις ἂν τοῦθ', ὁ δ' ἐχθρὸς εὐθὺς ἐξηνάγκασεν. 375
Αὐτίχ' αἱ πόλεις παρ' ἀνδρῶν γ' ἔμαθον ἐχθρῶν κοὐ
    φίλων
Ἐκπονεῖν θ' ὑψηλὰ τείχη ναῦς τε κεκτῆσθαι μακράς.
Τὸ δὲ μάθημα τοῦτο σώζει παῖδας, οἶκον, χρήματα.

ΧΟΡΟΣ.

Ἔστι μὲν λόγων ἀκοῦσαι πρῶτον, ὡς ἡμῖν δοκεῖ,
Χρήσιμον· μάθοι γὰρ ἄν τις κἀπὸ τῶν ἐχθρῶν σο-
    φόν. 380

ΠΕΙΣΘΕΤΑΙΡΟΣ.

Οἵδε τῆς ὀργῆς χαλᾶν εἴξασιν. Ἄναγ' ἐπὶ σκέλος.

ΕΠΟΨ.

Καὶ δίκαιόν γ' ἐστὶ, κἀμοὶ δεῖ νέμειν ὑμᾶς χάριν.

ΧΟΡΟΣ.

Ἀλλὰ μὴν οὐδ' ἄλλο σοί πω πρᾶγμ' ἐνηντιώμεθα.

ΠΕΙΣΘΕΤΑΙΡΟΣ.

Μᾶλλον εἰρήνην ἄγουσιν ἡμῖν· ὥστε τὴν χύτραν
Τώ τε τρυβλίω καθίει· 385
Καὶ τὸ δόρυ χρὴ, τὸν ὀβελίσκον,
Περιπατεῖν ἔχοντας ἡμᾶς
Τῶν ὅπλων ἐντὸς, παρ' αὐτὴν
Τὴν χύτραν ἄκραν ὁρῶντας
Ἐγγύς· ὡς οὐ φευκτέον νῷν. 390

ΕΥΕΛΠΙΔΗΣ.

Ἐτεὸν, ἢν δ' ἄρ' ἀποθάνωμεν,
Κατορυχησόμεσθα ποῦ γῆς ;

ΠΕΙΣΘΕΤΑΙΡΟΣ.

Ὁ Κεραμεικὸς δέξεται νώ.
Δημόσια γὰρ ἵνα ταφῶμεν,
Φήσομεν πρὸς τοὺς στρατηγοὺς 395
Μαχομένω τοῖς πολεμίοισιν
Ἀποθανεῖν ἐν Ὀρνεαῖς.

ΧΟΡΟΣ.

Ἄναγ' ἐς τάξιν πάλιν ἐς ταυτοὶ.
Καὶ τὸν θυμὸν κατάθου κύψας
Παρὰ τὴν ὀργὴν ὥσπερ ὁπλίτης· 400
Κἀναπυθώμεθα τούσδε, τίνες ποτὲ,
Καὶ πόθεν ἔμολον,
Ἐπὶ τίνα τ' ἐπίνοιαν.
Ἰὼ ἔποψ, σέ τοι καλῶ.

ΕΠΟΨ.

Καλεῖς δὲ τοῦ κλύειν θέλων ; 405

ΧΟΡΟΣ.
Τίνες ποθ' οἵδε καὶ πόθεν ;

ΕΠΟΨ.
Ξένω σοφῆς ἀφ' Ἑλλάδος.

ΧΟΡΟΣ.
Τύχη δὲ ποία κομί-
  ζει ποτ' αὐτὼ πρὸς ὄρ-
  νιθας ἐλθεῖν ;

ΕΠΟΨ.
  ῎Ερως   410
Βίου διαίτης τε καὶ
Σοῦ ξυνοικεῖν τέ σοι
Καὶ ξυνεῖναι τὸ πᾶν.

ΧΟΡΟΣ.
Τί φῄς ;
Λέγουσι δὲ δὴ τίνας λόγους ;   415

ΕΠΟΨ.
῎Απιστα καὶ πέρα κλύειν.

ΧΟΡΟΣ.
Ὁρᾷ τι κέρδος ἐνθάδ' ἄξιον μονῆς,
Ὅτῳ πέποιθέ μοι ξυνὼν
Κρατεῖν ἂν ἢ τὸν ἐχθρὸν ἢ
Φίλοισιν ὠφελεῖν ἔχειν ;   420

ΕΠΟΨ.
Λέγει μέγαν τιν' ὄλβον οὔ-
  τε λεκτὸν οὔτε πιστὸν, ὡς
Σὰ ταῦτα πάντα καὶ

Τὸ τῇδε καὶ τὸ κεῖσε, καὶ
Τὸ δεῦρο προσβιβᾷ λέγων.

ΧΟΡΟΣ.
Πότερα μαινόμενος;

ΕΠΟΨ.
Ἄφατον ὡς φρόνιμος.

ΧΟΡΟΣ.
Ἔνι σοφόν τι φρενί;

ΕΠΟΨ.
Πυκνότατον κίναδος,
Σόφισμα, κύρμα, τρίμμα, παιπάλημ' ὅλον.

ΧΟΡΟΣ.
Λέγειν λέγειν κέλευέ μοι.
Κλύων γὰρ ὧν σύ μοι λέγεις
Λόγων ἀνεπτέρωμαι.

ΕΠΟΨ.
Ἄγε δὴ σὺ καὶ σὺ τὴν πανοπλίαν μὲν πάλιν
Ταύτην λαβόντε κρεμάσατον τύχἀγαθῇ
Εἰς τὸν ἰπνὸν εἴσω, πλησίον τοὐπιστάτου·
Σὺ δὲ τούσδ' ἐφ' οἷσπερ τοῖς λόγοις συνέλεξ' ἐγώ,
Φράσον, δίδαξον.

ΠΕΙΣΘΕΤΑΙΡΟΣ.
Μὰ τὸν Ἀπόλλω 'γὼ μὲν οὔ,
Ἢν μὴ διάθωνταί γ' οἵδε διαθήκην ἐμοὶ
Ἥνπερ ὁ πίθηκος τῇ γυναικὶ διέθετο,
Ὁ μαχαιροποιός, μήτε δάκνειν τούτους ἐμὲ
Μήτ' ὀρχίπεδ' ἕλκειν μήτ' ὀρύττειν

ΧΟΡΟΣ.
Οὔ τί που
Τόν; Οὐδαμῶς.

ΠΕΙΣΘΕΤΑΙΡΟΣ.
Οὔκ, ἀλλὰ τὠφθαλμὼ λέγω.

ΧΟΡΟΣ.
Διατίθεμαι 'γώ.

ΠΕΙΣΘΕΤΑΙΡΟΣ.
Κατόμοσόν νυν ταῦτά μοι.

ΧΟΡΟΣ.
Ὄμνυμ' ἐπὶ τούτοις πᾶσι νικᾶν τοῖς κριταῖς   445
Καὶ τοῖς θεαταῖς πᾶσιν.

ΠΕΙΣΘΕΤΑΙΡΟΣ.
Ἔσται ταυταγί.

ΧΟΡΟΣ.
Εἰ δὲ παραβαίην, ἑνὶ κριτῇ νικᾶν μόνον.

ΚΗΡΥΞ.
Ἀκούετε λεῴ· τοὺς ὁπλίτας νυνμενὶ
Ἀνελομένους θὤπλ' ἀπιέναι πάλιν οἴκαδε,
Σκοπεῖν δ' ὅ τι ἂν προγράφωμεν ἐν τοῖς πινακίοις.   450

ΧΟΡΟΣ.
Στροφή.
Δολερὸν μὲν ἀεὶ κατὰ πάντα δὴ τρόπον
Πέφυκεν ἄνθρωπος· σὺ δ' ὅμως λέγε μοι.
Τάχα γὰρ τύχοις ἂν
Χρηστὸν ἐξειπὼν ὅ τι μοί παρορᾷς, ἢ
Δύναμίν τινα μείζω   455

ΟΡΝΙΘΕΣ.

Παραλειπομένην ὑπ' ἐμῆς φρενὸς ἀξυνέτου·
Σὺ δὲ τοῦθ' ὁρᾷς. Λέγ' εἰς κοινόν.
Ὁ γὰρ ἂν σὺ τύχῃς μοι
Ἀγαθὸν πορίσας, τοῦτο κοινὸν ἔσται.

Ἀλλ' ἐφ' ὅτῳπερ πράγματι τὴν σὴν ἥκεις γνωμην
ἀναπείσας,   460
Λέγε θαρρήσας· ὡς τὰς σπονδὰς οὐ μὴ πρότερον παραβῶμεν.

ΠΕΙΣΘΕΤΑΙΡΟΣ.
Καὶ μὴν ὀργῶ νὴ τὸν Δία καὶ προπεφύραται λόγος εἷς μοι,
Ὃν διαμάττειν οὐ κωλύει· φέρε παῖ στέφανον καταχεῖσθαι
Κατὰ χειρὸς ὕδωρ φερέτω ταχύ τις.

ΧΟΡΟΣ.
            Δειπνήσειν μέλλομεν, ἤ τι;

ΠΕΙΣΘΕΤΑΙΡΟΣ.
Μὰ Δί', ἀλλὰ λέγειν ζητῶ τι πάλαι μέγα καὶ λαρινὸν
ἔπος τι,   465
Ὅ τι τὴν τούτων θραύσει ψυχήν· οὕτως ὑμῶν ὑπεραλγῶ,
Οἵτινες ὄντες πρότερον βασιλῆς

ΧΟΡΟΣ.
            Ἡμεῖς βασιλῆς; Τίνος;

ΠΕΙΣΘΕΤΑΙΡΟΣ.
                        Ὑμεῖς

Πάντων ὁπόσ' ἔστιν, ἐμοῦ πρῶτον, τουδί, καὶ τοῦ Διὸς
αὐτοῦ,
Αρχαιότεροι πρότεροί τε Κρόνου καὶ Τιτάνων ἐγένεσθε
Καὶ γῆς.

ΧΟΡΟΣ.

Καὶ γῆς ;

ΠΕΙΣΘΕΤΑΙΡΟΣ.
Νὴ τὸν Ἀπόλλω.

ΧΟΡΟΣ.
Τουτὶ μὰ Δί' οὐκ ἐπεπύσμην. 470

ΠΕΙΣΘΕΤΑΙΡΟΣ.
Ἀμαθὴς γὰρ ἔφυς κοὐ πολυπράγμων, οὐδ' Αἴσωπον
πεπάτηκας,
Ὅς ἔφασκε λέγων κορυδὸν πάντων πρώτην ὄρνιθα
γενέσθαι,
Προτέραν τῆς γῆς, κἄπειτα νόσῳ τὸν πατέρ' αὐτῆς
ἀποθνήσκειν·
Γῆν δ' οὐκ εἶναι, τὸν δὲ προκεῖσθαι πεμπταῖον· τὴν δ'
ἀποροῦσαν
Ὑπ' ἀμηχανίας τὸν πατέρ' αὐτῆς ἐν τῇ κεφαλῇ κατορύξαι. 475

ΕΥΕΛΠΙΔΗΣ.
Ὁ πατὴρ ἄρα τῆς κορυδοῦ νυνὶ κεῖται τεθνεὼς Κεφα-
λῇσιν.

ΕΠΟΨ.
Οὔκουν δῆτ' εἰ πρότεροι μὲν γῆς, πρότεροι δὲ θεῶν
ἐγένοντο,

ΟΡΝΙΘΕΣ.

Ὡς πρεσβυτάτων αὐτῶν ὄντων ὀρθῶς ἔσθ᾽ ἡ βασιλεία;

ΕΥΕΛΠΙΔΗΣ.

Νὴ τὸν Ἀπόλλω · πάνυ τοίνυν χρὴ ῥύγχος βόσκειν σε
τὸ λοιπόν ·
ἀποδώσει ταχέως ὁ Ζεὺς τὸ σκῆπτρον τῷ δρυκολάπτῃ. 480

ΠΕΙΣΘΕΤΑΙΡΟΣ.

Ὡς οὐχὶ θεοὶ τοίνυν ἦρχον τῶν ἀνθρώπων τὸ παλαιόν,
Ἀλλ᾽ ὄρνιθες, κἀβασίλευον, πόλλ᾽ ἐστὶ τεκμήρια τούτων.
Αὐτίκα δ᾽ ὑμῖν πρῶτ᾽ ἐπιδείξω τὸν ἀλεκτρυόν᾽, ὡς ἐτυ-
ράννει
Ἦρχέ τε Περσῶν πρῶτον πάντων, Δαρείου καὶ Μεγα-
βάζου,
Ὥστε καλεῖται Περσικὸς ὄρνις ἀπὸ τῆς ἀρχῆς ἔτ᾽
ἐκείνης. 485

ΕΥΕΛΠΙΔΗΣ.

Διὰ ταῦτ᾽ ἄρ᾽ ἔχων καὶ νῦν ὥσπερ βασιλεὺς ὁ μέγας
διαβάσκει
Ἐπὶ τῆς κεφαλῆς τὴν κυρβασίαν τῶν ὀρνίθων μόνος
ὀρθήν.

ΠΕΙΣΘΕΤΑΙΡΟΣ.

Οὕτω δ᾽ ἴσχυέ τε καὶ μέγας ἦν τότε καὶ πολὺς, ὥστ᾽
ἔτι καὶ νῦν
Ὑπὸ τῆς ῥώμης τῆς τότ᾽ ἐκείνης, ὁπόταν μόνον ὄρθριον
ᾄσῃ,
Ἀναπηδῶσιν πάντες ἐπ᾽ ἔργον, χαλκῆς, κεραμῆς, σκυ-
λοδέψαι· 490

ΑΡΙΣΤΟΦΑΝΟΥΣ

Σκυτῆς, βαλανῆς, ἀλφιταμοιβοί, τορνευτολυρασπιδοπηγοί.
Οἱ δὲ βαδίζουσ᾽ ὑποδησάμενοι νύκτωρ.

ΕΥΕΛΠΙΔΗΣ.
Ἐμὲ τοῦτό γ᾽ ἐρώτα.
Χλαῖναν γὰρ ἀπώλεσ᾽ ὁ μοχθηρὸς Φρυγίων ἐρίων διὰ τοῦτον.
Ἐς δεκάτην γάρ ποτε παιδαρίου κληθεὶς ὑπέπινον ἐν ἄστει,
Κἄρτι καθεῦδον· καὶ πρὶν δειπνεῖν τοὺς ἄλλους, οὗτος ἄρ᾽ ᾖσε,   495
Κἀγὼ νομίσας ὄρθρον ἐχώρουν Ἁλιμουντάδε, κἄρτι προκύπτω
Ἔξω τείχους, καὶ λωποδύτης παίει ῥοπάλῳ με τὸ νῶτον·
Κἀγὼ πίπτω, μέλλω τε βοᾶν· ὁ δ᾽ ἀπέβλισε θοἰμάτιόν μου.

ΠΕΙΣΘΕΤΑΙΡΟΣ.
Ἰκτῖνος δ᾽ οὖν τῶν Ἑλλήνων ἦρχεν τότε κἀβασίλευε.

ΕΠΟΨ.
Τῶν Ἑλλήνων;

ΠΕΙΣΘΕΤΑΙΡΟΣ.
Καὶ κατέδειξέν γ᾽ οὗτος πρῶτος βασιλεύων   500
Προκυλινδεῖσθαι τοῖς ἰκτίνοις.

ΕΥΕΛΠΙΔΗΣ.
Νὴ τὸν Διόνυσον, ἐγὼ γοῦν
Ἐκυλινδούμην ἰκτῖνον ἰδών· κᾆθ᾽ ὕπτιος ὢν ἀναχάσκων

ΟΡΝΙΘΕΣ.

Οβολὸν κατεβρόχθισα· κᾶτα κενὸν τὸν θύλακον οἴκαδ' ἀφεῖλκον.

ΠΕΙΣΘΕΤΑΙΡΟΣ.

Αἰγύπτου δ' αὖ καὶ Φοινίκης πάσης κόκκυξ βασιλεὺς ἦν·
Χὠπόθ' ὁ κόκκυξ εἴποι κόκκυ, τότε γ' οἱ Φοίνικες
   ἅπαντες   505
Τοὺς πυροὺς ἂν καὶ τὰς κριθὰς ἐν τοῖς πεδίοις ἐθέριζον.

ΕΥΕΛΠΙΔΗΣ.

Τοῦτ' ἄρ' ἐκεῖν' ἦν τοὔπος ἀληθῶς· "κόκκυ, ψωλοὶ πεδίονδε."

ΠΕΙΣΘΕΤΑΙΡΟΣ.

Ἦρχον δ' οὕτω σφόδρα τὴν ἀρχήν, ὥστ' εἴ τις καὶ βασιλεύοι
Ἐν ταῖς πόλεσιν τῶν Ἑλλήνων, Ἀγαμέμνων ἢ Μενέλαος,
Ἐπὶ τῶν σκήπτρων ἐκάθητ' ὄρνις, μετέχων ὅ τι δωροδοκοίη. 510

ΕΥΕΛΠΙΔΗΣ.

Τουτὶ τοίνυν οὐκ ᾔδη 'γώ· καὶ δῆτά μ' ἐλάμβανε θαῦμα,
Ὁπότ' ἐξέλθοι Πρίαμός τις ἔχων ὄρνιν ἐν τοῖσι τραγῳδοῖς·
Ὁ δ' ἄρ' εἱστήκει τὸν Λυσικράτη τηρῶν ὅ τι δωροδοκοίη.

ΠΕΙΣΘΕΤΑΙΡΟΣ.

Ὃ δὲ δεινότατόν γ' ἐστὶν ἁπάντων, ὁ Ζεὺς γὰρ ὁ νῦν βασιλεύων
Ἀετὸν ὄρνιν ἕστηκεν ἔχων ἐπὶ τῆς κεφαλῆς, βασιλεὺς ὤν· 515

Ἡ δ' αὖ θυγάτηρ γλαῦχ', ὁ δ' Ἀπολλων ὥσπερ θεράπων ἱέρακα.

ΕΥΕΛΠΙΔΗΣ.

Νὴ τὴν Δήμητρ' εὖ ταῦτα λέγεις. Τίνος οὕνεκα ταῦτ
ἄρ' ἔχουσιν;

ΠΕΙΣΘΕΤΑΙΡΟΣ.

Ἵν' ὅταν θύων τις ἔπειτ' αὐτοῖς εἰς τὴν χεῖρ', ὡς νόμος
ἐστί,
Τὰ σπλάγχνα διδῷ, τοῦ Διὸς αὐτοὶ πρότεροι τὰ
σπλάγχνα λάβωσιν.
Ὤμνυ τ' οὐδεὶς τότ' ἂν ἀνθρώπων θεόν, ἀλλ' ὄρνιθας
ἅπαντες.   520
Λάμπων δ' ὄμνυσ' ἔτι καὶ νυνὶ τὸν χῆν', ὅταν ἐξα-
πατᾷ τι·
Οὕτως ὑμᾶς πάντες πρότερον μεγάλους ἁγίους τ' ἐνό-
μιζον,
Νῦν δ' ἀνδράποδ', ἠλιθίους, Μανᾶς.
Ὥσπερ δ' ἤδη τοὺς μαινομένους
Βάλλουσ' ὑμᾶς, κἀν τοῖς ἱεροῖς   525
Πᾶς τις ἐφ' ὑμῖν ὀρνιθευτὴς
Ἵστησι βρόχους, παγίδας, ῥάβδους,
Ἕρκη, νεφέλας, δίκτυα, πηκτάς·
Εἶτα λαβόντες πωλοῦσ' ἀθρόους·
Οἱ δ' ὠνοῦνται βλιμάζοντες·   530
Κοὐδ' οὖν, εἴπερ ταῦτα δοκεῖ δρᾶν,
Ὀπτήσαμενοι παρέθενθ' ὑμᾶς,
Ἀλλ' ἐπικνῶσιν τυρόν, ἔλαιον,

ΟΡΝΙΘΕΣ.

Σίλφιον, ὄξος, καὶ τρίψαντες
Κατάχυσμ᾽ ἕτερον γλυκὺ καὶ λιπαρόν, 535
Κᾆπειτα κατεσκέδασαν θερμὸν
Τοῦτο καθ᾽ ὑμῶν
Αὐτῶν ὥσπερ κενεβρείων.

ΧΟΡΟΣ.

Ἀντιστροφή.

Πολὺ δὴ πολὺ δὴ χαλεπωτάτους λόγους
Ἤνεγκας, ἄνθρωφ᾽· ὡς ἐδάκρυσά γ᾽ ἐμῶν 540
Πατέρων κάκην, οἳ
Τίσδε τὰς τιμὰς προγόνων παραδόντων,
Ἐπ᾽ ἐμοῦ κατέλυσαν.
Σὺ δέ μοι κατὰ δαίμονα καὶ κατὰ συντυχίαν
Ἀγαθὴν ἥκεις ἐμοὶ σωτήρ. 545
Ἀναθεὶς γὰρ ἐγώ σοι
Τά τε νοττία κἀμαυτὸν οἰκήσω.

Ἀλλ᾽ ὅ τι χρὴ δρᾶν, σὺ δίδασκε παρών· ὡς ζῆν οὐκ
ἄξιον ἡμῖν,
Εἰ μὴ κομιούμεθα παντὶ τρόπῳ τὴν ἡμετέραν βασιλείαν.

ΠΕΙΣΘΕΤΑΙΡΟΣ.

Καὶ δὴ τοίνυν πρῶτα διδάσκω μίαν ὀρνίθων πόλιν
εἶναι, 550
Κᾆπειτα τὸν ἀέρα πάντα κύκλῳ καὶ πᾶν τουτὶ τὸ
μεταξὺ
Περιτειχίζειν μεγάλαις πλίνθοις ὀπταῖς ὥσπερ Βαβυλῶνα.

ΕΠΟΨ.

Ὦ Κεβριόνα καὶ Πορφυρίων, ὡς σμερδαλεοι τὸ πόλισμα.

ΠΕΙΣΘΕΤΑΙΡΟΣ.

Κἄπειτ' ἢν τοῦτ' ἐπανεστήκῃ, τὴν ἀρχὴν τὸν Δί' απαιτεῖν·
Κἂν μὲν μὴ φῇ μηδ' ἐθελήσῃ μηδ' εὐθὺς γνωσιμαχήσῃ, 555
Ιεροὶ πόλεμον πρωυδᾶν αὐτῷ, καὶ τοῖσι θεοῖσιν ἀπειπεῖν
Διὰ τῆς χώρας τῆς ὑμετέρας ἐστυκόσι μὴ διαφοιτᾶν,
Ὥσπερ πρότερον μοιχεύσοντες τὰς Ἀλκμήνας κατέβαινον
Καὶ τὰς Ἀλόπας καὶ τὰς Σεμέλας· ἤνπερ δ' ἐπίωσ',
ἐπιβάλλειν
Σφραγῖδ' αὐτοῖς ἐπὶ τὴν ψωλὴν, ἵνα μὴ βινῶσ' ἔτ'
ἐκείνας. 560
Τοῖς δ' ἀνθρώποις ὄρνιν ἕτερον πέμψαι κήρυκα κελεύω,
Ὡς ὀρνίθων βασιλευόντων θύειν ὄρνισι τὸ λοιπόν·
Κἄπειτα θεοῖς ὕστερον αὖθις· προσνείμασθαι δὲ πρεπόντως
Τοῖσι θεοῖσιν τῶν ὀρνίθων ὃς ἂν ἁρμόζῃ καθ' ἕκαστον·
Ἢν Ἀφροδίτῃ θύῃ, πυροὺς ὄρνιθι φαληρίδι θύειν· 565
Ἢν δὲ Ποσειδῶνί τις οἶν θύῃ, νήττῃ πυροὺς καθαγίζειν·
Ἢν δ' Ἡρακλέει θύῃ τις βοῦν, λάρῳ ναστοὺς μέλι
τούττας·
Κἂν Διὶ θύῃ βασιλεῖ κριόν, βασιλεύς ἐστ' ὀρχίλος ὄρνις,

ΟΡΝΙΘΕΣ.

Ὧι προτέρῳ δεῖ τοῦ Διὸς αὐτοῦ σέρφον ἐνόρχην σφα-
γιάζειν.

ΕΥΕΛΠΙΔΗΣ.
Ἥσθην σέρφῳ σφαγιαζομένῳ. Βροντάτω νῦν ὁ μέγας
Ζάν. 570

ΕΠΟΨ.
Καὶ πῶς ἡμᾶς νομιοῦσι θεοὺς ἄνθρωποι κοὐχὶ κολοιους,
Οἳ πετόμεσθα πτέρυγάς τ᾽ ἔχομεν;

ΠΕΙΣΘΕΤΑΙΡΟΣ.
Ληρεῖς· καὶ νὴ Δί᾽ ὅ γ᾽ Ἑρμῆς
Πέτεται θεὸς ὢν πτέρυγάς τε φορεῖ κἄλλοι γε θεοὶ
πάνυ πολλοί.
Αὐτίκα Νίκη πέτεται πτερύγοιν χρυσαῖν, καὶ νὴ Δί᾽
Ἔρως γε·
Ἶριν δέ γ᾽ Ὅμηρος ἔφασκ᾽ ἰκέλην εἶναι τρήρωνι πε-
λείῃ. 575

ΕΠΟΨ.
Ὁ Ζεὺς δ᾽ ἡμῖν οὐ βροντήσας πέμπει πτερόεντα κεραυνόν;

ΠΕΙΣΘΕΤΑΙΡΟΣ.
Ἢν δ᾽ οὖν ὑμᾶς μὲν ὑπ᾽ ἀγνοίας εἶναι νομίσωσι τι
μηδέν,
Τούτους δὲ θεοὺς τοὺς ἐν Ὀλύμπῳ, τότε χρὴ στρουθῶ;
νέφος ἀρθὲν
Καὶ σπερμολόγων ἐκ τῶν ἀγρῶν τὸ σπέρμ᾽ αὐτῶν ἀνα-
κάψαι·
Κἄπειτ᾽ αὐτοῖς ἡ Δημήτηρ πυροὺς πεινῶσι μετρείτω. 580

ΕΥΕΛΠΙΔΗΣ.
Οὐκ ἐθελήσει μὰ Δί', ἀλλ' ὄψει προφάσεις αὐτὴν πα-
ρέχουσαν.

ΠΕΙΣΘΕΤΑΙΡΟΣ.
Οἱ δ' αὖ κόρακες τῶν ζευγαρίων, οἶσιν τὴν γῆν κατα-
ροῦσιν,
Καὶ τῶν προβάτων τοὺς ὀφθαλμοὺς ἐκκοψάντων ἐπὶ
πείρᾳ·
Εἶθ' ὅ γ' Ἀπόλλων ἰατρός γ' ὢν ἰάσθω· μισθοφορεῖ δέ.

ΕΥΕΛΠΙΔΗΣ.
Μή, πρίν γ' ἂν ἐγὼ τὼ βοιδαρίω τὠμὼ πρώτιστ' ἀπο-
δῶμαι.   585

ΠΕΙΣΘΕΤΑΙΡΟΣ.
Ἢν δ' ἡγῶνται σὲ θεόν, σὲ βίον, σὲ δὲ Γῆν, σὲ Κρόνον,
σὲ Ποσειδῶ,
Ἀγάθ' αὐτοῖσιν πάντα παρέσται.

ΕΠΟΨ.
Λέγε δή μοι τῶν ἀγαθῶν ἕν.

ΠΕΙΣΘΕΤΑΙΡΟΣ.
Πρῶτα μὲν αὐτῶν τὰς οἰνάνθας οἱ πάρνοπες οὐ κατέ-
δονται,
Ἀλλὰ γλαυκῶν λόχος εἰς αὐτοὺς καὶ κερχνῄδων ἐπι-
τρίψει.
Εἶθ' οἱ κνῖπες καὶ ψῆνες ἀεὶ τὰς συκᾶς οὐ κατέδον-
ται,   590
Ἀλλ' ἀναλέξει πάντας καθαρῶς αὐτοὺς ἀγέλη μία
κιχλῶν.

ΕΠΟΨ.
Πλουτεῖν δὲ πόθεν δώσομεν αὐτοῖς ; καὶ γὰρ τούτοι
σφόδρ' ἐρῶσι.

ΠΕΙΣΘΕΤΑΙΡΟΣ.
Τὰ μέταλλ' αὐτοῖς μαντευομένοις οὗτοι δώσουσι τὰ
χρηστὰ
Τάς τ' ἐμπορίας τὰς κερδαλέας πρὸς τὸν μάντιν κατε-
ροῦσιν,
Ὥστ' ἀπολεῖται τῶν ναυκλήρων οὐδείς.

ΕΠΟΨ.
Πῶς οὐκ ἀπολεῖται ; 595

ΠΕΙΣΘΕΤΑΙΡΟΣ.
Προερεῖ τις ἀεὶ τῶν ὀρνίθων μαντευομένῳ περὶ τοῦ
πλοῦ·
Νυνὶ μὴ πλεῖ, χειμὼν ἔσται· νυνὶ πλεῖ, κέρδος ἐπέσται.

ΕΥΕΛΠΙΔΗΣ.
Γαῦλον κτῶμαι καὶ ναυκληρῶ, κοὐκ ἂν μείναιμι παρ'
ὑμῖν.

ΠΕΙΣΘΕΤΑΙΡΟΣ.
Τοὺς θησαυρούς τ' αὐτοῖς δείξουσ' οὓς οἱ πρότερον κα-
τέθεντο
Τῶν ἀργυρίων· οὗτοι γὰρ ἴσασι· λέγουσι δέ τοι τάδε
πάντες, 600
Οὐδεὶς οἶδεν τὸν θησαυρὸν τὸν ἐμὸν πλὴν εἴ τις ἄρ'
ὄρνις.

ΕΥΕΛΠΙΔΗΣ.
Πωλῶ γαῦλον, κτῶμαι σμινύην, καὶ τὰς ὑδρίας ἀνο-
ρύττω.

ΕΠΟΨ.
Πῶς δ' ὑγίειαν δώσουσ' αὐτοῖς, οὖσαν παρ.. ~οῖσι θεοῖσιν;

ΠΕΙΣΘΕΤΑΙΡΟΣ.
Ἢν εὖ πράττωσ', οὐχ ὑγιεία μεγάλη τοῦτ' ἐστί; σάφ' ἴσθι,
Ὡς ἄνθρωπός γε κακῶς πράττων ἀτεχνῶς οὐδεὶς ὑγιαίνει. 605

ΕΠΟΨ.
Πῶς δ' εἰς γῆράς ποτ' ἀφίξονται; Καὶ γὰρ τοῦτ' ἔστ' ἐν Ὀλύμπῳ·
Ἢ παιδάρι' ὄντ' ἀποθνήσκειν δεῖ;

ΠΕΙΣΘΕΤΑΙΡΟΣ.
Μὰ Δί', ἀλλὰ τριακόσι' αὐτοῖς
Ἔτι προσθήσουσ' ὄρνιθες ἔτη.

ΕΠΟΨ.
Παρὰ τοῦ;

ΠΕΙΣΘΕΤΑΙΡΟΣ.
Παρὰ τοῦ; Παρ' ἑαυτῶν.
Οὐκ οἶσθ' ὅτι πέντ' ἀνδρῶν γενεὰς ζώει λακέρυζα κορώνη;

ΕΥΕΛΠΙΔΗΣ.
Ἀιβοῖ, ὡς πολλῷ κρείττους οὗτοι τοῦ Διὸς ἡμῖν βασιλεύειν. 610

ΠΕΙΣΘΕΤΑΙΡΟΣ.
Οὐ γὰρ πολλῷ; ....
Καὶ πρῶτα μὲν οὐχὶ νεὼς ἡμᾶς

ΟΡΝΙΘΕΣ. 47

Οἰκοδομεῖν δεῖ λιθίνους αὐτοῖς,
Οὐδὲ θυρῶσαι χρυσαῖσι θύραις,
Ἀλλ' ὑπὸ θάμνοις καὶ πρινιδίοις 615
Οἰκήσουσιν. Τοῖς δ' αὖ σεμνοῖς
Τῶν ὀρνίθων δένδρον ἐλαίας
Ὁ νεὼς ἔσται· κοὐκ εἰς Δελφοὺς
Οὐδ' εἰς Ἄμμων' ἐλθόντες ἐκεῖ
Θύσομεν, ἀλλ' ἐν ταῖσιν κομάροις 620
Καὶ τοῖς κοτίνοις στάντες ἔχοντες
Κριθάς, πυρούς, εὐξόμεθ' αὐτοῖς
Ἀνατείνοντες τὼ χεῖρ' ἀγαθῶν
Διδόναι τι μέρος· καὶ ταῦθ' ἡμῖν
Παραχρῆμ' ἔσται 625
Πυροὺς ὀλίγους προβαλοῦσιν.

ΧΟΡΟΣ.

Ὦ φίλτατ' ἐμοὶ πολὺ πρεσβυτῶν ἐξ ἐχθίστου μετα-
πίπτων,
Οὐκ ἔστιν ὅπως ἂν ἐγώ ποθ' ἑκὼν τῆς σῆς γνώμης ἔτ'
ἀφείμην.
Ἐπαυχήσας δὲ τοῖσι σοῖς λόγοις
Ἐπηπείλησα καὶ κατώμοσα, 530
Ἢν σὺ παρ' ἐμὲ θέμενος
Ὁμόφρονας λόγους δικαίους,
Ἀδόλοψ, ὁσίους,
Ἐπὶ θεοὺς ἴῃς,
Ἐμοὶ φρονῶν ξυνῳδά, μὴ 535
Πολὺν χρόνον θεοὺς ἔτι

Σκῆπτρα τἀμὰ τρίψειν.
Ἀλλ' ὅσα μὲν δεῖ ῥώμῃ πράττειν, ἐπὶ ταῦτα τεταξόμεθ'
ἡμεῖς·
Ὅσα δὲ γνώμῃ δεῖ βουλεύειν, ἐπὶ σοὶ τάδε πάντ' ἀνά-
κειται.

ΕΠΟΨ.

Καὶ μὴν μὰ τὸν Δί' οὐχὶ νυστάζειν γ' ἔτι   640
Ὥρα 'στὶν ἡμῖν οὐδὲ μελλονικιᾶν,
Ἀλλ' ὡς τάχιστα δεῖ τι δρᾶν· πρῶτον δέ τε
Εἰσέλθετ' εἰς νεοττιάν γε τὴν ἐμὴν
Καὶ τἀμὰ κάρφη καὶ τὰ παρόντα φρύγανα,
Καὶ τοὔνομ' ἡμῖν φράσατον.

ΠΕΙΣΘΕΤΑΙΡΟΣ.
                        Ἀλλὰ ῥᾴδιον.   645
Ἐμοὶ μὲν ὄνομα Πεισθέταιρος.

ΕΠΟΨ.
                Τῳδεδί ;

ΠΕΙΣΘΕΤΑΙΡΟΣ
Εὐελπίδης Κριῶθεν.

ΕΠΟΨ.
            Ἀλλὰ χαίρετον
Ἄμφω.

ΠΕΙΣΘΕΤΑΙΡΟΣ.
    Δεχόμεσθα.

ΕΠΟΨ.
    Δεῦρο τοίνυν εἴσιτον.

ΠΕΙΣΘΕΤΑΙΡΟΣ.
Ἴωμεν· εἰσηγοῦ σὺ λαβὼν ἡμᾶς.

ΟΡΝΙΘΕΣ.

ΕΠΟΨ.
῎Ιθι.

ΠΕΙΣΘΕΤΑΙΡΟΣ.
Ἀτὰρ τὸ δεῖνα·δεῦρ᾿ ἐπανάκρουσαι πάλιν. 650
Φέρ᾿ ἴδω, φράσον νῷν, πῶς ἐγώ τε χοὑτοσὶ
Ξυνεσόμεθ᾿ ὑμῖν πετομένοις οὐ πετομένῳ;

ΕΠΟΨ.
Καλῶς.

ΠΕΙΣΘΕΤΑΙΡΟΣ.
῞Ορα νυν ὡς ἐν Αἰσώπου λόγοις
Ἐστὶν λεγόμενον δή τι, τὴν ἀλώπεχ᾿, ὡς
Φλαύρως ἐκοινώνησεν ἀετῷ ποτέ. 655

ΕΠΟΨ.
Μηδὲν φοβηθῇς· ἔστι γάρ τι ῥίζιον,
῝Ο διατραγόντ᾿ ἔσεσθον ἐπτερωμένω.

ΠΕΙΣΘΕΤΑΙΡΟΣ.
Οὕτω μὲν εἰσίωμεν. ῎Αγε δή, Ξανθία
Καὶ Μανόδωρε, λαμβάνετε τὰ στρώματα.

ΧΟΡΟΣ.
Οὗτος, σε καλῶ σὲ καλῶ.

ΕΠΟΨ.
Τί καλεῖς;

ΧΟΡΟΣ.
Τούτους μὲν ἄγων μετὰ σαυτοῦ 660
Ἀρίστισον εὖ· τὴν δ᾿ ἡδυμελῆ ξύμφωνον ἀηδόνα Μούσαις
Κατάλειφ᾿ ἡμῖν δεῦρ᾿ ἐκβιβάσας, ἵνα παίσωμεν μετ᾿
ἐκείνης.

ΠΕΙΣΘΕΤΑΙΡΟΣ.
Ὦ τοῦτο μέντοι νὴ Δί᾽ αὐτοῖσιν πιθοῦ·
Ἐκβίβασον ἐκ τοῦ βουτόμου τοὐρνίθιον,
Ἐκβίβασον αὐτοῦ πρὸς θεῶν αὐτήν, ἵνα   665
Καὶ νὼ θεασώμεσθα τὴν ἀηδόνα.

ΕΠΟΨ.
Ἀλλ᾽ εἰ δοκεῖ σφῷν, ταῦτα χρὴ δρᾶν. Ἡ Πρόκνη
Ἔκβαινε, καὶ σαυτὴν ἐπιδείκνυ τοῖς ξένοις.

ΠΕΙΣΘΕΤΑΙΡΟΣ.
Ὦ Ζεῦ πολυτίμηθ᾽, ὡς καλὸν τοὐρνίθιον,
Ὡς δ᾽ ἁπαλόν, ὡς δὲ λευκόν.

ΕΥΕΛΠΙΔΗΣ.
                              Ἆρά γ᾽ οἶσθ᾽ ὅτι   670
Ἐγὼ διαμηρίζοιμ᾽ ἂν αὐτὴν ἡδέως ;

ΠΕΙΣΘΕΤΑΙΡΟΣ.
Ὅσον δ᾽ ἔχει τὸν χρυσόν, ὥσπερ παρθένος.

ΕΥΕΛΠΙΔΗΣ.
Ἐγὼ μὲν αὐτὴν καὶ φιλῆσαί μοι δοκῶ.

ΠΕΙΣΘΕΤΑΙΡΟΣ.
Ἀλλ᾽, ὦ κακόδαιμον, ῥύγχος ὀβελίσκοιν ἔχει.

ΕΥΕΛΠΙΔΗΣ.
Ἀλλ᾽ ὥσπερ ᾠὸν νὴ Δί᾽ ἀπολέψαντα χρὴ   675
Ἀπὸ τῆς κεφαλῆς τὸ λέμμα κᾆθ᾽ οὕτω φιλεῖν.

ΕΠΟΨ.
Ἴωμεν.

ΠΕΙΣΘΕΤΑΙΡΟΣ.
Ἡγοῦ δὴ σὺ νῷν τύχἀγαθῇ.

ΟΡΝΙΘΕΣ.

ΧΟΡΟΣ.

Ὦ φίλη, ὦ ξουθή,
Ὦ φίλτατον ὀρνέων,
Πάντων ξύννομε τῶν ἐμῶν
Ὕμνων ξύντροφ᾽ ἀηδοῖ,
Ἦλθες ἦλθες, ὤφθης,
Ἡδὺν φθόγγον ἐμοὶ φέρουσ᾽.
Ἀλλ᾽, ὦ καλλιβόαν κρέκουσ᾽
Αὐλὸν φθέγμασιν ἠρινοῖς,
Ἄρχου τῶν ἀναπαίστων.
Ἄγε δὴ φύσιν ἄνδρες ἀμαυρόβιοι, φύλλων γενεᾷ προσόμοιοι,
Ὀλιγοδρανέες, πλάσματα πηλοῦ, σκιοειδέα φῦλ᾽ ἀμενηνά,
Ἀπτῆνες ἐφημέριοι, ταλαοὶ βροτοί, ἀνέρες εἰκελόνειροι,
Πρόσχετε τὸν νοῦν τοῖς ἀθανάτοις ἡμῖν, τοῖς αἰὲν ἐοῦσι,
Τοῖς αἰθερίοις, τοῖσιν ἀγήρῳς, τοῖς ἄφθιτα μηδομένοισιν·
Ἵν᾽ ἀκούσαντες πάντα παρ᾽ ἡμῶν ὀρθῶς περὶ τῶν μετεώρων,
Φύσιν οἰωνῶν γένεσίν τε θεῶν ποταμῶν τ᾽ Ἐρέβους τε Χάους τε
Εἰδότες ὀρθῶς παρ᾽ ἐμοῦ Προδίκῳ κλάειν εἴπητε τὸ λοιπόν.
Χάος ἦν καὶ Νὺξ Ἔρεβός τε μέλαν πρῶτον καὶ Τάρταρος εὐρύς·
Γῆ δ᾽ οὐδ᾽ ἀὴρ οὐδ᾽ οὐρανὸς ἦν· Ἐρέβους δ᾽ ἐν ἀπείροσι κόλποις

Τίκτει πρώτιστον ὑπηνέμιον Νὺξ ἡ μελανόπτερος ᾠόν,
Ἐξ οὗ περιτελλομέναις ὥραις ἔβλαστεν Ἔρως ὁ ποθεινός,
Στίλβων νῶτον πτερύγοιν χρυσαῖν, εἰκὼς ἀνεμώκεσι δίναις.
Οὗτος δὲ Χάει πτερόεντι μιγεὶς νυχίῳ κατὰ Τάρταρον εὐρὺν   700
Ἐνεόττευσεν γένος ἡμέτερον, καὶ πρῶτον ἀνήγαγεν ἐς φῶς.
Πρότερον δ' οὐκ ἦν γένος ἀθανάτων, πρὶν Ἔρως ξυνέμιξεν ἅπαντα·
Ξυμμιγνυμένων δ' ἑτέρων ἑτέροις γένετ' οὐρανὸς ὠκεανός τε
Καὶ γῆ πάντων τε θεῶν μακάρων γένος ἄφθιτον. Ὧδε μέν ἐσμεν
Πολὺ πρεσβύτατοι πάντων μακάρων. Ἡμεῖς δ' ὡς ἐσμὲν Ἔρωτος   705
Πολλοῖς δῆλον· πετόμεσθά τε γὰρ καὶ τοῖσιν ἐρῶσι σύνεσμεν·
Πολλοὺς δὲ καλοὺς ἀπομωμοκότας παῖδας πρὸς τέρμασιν ὥρας
Διὰ τὴν ἰσχὺν τὴν ἡμετέραν διεμήρισαν ἄνδρες ἐρασταί,
Ὁ μὲν ὄρτυγα δούς, ὁ δὲ πορφυρίων', ὁ δὲ χῆν', ὁ δὲ Περσικὸν ὄρνιν.
Πάντα δὲ θνητοῖς ἐστὶν ἀφ' ἡμῶν τῶν ὀρνίθων τὰ μέγιστα.   710
Πρῶτα μὲν ὥρας φαίνομεν ἡμεῖς ἦρος, χειμῶνος, ὀπώρας·

Σπείρειν μέν, όταν γέρανος κρώζουσ' ἐς τὴν Λιβύην
μεταχωρῇ·
Καὶ πηδάλιον τότε ναυκλήρῳ φράζει κρεμάσαντι καθεύ-
δειν,
Εἶτα δ' Ὀρέστῃ χλαῖναν ὑφαίνειν, ἵνα μὴ ῥιγῶν ἀπο-
δύῃ.
Ἰκτῖνος δ' αὖ μετὰ ταῦτα φανεὶς ἑτέραν ὥραν ἀπο-
φαίνει, 715
Ἡνίκα πεκτεῖν ὥρα προβάτων πόκον ἠρινόν· εἶτα χε-
λιδών,
Ὅτε χρὴ χλαῖναν πωλεῖν ἤδη καὶ ληδάριόν τι πρίασθαι.
Ἐσμὲν δ' ὑμῖν Ἄμμων, Δελφοί, Δωδώνη, Φοῖβος Ἀπόλ-
λων.
Ἐλθόντες γὰρ πρῶτον ἐπ' ὄρνις, οὕτω πρὸς ἅπαντα
τρέπεσθε,
Πρός τ' ἐμπορίαν καὶ πρὸς βιότου κτῆσιν καὶ πρὸς
γάμον ἀνδρός· 720
Ὄρνιν τε νομίζετε πάνθ' ὅσαπερ περὶ μαντείας δια-
κρίνει·
Φήμη γ' ὑμῖν ὄρνις ἐστί, πταρμόν τ' ὄρνιθα καλεῖτε,
Ξύμβολον ὄρνιν, φωνὴν ὄρνιν, θεράποντ' ὄρνιν, ὄνον
ὄρνιν.
Ἆρ οὐ φανερῶς ἡμεῖς ὑμῖν ἐσμὲν μαντεῖος Ἀπόλλων;
Ἢν οὖν ἡμᾶς νομίσητε θεούς, 725
Ἕξετε χρῆσθαι μάντεσι Μούσαις,
Αὔραις, ὥραις, χειμῶνι, θέρει,
Μετρίῳ πνίγει· κοὐκ ἀποδράντες

Καθεδούμεθ' άνω σεμνυνόμενοι
Παρὰ ταῖς νεφέλαις ὥσπερ χὼ Ζεύς·   730
Ἀλλὰ παρόντες δώσομεν ὑμῖν,
Αὑτοῖς, παισίν, παίδων παισίν,
Πλουθυγιείαν,
Εὐδαιμονίαν, βίον, εἰρήνην,
Νεότητα, γέλωτα, χορούς, θαλίας,   735
Γάλα τ' ὀρνίθων.
Ὥστε παρέσται κοπιᾶν ὑμῖν
Ὑπὸ τῶν ἀγαθῶν·
Οὕτω πλουτήσετε πάντες.

Στροφή.

Μοῦσα λοχμαία,   740
Τιὸ τιὸ τιὸ τιὸ τιὸ τιὸ τιοτίγξ,
Ποικίλη, μεθ' ἧς ἐγὼ
Νάπαισι καὶ κορυφαῖς ἐν ὀρείαις,
Τιὸ τιὸ τιὸ τιοτίγξ,
Ἱζόμενος μελίας ἐπὶ φυλλοκόμου,   745
Τιὸ τιὸ τιὸ τιοτίγξ,
Δι' ἐμῆς γένυος ξουθῆς μελέων
Πανὶ νόμους ἱεροὺς ἀναφαίνω
Σεμνά τε μητρὶ χορεύματ' ὀρεία,
Τοτοτοτοτοτοτοτοτοτίγξ,   750
Ἔνθεν ὥσπερ ἡ μέλιττα
Φρύνιχος ἀμβροσίων μελέων ἀπεβόσκετο καρπόν, ἀεὶ
       φέ-
 ρων γλυκεῖαν ᾠδάν.

Γιο τιὸ τιὸ τιοτίγξ.
Εἰ μετ' ὀρνίθων τις ὑμῶν, ὦ θεαταί, βούλεται   755
Διαπλέκειν ζῶν ἡδέως τὸ λοιπόν, ὡς ἡμᾶς ἴτω.
Ὅσα γάρ ἐστιν ἐνθάδ' αἰσχρὰ τῷ νόμῳ κρατούμενα,
Ταῦτα πάντ' ἐστὶν παρ' ἡμῖν τοῖσιν ὄρνισιν καλά.
Εἰ γὰρ ἐνθάδ' ἐστὶν αἰσχρὸν τὸν πατέρα τύπτειν νόμῳ,
Τοῦτ' ἐκεῖ καλὸν παρ' ἡμῖν ἐστιν, ἤν τις τῷ πατρὶ   760
Προσδραμὼν εἴπῃ πατάξας, " αἶρε πλῆκτρον, εἰ μαχεῖ."
Εἰ δὲ τυγχάνει τις ὑμῶν δραπέτης ἐστιγμένος,
Ἀτταγᾶς οὗτος παρ' ἡμῖν ποικίλος κεκλήσεται.
Εἰ δὲ τυγχάνει τις ὢν Φρὺξ μηδὲν ἧττον Σπινθάρου,
Φρυγίλος ὄρνις ἐνθάδ' ἔσται, τοῦ Φιλήμονος γένους.   765
Εἰ δὲ δοῦλός ἐστι καὶ Κὰρ ὥσπερ Ἐξηκεστίδης,
Φυσάτω πάππους παρ' ἡμῖν, καὶ φανοῦνται φράτορες.
Εἰ δ' ὁ Πισίου προδοῦναι τοῖς ἀτίμοις τὰς πύλας
Βούλεται, πέρδιξ γενέσθω, τοῦ πατρὸς νεοττίον·
Ὡς παρ' ἡμῖν οὐδὲν αἰσχρόν ἐστιν ἐκπερδικίσαι.   770

Ἀντιστροφή.

Τοιάδε κύκνοι,
Τιὸ τιὸ τιὸ τιὸ τιὸ τιὸ τιοτίγξ,
Συμμιγῆ βοὴν ὁμοῦ
Πτεροῖς κρέκοντες ἴαχον Ἀπόλλω,
Τιὸ τιὸ τιὸ τιοτίγξ,   775
Ὄχθῳ ἐφεζόμενοι παρ' Ἕβρον ποταμόν,
Τιὸ τιὸ τιὸ τιοτίγξ,
Διὰ δ' αἰθέριον νέφος ἦλθε βοά·
Πτῆξε δὲ ποικίλα φῦλά τε θηρῶν,

Κύματά τ' ἔσβεσε νήνεμος αἴθρη, 780
Τοτοτοτοτοτοτοτοτίγξ·
Πᾶς δ' ἐπεκτύπησ' Ὄλυμπος·
Εἷλε δὲ θάμβος ἄνακτας· Ὀλυμπιάδες δὲ μέλος Χα-
      ριτες Μοῦ-
σαί τ' ἐπωλόλυξαν.
Τιὸ τιὸ τιὸ τιοτίγξ. 785
Οὐδέν ἐστ' ἄμεινον οὐδ' ἥδιον ἢ φῦσαι πτερά.
Αὐτίχ' ὑμῶν τῶν θεατῶν εἴ τις ἦν ὑπόπτερος,
Εἶτα πεινῶν τοῖς χοροῖσι τῶν τραγῳδῶν ἤχθετο,
Ἐκπτόμενος ἂν οὗτος ἠρίστησεν ἐλθὼν οἴκαδε,
Κᾆτ' ἂν ἐμπλησθεὶς ἐφ' ἡμᾶς αὖθις αὖ κατέπτατο. 790
Εἴ τε Πατροκλείδης τις ὑμῶν τυγχάνει χεζητιῶν,
Οὐκ ἂν ἐξίδισεν ἐς θοἰμάτιον, ἀλλ' ἀνέπτατο,
Κἀποπαρδὼν κἀναπνεύσας αὖθις αὖ κατέπτατο·
Εἴ τε μοιχεύων τις ὑμῶν ἐστιν ὅστις τυγχάνει,
Κᾆθ' ὁρᾷ τὸν ἄνδρα τῆς γυναικὸς ἐν βουλευτικῷ, 795
Οὗτος ἂν πάλιν παρ' ὑμῶν πτερυγίσας ἀνέπτατο,
Εἶτα βινήσας ἐκεῖθεν αὖθις αὖ καθέζετο.
Ἆρ' ὑπόπτερον γενέσθαι παντός ἐστιν ἄξιον;
Ὡς Διιτρέφης γε πυτιναῖα μόνον ἔχων πτερὰ
Ἡιρέθη φύλαρχος, εἶθ' ἵππαρχος, εἶτ' ἐξ οὐδενὸς 800
Μεγάλα πράττει, κἀστὶ νυνὶ ξουθὸς ἱππαλεκτρυών.

ΠΕΙΣΘΕΤΑΙΡΟΣ.

Ταυτὶ τοιαυτί· μὰ Δί' ἐγὼ μὲν πρᾶγμά πω
Γελοιότερον οὐκ εἶδον οὐδεπώποτε.

ΕΥΕΛΠΙΔΗΣ.

Ἐπὶ τῷ γελᾷς;

ΠΕΙΣΘΕΤΑΙΡΟΣ.
Ἐπὶ τοῖσι σοῖς ὠκυπτέροις.
Οἶσθ᾽ ᾧ μάλιστ᾽ ἔοικας ἐπτερωμένος; 805
Εἰς εὐτέλειαν χηνὶ συγγεγραμμένῳ.

ΕΥΕΛΠΙΔΗΣ.
Σὺ δὲ κοψίχῳ γε σκάφιον ἀποτετιλμένῳ.

ΠΕΙΣΘΕΤΑΙΡΟΣ.
Ταυτὶ μὲν ἠκάσμεσθα κατὰ τὸν Αἰσχύλον·
" Τάδ᾽ οὐχ ὑπ᾽ ἄλλων, ἀλλὰ τοῖς αὑτῶν πτεροῖς."

ΕΠΟΨ.
Ἄγε δὴ τί χρὴ δρᾶν;

ΠΕΙΣΘΕΤΑΙΡΟΣ.
Πρῶτον ὄνομα τῇ πόλει 810
Θέσθαι τι μέγα καὶ κλεινόν, εἶτα τοῖς θεοῖς
Θῦσαι μετὰ τοῦτο.

ΕΥΕΛΠΙΔΗΣ.
Ταῦτα κἀμοὶ συνδοκεῖ.

ΕΠΟΨ.
Φέρ᾽ ἴδω, τί δ᾽ ἡμῖν τοὔνομ᾽ ἔσται τῇ πόλει;

ΠΕΙΣΘΕΤΑΙΡΟΣ.
Βούλεσθε τὸ μέγα τοῦτο τοὐκ Λακεδαίμονος
Σπάρτην ὄνομα καλῶμεν αὐτήν;

ΕΥΕΛΠΙΔΗΣ.
Ἡράκλεις· 815
Σπάρτην γὰρ ἂν θείμην ἐγὼ τἠμῇ πόλει;

Οὐδ' ἂν χαμεύνῃ πάνυ γε κειρίαν γ' ἔχων.

ΠΕΙΣΘΕΤΑΙΡΟΣ.
Τί δῆτ' ὄνομ' αὐτῇ θησόμεσθ';

ΕΥΕΛΠΙΔΗΣ.
      Ἐντευθενὶ
Ἐκ τῶν νεφελῶν καὶ τῶν μετεώρων χωρίων
Χαῦνόν τι πάνυ.

ΠΕΙΣΘΕΤΑΙΡΟΣ.
   Βούλει Νεφελοκοκκυγίαν;   820

ΕΠΟΨ.
Ἰοὺ ἰού·
Καλὸν γὰρ ἀτεχνῶς καὶ μέγ' εὗρες τοὔνομα.

ΕΥΕΛΠΙΔΗΣ.
Ἆρ' ἐστὶν αὑτηγὶ Νεφελοκοκκυγία,
Ἵνα καὶ τὰ Θεογένους τὰ πολλὰ χρήματα
Τά τ' Αἰσχίνου γ' ἅπαντα;

ΠΕΙΣΘΕΤΑΙΡΟΣ.
     Καὶ λῷστον μὲν οὖν   825
Τὸ Φλέγρας πεδίον, ἵν' οἱ θεοὶ τοὺς Γηγενεῖς
Ἀλαζονευόμενοι καθυπερηκόντισαν.

ΕΥΕΛΠΙΔΗΣ.
Λιπαρὸν τὸ χρῆμα τῆς πόλεως. Τίς δαὶ θεὸς
Πολιοῦχος ἔσται; τῷ ξανοῦμεν τὸν πέπλον;

ΠΕΙΣΘΕΤΑΙΡΟΣ.
Τί δ' οὐκ Ἀθηναίαν ἐῶμεν πολιάδα;   830

ΕΥΕΛΠΙΔΗΣ.
Καὶ πῶς ἂν ἔτι γένοιτ' ἂν εὔτακτος πόλις,

Ὅπου θεός, γυνὴ γεγονυῖα, πανοπλίαν
Ἔστηκ' ἔχουσα, Κλεισθένης δὲ κερκίδα;

ΠΕΙΣΘΕΤΑΙΡΟΣ.
Τίς δαὶ καθέξει τῆς πόλεως τὸ Πελαργικόν;

ΕΠΟΨ.
Ὄρνις ἀφ' ἡμῶν τοῦ γένους τοῦ Περσικοῦ, 835
Ὅσπερ λέγεται δεινότατος εἶναι πανταχοῦ
Ἄρεως νεοττός.

ΕΥΕΛΠΙΔΗΣ.
Ὦ νεοττὲ δέσποτα·
Ὡς δ' ὁ θεὸς ἐπιτήδειος οἰκεῖν ἐπὶ πετρῶν.

ΠΕΙΣΘΕΤΑΙΡΟΣ.
Ἄγε νυν, σὺ μὲν βάδιζε πρὸς τὸν ἀέρα,
Καὶ τοῖσι τειχίζουσι παραδιακόνει, 840
Χάλικας παραφόρει, πηλὸν ἀποδὺς ὄργασον,
Λεκάνην ἀνένεγκε, κατάπεσ' ἀπὸ τῆς κλίμακος,
Φύλακας καταστῆσαι, τὸ πῦρ ἔγκρυπτ' ἀεί,
Κωδωνοφορῶν περίτρεχε, καὶ κάθευδ' ἐκεῖ·
Κήρυκα δὲ πέμψον τὸν μὲν εἰς θεοὺς ἄνω, 845
Ἕτερον δ' ἄνωθεν αὖ παρ' ἀνθρώπους κάτω,
Κἀκεῖθεν αὖθις παρ' ἐμέ.

ΕΥΕΛΠΙΔΗΣ.
   Σὺ δέ γ' αὐτοῦ μένων
Οἴμωζε παρ' ἔμ'.

ΠΕΙΣΘΕΤΑΙΡΟΣ.
  Ἴθ', ὠγάθ', οἷ πέμπω σ' ἐγώ.

Οὐδὲν γὰρ ἄνευ σοῦ τῶνδ᾽ ἃ λέγω πεπράξεται.
Ἐγὼ δ᾽ ἵνα θύσω τοῖσι καινοῖσιν θεοῖς, 850
Τὸν ἱερέα πέμψοντα τὴν πομπὴν καλῶ.
Παῖ παῖ, τὸ κανοῦν αἴρεσθε καὶ τὴν χέρνιβα.

ΧΟΡΟΣ.

Στροφή.

Ὁμορροθῶ, συνθέλω,
Συμπαραινέσας ἔχω
Προσόδια μεγάλα 855
Σεμνὰ προσιέναι θεοῖσιν·
Ἅμα δὲ προσέτι χάριτος ἕνεκα
Προβάτιόν τι θύειν.
Ἴτω ἴτω, ἴτω δὲ Πυθιὰς βοά·
Συνᾳδέτω δὲ Χαῖρις ᾠδάν. 860

ΠΕΙΣΘΕΤΑΙΡΟΣ.

Παῦσαι σὺ φυσῶν. Ἡράκλεις, τουτὶ τί ἦν;
Τουτὶ μὰ Δί᾽ ἐγὼ πολλὰ δὴ καὶ δείν᾽ ἰδών,
Οὔπω κόρακ᾽ εἶδον ἐμπεφορβιωμένον.
Ἱερεῦ, σὸν ἔργον, θῦε τοῖς καινοῖς θεοῖς.

ΙΕΡΕΥΣ.

Δράσω τάδ᾽· ἀλλὰ ποῦ 'στιν ὁ τὸ κανοῦν ἔχων; 865
εὔχεσθε τῇ Ἑστίᾳ τῇ ὀρνιθείῳ, καὶ τῷ ἰκτίνῳ τῷ
ἑστιούχῳ, καὶ ὄρνισιν Ὀλυμπίοις καὶ Ὀλυμπίῃσι
πᾶσι καὶ πάσῃσιν,

ΠΕΙΣΘΕΤΑΙΡΟΣ.

Ὦ Σουνιέρακε, χαῖρ᾽ ἄναξ Πελαργικέ.

ΟΡΝΙΘΕΣ.

ΙΕΡΕΥΣ.
Καὶ κύκνῳ Πυθίῳ καὶ Δηλίῳ, καὶ Λητοῖ Ὀρτυ- 870
γομήτρᾳ, καὶ Ἀρτέμιδι Ἀκαλανθίδι,

ΠΕΙΣΘΕΤΑΙΡΟΣ.
Οὐκέτι Κολαινίς, ἀλλ᾽ Ἀκαλανθὶς Ἄρτεμις.

ΙΕΡΕΥΣ.
Καὶ φρυγίλῳ Σαβαζίῳ, καὶ στρουθῷ μεγάλῃ
μητρὶ θεῶν καὶ ἀνθρώπων,

ΠΕΙΣΘΕΤΑΙΡΟΣ.
Δέσποινα Κυβέλη, στρουθέ, μῆτερ Κλεοκρίτου. 875

ΙΕΡΕΥΣ.
Διδόναι Νεφελοκοκκυγιεῦσιν ὑγίειαν καὶ σωτη-
ρίαν, αὐτοῖσι καὶ Χίοισι,

ΠΕΙΣΘΕΤΑΙΡΟΣ.
Χίοισιν ἥσθην πανταχοῦ προσκειμένοις.

ΙΕΡΕΥΣ.
Καὶ ἥρωσι [καὶ ὄρνισι] καὶ ἡρώων παισί, πορφυρίωνι, καὶ πελεκᾶντι, καὶ πελεκίνῳ, καὶ φλέξι- 880
δι, καὶ τέτρακι, καὶ ταῶνι, καὶ ἐλεᾷ, καὶ βάσκᾳ,
καὶ ἐλασᾷ, καὶ ἐρωδιῷ, καὶ καταράκτῃ, καὶ μελαγκορύφῳ, καὶ αἰγιθάλλῳ·

ΠΕΙΣΘΕΤΑΙΡΟΣ.
Παῦ᾽ ἐς κόρακας· παῦσαι καλῶν ἰοὺ ἰού.
Ἐπὶ ποῖον, ὦ κακόδαιμον, ἱερεῖον καλεῖς 885
Ἁλιαέτους καὶ γῦπας;   Οὐχ ὁρᾷς ὅτι
Ἰκτῖνος εἷς ἂν τουτό γ᾽ οἴχοιθ᾽ ἁρπάσας;
Ἄπελθ᾽ ἀφ᾽ ἡμῶν καὶ σὺ καὶ τὰ στέμματα·

ΑΡΙΣΤΟΦΑΝΟΥΣ

Ἐγὼ γὰρ αὐτὸς τουτογὶ θύσω μόνος.

ΙΕΡΕΥΣ.

Ἀντιστροφή.

Εἶτ' αὖθις αὖ τἄρα σοι
Δεῖ με δεύτερον μέλος
Χέρνιβι θεοσεβὲς
Ὅσιον ἐπιβοᾶν, καλεῖν δὲ
Μάκαρας, ἕνα τινὰ μόνον, εἴπερ
Ἱκανὸν ἕξετ' ὄψον.
Τὰ γὰρ παρόντα θύματ' οὐδὲν ἄλλο πλὴν
Γένειόν ἐστι καὶ κέρατα.

ΠΕΙΣΘΕΤΑΙΡΟΣ.

Θύοντες εὐξώμεσθα τοῖς πτερίνοις θεοῖς.

ΠΟΙΗΤΗΣ.

Νεφελοκοκκυγίαν τὰν εὐδαίμονα
Κλῇσον, ὦ Μοῦσα,
Τεαῖς ἐν ὕμνων ἀοιδαῖς.

ΠΕΙΣΘΕΤΑΙΡΟΣ.

Τουτὶ τὸ πρᾶγμα ποδαπόν ; Εἰπέ μοι, τίς εἶ ;

ΠΟΙΗΤΗΣ.

Ἐγὼ μελιγλώσσων ἐπέων ἱεὶς ἀοιδάν,
Μουσάων θεράπων ὀτρηρός,
Κατὰ τὸν Ὅμηρον.

ΠΕΙΣΘΕΤΑΙΡΟΣ.

Ἔπειτα δῆτα δοῦλος ὢν κόμην ἔχεις ;

ΠΟΙΗΤΗΣ.

Οὔκ, ἀλλὰ πάντες ἐσμὲν οἱ διδάσκαλοι

ΟΡΝΙΘΕΣ.

Μουσάων θεράποντες ὀτρηροί,
Κατὰ τὸν Ὅμηρον.

ΠΕΙΣΘΕΤΑΙΡΟΣ.
Οὐκ ἔτος ὀτρηρὸν καὶ τὸ ληδάριον ἔχεις.
Ἀτὰρ, ὦ ποιητά, κατὰ τί δεῦρ᾽ ἀνεφθάρης ;

ΠΟΙΗΤΗΣ.
Μέλη πεποίηκ᾽ ἐς τὰς Νεφελοκοκκυγίας
Τὰς ὑμετέρας κύκλιά τε πολλὰ καὶ καλά,
Καὶ παρθένεια, καὶ κατὰ τὰ Σιμωνίδου.

ΠΕΙΣΘΕΤΑΙΡΟΣ.
Ταυτὶ σὺ πότ᾽ ἐποίησας ἀπὸ ποίου χρόνου ;

ΠΟΙΗΤΗΣ.
Πάλαι πάλαι δὴ τήνδ᾽ ἐγὼ κλῄζω πόλιν.

ΠΕΙΣΘΕΤΑΙΡΟΣ.
Οὐκ ἄρτι θύω τὴν δεκάτην ταύτης ἐγώ,
Καὶ τοὔνομ᾽ ὥσπερ παιδίῳ νῦν δὴ ᾽θέμην ;

ΠΟΙΗΤΗΣ.
Ἀλλά τις ὠκεῖα Μουσάων φάτις
Οἷάπερ ἵππων ἀμαρυγά.
Σὺ δὲ πάτερ κτίστορ Αἴτνας,
Ζαθέων ἱερῶν ὁμώνυμε,
Δὸς ἐμὶν ὅ τι περ
Τεᾷ κεφαλᾷ θέλεις
Πρόφρων δόμεν ἐμὶν τεΐν.

ΠΕΙΣΘΕΤΑΙΡΟΣ.
Τουτὶ παρέξει τὸ κακὸν ἡμῖν πράγματα,
Εἰ μή τι τούτῳ δόντες ἀποφευξούμεθα.

Οὗτος, σὺ μέντοι σπολάδα καὶ χιτῶν' ἔχεις,
Ἀπόδυθι καὶ δὸς τῷ ποιητῇ τῷ σοφῷ.
Ἔχε τὴν σπολάδα· πάντως δέ μοι ῥιγῶν δοκεῖς.   930

ΠΟΙΗΤΗΣ.
Τόδε μὲν οὐκ ἀέκουσα φίλα
Μοῦσα τόδε δῶρον δέχεται·
Τὺ δὲ τεᾷ φρενὶ μάθε
Πινδάρειον ἔπος·

ΠΕΙΣΘΕΤΑΙΡΟΣ.
Ἄνθρωπος ἡμῶν οὐκ ἀπαλλαχθήσεται.   935

ΠΟΙΗΤΗΣ.
Νομάδεσσι γὰρ ἐν Σκύθαις
Ἀλᾶται Στράτων,
Ὃς ὑφαντοδόνητον ἔσθος οὐ πέπαται·
Ἀκλεὴς δ' ἔβα σπολὰς ἄνευ χιτῶνος.
Ξύνες ὅ τοι λέγω.   940

ΠΕΙΣΘΕΤΑΙΡΟΣ.
Ξυνίημ' ὅτι βούλει τὸν χιτωνίσκον λαβεῖν.
Ἀπόδυθι· δεῖ γὰρ τὸν ποιητὴν ὠφελεῖν.
Ἄπελθε τουτονὶ λαβών.

ΠΟΙΗΤΗΣ.
                Ἀπέρχομαι,
Κἀς τὴν πόλιν γ' ἐλθὼν ποιήσω δὴ ταδί·
Κλῇσον, ὦ χρυσόθρονε, τὰν   945
Τρομεράν, κρυεράν·
Νιφόβολα πεδία πολύσπορά τ'
Ἤλυθον· ἀλαλάν.

ΠΕΙΣΘΕΤΑΙΡΟΣ.
Νὴ τὸν Δί', ἀλλ' ἤδη πέφευγας ταυταγὶ
Τὰ κρυερὰ τονδὶ τὸν χιτωνίσκον λαβών.   950
Τουτὶ μὰ Δί' ἐγὼ τὸ κακὸν οὐδέποτ' ἤλπισα,
Οὕτω ταχέως τοῦτον πεπύσθαι τὴν πόλιν.
Αὖθις σὺ περιχώρει λαβὼν τὴν χέρνιβα.

ΙΕΡΕΥΣ.
Εὐφημία 'στω.

ΧΡΗΣΜΟΛΟΓΟΣ.
Μὴ κατάρξῃ τοῦ τράγου.

ΠΕΙΣΘΕΤΑΙΡΟΣ.
Σὺ δ' εἶ τίς;

ΧΡΗΣΜΟΛΟΓΟΣ.
Ὅστις; Χρησμολόγος.

ΠΕΙΣΘΕΤΑΙΡΟΣ.
Οἴμωζέ νυν.   955

ΧΡΗΣΜΟΛΟΓΟΣ.
Ὦ δαιμόνιε, τὰ θεῖα μὴ φαύλως φέρε·
Ὡς ἔστι Βάκιδος χρησμὸς ἄντικρυς λέγων
Ἐς τὰς Νεφελοκοκκυγίας.

ΠΕΙΣΘΕΤΑΙΡΟΣ.
Κἄπειτα πῶς
Ταῦτ' οὐκ ἐχρησμολόγεις σὺ πρὶν ἐμὲ τὴν πόλιν
Τήνδ' οἰκίσαι;

ΧΡΗΣΜΟΛΟΓΟΣ.
Τὸ θεῖον ἐνεπόδιζέ με.   960

ΠΕΙΣΘΕΤΑΙΡΟΣ.
Ἀλλ' οὐδὲν οἷόν ἐστ' ἀκοῦσαι τῶν ἐπῶν.

ΧΡΗΣΜΟΛΟΓΟΣ.
Ἀλλ' ὅταν οἰκήσωσι λύκοι πολιαί τε κορῶναι
Ἐν ταὐτῷ τὸ μεταξὺ Κορίνθου καὶ Σικυῶνος,

ΠΕΙΣΘΕΤΑΙΡΟΣ.
Τί οὖν προσήκει δῆτ' ἐμοὶ Κορινθίων ;

ΧΡΗΣΜΟΛΟΓΟΣ.
Ἠνίξαθ' ὁ Βάκις τοῦτο πρὸς τὸν ἀέρα. 965
Πρῶτον Πανδώρᾳ θῦσαι λευκότριχα κριόν·
Ὃς δέ κ' ἐμῶν ἐπέων ἔλθῃ πρώτιστα προφήτης,
Τῷ δόμεν ἱμάτιον καθαρὸν καὶ καινὰ πέδιλα,

ΠΕΙΣΘΕΤΑΙΡΟΣ.
Ἔνεστι καὶ τὰ πέδιλα ;

ΧΡΗΣΜΟΛΟΓΟΣ.
Λαβὲ τὸ βιβλίον.
Καὶ φιάλην δοῦναι, καὶ σπλάγχνων χεῖρ' ἐπιπλῆσαι. 970

ΠΕΙΣΘΕΤΑΙΡΟΣ.
Καὶ σπλάγχνα διδόν' ἔνεστι ;

ΧΡΗΣΜΟΛΟΓΟΣ.
Λαβὲ τὸ βιβλίον.
Κἂν μὲν, θέσπιε κοῦρε, ποιῇς ταῦθ' ὡς ἐπιτέλλω,
Αἰετὸς ἐν νεφέλῃσι γενήσεαι· αἰ δέ κε μὴ δῷς,
Οὐκ ἔσει οὐ τρυγὼν οὐδ' αἰετός, οὐ δρυκολάπτης.

ΠΕΙΣΘΕΤΑΙΡΟΣ
Καὶ ταῦτ' ἔνεστ' ἐνταῦθα;

ΟΡΝΙΘΕΣ.

ΧΡΗΣΜΟΛΟΓΟΣ.
    Λαβὲ τὸ βιβλίον.   975

ΠΕΙΣΘΕΤΑΙΡΟΣ.
Οὐδὲν ἄρ' ὅμοιώς ἐσθ' ὁ χρησμὸς τουτῳί,
"Ὃν ἐγὼ παρὰ τἀπόλλωνος ἐξεγραψάμην·
Αὐτὰρ ἐπὴν ἄκλητος ἰὼν ἄνθρωπος ἀλαζὼν
Λυπῇ θύοντας καὶ σπλαγχνεύειν ἐπιθυμῇ,
Δὴ τότε χρὴ τύπτειν αὐτὸν πλευρῶν τὸ μεταξύ,   980

ΧΡΗΣΜΟΛΟΓΟΣ.
Οὐδὲν λεγειν οἶμαί σε.

ΠΕΙΣΘΕΤΑΙΡΟΣ.
    Λαβὲ τὸ βιβλίον.
Καὶ φείδου μηδὲν μηδ' αἰετοῦ ἐν νεφέλῃσι,
Μήτ' ἢν Λάμπων ᾖ μήτ' ἢν ὁ μέγας Διοπείθης.

ΧΡΗΣΜΟΛΟΓΟΣ.
Καὶ ταῦτ' ἔνεστ' ἐνταῦθα;

ΠΕΙΣΘΕΤΑΙΡΟΣ.
    Λαβὲ τὸ βιβλίον.
Οὐκ εἶ θύραζ' ἐς κόρακας;

ΧΡΗΣΜΟΛΟΓΟΣ.
    Οἴμοι δείλαιος.   985

ΠΕΙΣΘΕΤΑΙΡΟΣ.
Οὔκουν ἑτέρωσε χρησμολογήσεις ἐκτρέχων;

ΜΕΤΩΝ.
Ἥκω παρ' ὑμᾶς

ΠΕΙΣΘΕΤΑΙΡΟΣ.
Ἕτερον αὖ τουτὶ κακόν.

Τί δ' αὖ σὺ δράσων; τίς δ' ἰδέα βουλήματος;
Τίς ἡ 'πίνοια τίς ὁ κόθορνος τῆς ὁδοῦ;

ΜΕΤΩΝ.

Γεωμετρῆσαι βούλομαι τὸν ἀέρα 990
Ὑμῖν, διελεῖν τε κατὰ γύας.

ΠΕΙΣΘΕΤΑΙΡΟΣ.
      Πρὸς τῶν θεῶν,
Σὺ δ' εἶ τίς ἀνδρῶν;

ΜΕΤΩΝ.
    Ὅστις εἴμ' ἐγώ; Μέτων,
Ὃν οἶδεν Ἑλλὰς χὠ Κολωνός.

ΠΕΙΣΘΕΤΑΙΡΟΣ.
       Εἰπέ μοι,
Ταυτὶ δέ σοι τί ἔστι;

ΜΕΤΩΝ.
    Κανόνες ἀέρος.
Αὐτίκα γὰρ ἀήρ ἐστι τὴν ἰδέαν ὅλος 995
Κατὰ πνιγέα μάλιστα. Προσθεὶς οὖν ἐγὼ
Τὸν κανόν', ἄνωθεν τουτονὶ τὸν καμπύλον
Ἐνθεὶς διαβήτην — μανθάνεις;

ΠΕΙΣΘΕΤΑΙΡΟΣ.
      Οὐ μανθάνω.

ΜΕΤΩΝ.
Ὀρθῷ μετρήσω κανόνι προστιθείς, ἵνα
Ὁ κύκλος γένηταί σοι τετράγωνος, κἀν μέσῳ 1000
Ἀγορά, φέρουσαι δ' ὦσιν εἰς αὐτὴν ὁδοὶ
Ὀρθαὶ πρὸς αὐτὸ τὸ μέσον, ὥσπερ δ' ἀστέρος,

ΟΡΝΙΘΕΣ. 69

Αὐτοῦ κυκλοτεροῦς ὄντος ὀρθαὶ πανταχῆ
Ἀκτῖνες ἀπολάμπωσιν.

ΠΕΙΣΘΕΤΑΙΡΟΣ.
Ἄνθρωπος Θαλῆς.
Μέτων,

ΜΕΤΩΝ.
Τί ἔστιν;

ΠΕΙΣΘΕΤΑΙΡΟΣ.
Οἶσθ' ὁτιὴ φιλῶ σ' ἐγώ; 1005
Κἀμοὶ πιθόμενος ὑπαποκίνει τῆς ὁδοῦ.

ΜΕΤΩΝ.
Τί δ' ἐστι δεινόν;

ΠΕΙΣΘΕΤΑΙΡΟΣ.
Ὥσπερ ἐν Λακεδαίμονι
Ξενηλατοῦνται καὶ κεκίνηνταί τινες
Πληγαὶ συχναὶ κατ' ἄστυ.

ΜΕΤΩΝ.
Μῶν στασιάζετε;

ΠΕΙΣΘΕΤΑΙΡΟΣ.
Μὰ τὸν Δί' οὐ δῆτ'.

ΜΕΤΩΝ.
Ἀλλὰ πῶς;

ΠΕΙΣΘΕΤΑΙΡΟΣ.
Ὁμοθυμαδὸν 1010
Σποδεῖν ἅπαντας τοὺς ἀλαζόνας δοκεῖ.

ΜΕΤΩΝ.
Ὑπάγοιμί τἄρ' ἄν.

ΠΕΙΣΘΕΤΑΙΡΟΣ.
     Νὴ Δί', ὡς οὐκ οἶδ' ἄρ' εἰ
Φθαίης ἄν· ἐπίκεινται γὰρ ἐγγὺς αὐταί.

            ΜΕΤΩΝ.
Οἴμοι κακοδαίμων.

        ΠΕΙΣΘΕΤΑΙΡΟΣ.
              Οὐκ ἔλεγον ἐγὼ πάλαι ;
Οὐκ ἀναμετρήσεις σαυτὸν ἀπιὼν ἀλλαχῇ ;   1015

            ΕΠΙΣΚΟΠΟΣ.
Ποῦ πρόξενοι ;

        ΠΕΙΣΘΕΤΑΙΡΟΣ.
           Τίς ὁ Σαρδανάπαλλος οὑτοσί ;

            ΕΠΙΣΚΟΠΟΣ.
Ἐπίσκοπος ἥκω δεῦρο τῷ κυάμῳ λαχὼν
Ἐς τὰς Νεφελοκοκκυγίας.

        ΠΕΙΣΘΕΤΑΙΡΟΣ.
                   Ἐπίσκοπος ;
Ἔπεμψε δὲ τίς σε δεῦρο ;

            ΕΠΙΣΚΟΠΟΣ.
                  Φαῦλον βιβλίον
Τελέου.

        ΠΕΙΣΘΕΤΑΙΡΟΣ.
        Τί ; βούλει δῆτα τὸν μισθὸν λαβὼν   1020
Μὴ πράγματ' ἔχειν, ἀλλ' ἀπιέναι ;

            ΕΠΙΣΚΟΠΟΣ.
                       Νὴ τοὺς θεούς.
Ἐκκλησιάσαι δ' οὖν ἐδεόμην οἴκοι μένων.

ΟΡΝΙΘΕΣ. 71

Ἔστιν γὰρ ἃ δι' ἐμοῦ πέπρακται Φαρνάκῃ.

ΠΕΙΣΘΕΤΑΙΡΟΣ.
Ἄπιθι λαβών· ἔστιν δ' ὁ μισθὸς οὑτοσί.

ΕΠΙΣΚΟΠΟΣ.
Τουτὶ τί ἦν;

ΠΕΙΣΘΕΤΑΙΡΟΣ.
Ἐκκλησία περὶ Φαρνάκου. 1025

ΕΠΙΣΚΟΠΟΣ.
Μαρτύρομαι τυπτόμενος ὢν ἐπίσκοπος.

ΠΕΙΣΘΕΤΑΙΡΟΣ.
Οὐκ ἀποσοβήσεις; Οὐκ ἀποίσεις τὼ κάδω;
Οὐ δεινά; Καὶ πέμπουσιν ἤδη 'πισκόπους
Ἐς τὴν πόλιν, πρὶν καὶ τεθύσθαι τοῖς θεοῖς.

ΨΗΦΙΣΜΑΤΟΠΩΛΗΣ.
Ἐὰν δ' ὁ Νεφελοκοκκυγιεὺς τὸν Ἀθηναῖον 1030
ἀδικῇ

ΠΕΙΣΘΕΤΑΙΡΟΣ.
Τουτὶ τί ἔστιν αὖ κακὸν τὸ βιβλίον;

ΨΗΦΙΣΜΑΤΟΠΩΛΗΣ.
Ψηφισματοπώλης εἰμί, καὶ νόμους νέους
Ἥκω παρ' ὑμᾶς δεῦρο πωλήσων.

ΠΕΙΣΘΕΤΑΙΡΟΣ.
Τὸ τί;

ΨΗΦΙΣΜΑΤΟΠΩΛΗΣ.
Χρῆσθαι Νεφελοκοκκυγιᾶς τοῖσδε τοῖς μέτροισι 1035
καὶ σταθμοῖσι καὶ ψηφίσμασι, καθάπερ Ὀλοφύξιοι.

ΠΕΙΣΘΕΤΑΙΡΟΣ.
Σὺ δέ γ' οἷσπερ ὠτοτύξιοι χρήσει τάχα.

ΨΗΦΙΣΜΑΤΟΠΩΛΗΣ.
Οὗτος, τί πάσχεις;

ΠΕΙΣΘΕΤΑΙΡΟΣ.
Οὐκ ἀποίσεις τοὺς νόμους;
Πικροὺς ἐγώ σοι τήμερον δείξω νόμους. 1040

ΕΠΙΣΚΟΠΟΣ.
Καλοῦμαι Πεισθέταιρον ὕβρεως ἐς τὸν μουνυ-
χιῶνα μῆνα.

ΠΕΙΣΘΕΤΑΙΡΟΣ.
Ἄληθες, οὗτος; Ἔτι γὰρ ἐνταῦθ' ἦσθα σύ;

ΨΗΦΙΣΜΑΤΟΠΩΛΗΣ.
Ἐὰν δέ τις ἐξελαύνῃ τοὺς ἄρχοντας, καὶ μὴ
δέχηται κατὰ τὴν στήλην, 1945

ΠΕΙΣΘΕΤΑΙΡΟΣ.
Οἴμοι κακοδαίμων, καὶ σὺ γὰρ ἐνταῦθ' ἦσθ' ἔτι;

ΕΠΙΣΚΟΠΟΣ.
Ἀπολῶ σε, καὶ γράφω σε μυρίας δραχμάς.

ΠΕΙΣΘΕΤΑΙΡΟΣ.
Ἐγὼ δὲ σοῦ γε τὼ κύδω διασκεδῶ.

ΕΠΙΣΚΟΠΟΣ.
Μέμνησ' ὅτε τῆς στήλης κατετίλας ἑσπέρας;

ΠΕΙΣΘΕΤΑΙΡΟΣ.
Αἰβοῖ· λαβέτω τις αὐτόν. Οὗτος, οὐ μενεῖς; 1050

ΙΕΡΕΥΣ.
Ἀπίωμεν ἡμεῖς ὡς τάχιστ' ἐντευθενὶ

ΟΡΝΙΘΕΣ.

Θύσοντες εἴσω τοῖς θεοῖσι τὸν τράγον.

ΧΟΡΟΣ.

Στροφή.

Ἤδη μοι τῷ παντόπτᾳ
Καὶ παντάρχᾳ θνητοὶ πάντες
Θύσουσ' εὐκταίαις εὐχαῖς. 1055
Πᾶσαν μὲν γὰρ γᾶν ὀπτεύω,
Σώζω δ' εὐθαλεῖς καρπούς,
Κτείνων παμφύλων γένναν
Θηρῶν, οἳ πάντ' ἐν γαίᾳ
Ἐκ κάλυκος αὐξανόμενα γένυσι πολυφάγοις, 1060
Δένδρεσί τ' ἐφεζόμενα καρπὸν ἀποβόσκεται·
Κτείνω δ' οἳ κήπους εὐώδεις
Φθείρουσιν λύμαις ἐχθίσταις·
Ἑρπετά τε καὶ δάκετα πάνθ' ὅσαπερ
Ἔστιν ὑπ' ἐμᾶς πτέρυγος ἐν φοναῖς ὄλλυται. 1065
Γῇδε μέντοι θἠμέρᾳ μάλιστ' ἐπαναγορεύεται,
Ἢν ἀποκτείνῃ τις ὑμῶν Διαγόραν τὸν Μήλιον,
Λαμβάνειν τάλαντον, ἤν τε τῶν τυράννων τίς τινα
Τῶν τεθνηκότων ἀποκτείνῃ, τάλαντον λαμβάνειν.
Βουλόμεσθ' οὖν νῦν ἀνειπεῖν ταῦτα χἠμεῖς ἐνθάδε· 1070
Ἢν ἀποκτείνῃ τις ὑμῶν Φιλοκράτη τὸν Στρούθιον,
Λήψεται τάλαντον· ἢν δὲ ζῶντά γ' ἀγάγῃ, τέτταρα,
Ὅτι συνείρων τοὺς σπίνους πωλεῖ καθ' ἑπτὰ τοὐβολοῦ,
Εἶτα φυσῶν τὰς κίχλας δείκνυσι καὶ λυμαίνεται,
Τοῖς τε κοψίχοισιν εἰς τὰς ῥῖνας ἐγχεῖ τὰ πτερά, 1075
Τὰς περιστεράς θ' ὁμοίως ξυλλαβὼν εἴρξας ἔχει,

Κἀπαναγκάζει παλεύειν δεδεμένας ἐν δικτύῳ.
Ταῦτα βουλόμεσθ' ἀνειπεῖν· κεἴ τις ὄρνιθας τρέφει
Εἰργμένους ὑμῶν ἐν αὐλῇ, φράζομεν μεθιέναι.
Ἢν δὲ μὴ πείθησθε, συλληφθέντες ὑπὸ τῶν ὀρνέων 1080
Αὖθις ὑμεῖς αὖ παρ' ἡμῖν δεδεμένοι παλεύσετε.

Ἀντιστροφή.

Εὔδαιμον φῦλον πτηνῶν
Οἰωνῶν, οἳ χειμῶνος μὲν
Χλαίνας οὐκ ἀμπισχοῦνται·
Οὐδ' αὖ θερμὴ πνίγους ἡμᾶς   1085
Ἀκτὶς τηλαυγὴς θάλπει·
Ἀλλ' ἀνθηρῶν λειμώνων
Φύλλων ἐν κόλποις ναίω,
Ἡνίκ' ἂν ὁ θεσπέσιος ὀξὺ μέλος ἀχέτας
Θάλπεσι μεσημβρινοῖς ἡλιομανὴς βοᾷ.   1090
Χειμάζω δ' ἐν κοίλοις ἄντροις,
Νύμφαις οὐρείαις ξυμπαίζων·
Ἠρινά τε βοσκόμεθα παρθένια
Λευκότροφα μύρτα, Χαρίτων τε κηπεύματα.
Τοῖς κριταῖς εἰπεῖν τι βουλόμεσθα τῆς νίκης πέρι, 1095
Ὅσ' ἀγάθ', ἢν κρίνωσιν ἡμᾶς, πᾶσιν αὐτοῖς δώσομεν,
Ὥστε κρείττω δῶρα πολλῷ τῶν Ἀλεξάνδρου λαβεῖν.
Πρῶτα μὲν γὰρ οὗ μάλιστα πᾶς κριτὴς ἐφίεται,
Γλαῦκες ὑμᾶς οὔποτ' ἐπιλείψουσι Λαυριωτικαί·
Ἀλλ' ἐνοικήσουσιν ἔνδον, ἔν τε τοῖς βαλαντίοις 1100
Ἐννεοττεύσουσι κἀκλέψουσι μικρὰ κέρματα.
Εἶτα πρὸς τούτοισιν ὥσπερ ἐν ἱεροῖς οἰκήσετε,

ΟΡΝΙΘΕΣ. 75

Τὰς γὰρ ὑμῶν οἰκίας ἐρέψομεν πρὸς ἀετόν·
Κἂν λαχόντες ἀρχίδιον εἶθ' ἁρπάσαι βούλησθέ τι,
Ὀξὺν ἱερακίσκον ἐς τὰς χεῖρας ὑμῖν δώσομεν. 1105
Ἢν δέ που δειπνῆτε, πρηγορῶνας ὑμῖν πέμψομεν.
Ἢν δὲ μὴ κρίνητε, χαλκεύεσθε μηνίσκους φορεῖν
Ὥσπερ ἀνδριάντες· ὡς ὑμῶν ὃς ἂν μὴ μῆν' ἔχῃ,
Ὅταν ἔχητε χλανίδα λευκήν, τότε μάλισθ' οὕτω δίκην
Δώσεθ' ἡμῖν, πᾶσι τοῖς ὄρνισι κατατιλώμενοι. 1110

ΠΕΙΣΘΕΤΑΙΡΟΣ.

Τὰ μὲν ἱέρ' ἡμῖν ἐστιν, ὤρνιθες, καλά·
Ἀλλ' ὡς ἀπὸ τοῦ τείχους πάρεστιν ἄγγελος
Οὐδεὶς ὅτου πευσόμεθα τἀκεῖ πράγματα, —
Ἀλλ' οὑτοσὶ τρέχει τις Ἀλφειὸν πνέων.

ΑΓΓΕΛΟΣ Α.

Ποῦ ποῦ 'στι, ποῦ ποῦ ποῦ 'στι, ποῦ ποῦ ποῦ 'στι,
ποῦ 1115
Ποῦ Πεισθέταιρός ἐστιν ἄρχων;

ΠΕΙΣΘΕΤΑΙΡΟΣ.

Οὑτοσί.

ΑΓΓΕΛΟΣ Α.

Ἐξῳκοδόμηταί σοι τὸ τεῖχος.

ΠΕΙΣΘΕΤΑΙΡΟΣ.

Εὖ λέγεις.

ΑΓΓΕΛΟΣ Α.

Κάλλιστον ἔργον καὶ μεγαλοπρεπέστατον·
Ὥστ' ἂν ἐπάνω μὲν Προξενίδης ὁ Κομπασεὺς
Καὶ Θεογένης ἐναντίω δύ' ἅρματε, 1120

Ἵππων ὑπόντων μέγεθος ὅσον ὁ δούριος,
Ὑπὸ τοῦ πλάτους ἂν παρελασαίτην.

ΠΕΙΣΘΕΤΑΙΡΟΣ.
Ἡράκλεις.

ΑΓΓΕΛΟΣ Α.
Τὸ δὲ μῆκός ἐστι, καὶ γὰρ ἐμέτρησ᾽ αὔτ᾽ ἐγώ,
Ἑκατοντορόγυιον.

ΠΕΙΣΘΕΤΑΙΡΟΣ.
Ὦ Πόσειδον, τοῦ μάκρους.
Τίνες ᾠκοδόμησαν αὐτὸ τηλικουτονί; 1125

ΑΓΓΕΛΟΣ Α.
Ὄρνιθες, οὐδεὶς ἄλλος, οὐκ Αἰγύπτιος
Πλινθοφόρος, οὐ λιθουργός, οὐ τέκτων παρῆν,
Ἀλλ᾽ αὐτόχειρες, ὥστε θαυμάζειν ἐμέ.
Ἐκ μέν γε Λιβύης ἧκον ὡς τρισμύριαι
Γέρανοι, θεμελίους καταπεπωκυῖαι λίθους. 1130
Τούτους δ᾽ ἐτύκιζον αἱ κρέκες τοῖς ῥύγχεσιν.
Ἕτεροι δ᾽ ἐπλινθοποίουν πελαργοὶ μύριοι·
Ὕδωρ δ᾽ ἐφόρουν κάτωθεν ἐς τὸν ἀέρα
Οἱ χαραδριοὶ καὶ τἄλλα ποτάμι᾽ ὄρνεα.

ΠΕΙΣΘΕΤΑΙΡΟΣ.
Ἐπηλοφόρουν δ᾽ αὐτοῖσι τίνες;

ΑΓΓΕΛΟΣ Α.
Ἐρῳδιοὶ 1135
Λεκάναισι.

ΠΕΙΣΘΕΤΑΙΡΟΣ.
Τὸν δὲ πηλὸν ἐνεβάλλοντο πῶς;

ΑΓΓΕΛΟΣ Α.

Τοῦτ', ὦγάθ', ἐξεύρητο καὶ σοφώτατα·
Οἱ χῆνες ὑποτύπτοντες ὥσπερ ταῖς ἅμαις
Ἐς τὰς λεκάνας ἐνέβαλλον αὐτὸν τοῖν ποδοῖν.

ΠΕΙΣΘΕΤΑΙΡΟΣ.
Τί δῆτα πόδες ἂν οὐκ ἂν ἐργασαίατο; 1140

ΑΓΓΕΛΟΣ Α.
Καὶ νὴ Δί' αἱ νῆτταί γε περιεζωσμέναι
Ἐπλινθοφόρουν· ἄνω δὲ τὸν ὑπαγωγέα
Ἐπέτοντ' ἔχουσαι κατόπιν, ὥσπερ παιδία,
Τὸν πηλὸν ἐν τοῖς στόμασιν αἱ χελιδόνες.

ΠΕΙΣΘΕΤΑΙΡΟΣ.
Τί δῆτα μισθωτοὺς ἂν ἔτι μισθοῖτο τις; 1145
Φέρ' ἴδω, τί δαί; Τὰ ξύλινα τοῦ τείχους τίνες
Ἀπειργάσαντ';

ΑΓΓΕΛΟΣ Α.
Ὄρνιθες ἦσαν τέκτονες
Σοφώτατοι πελεκᾶντες, οἳ τοῖς ῥύγχεσιν
Ἀπεπελέκησαν τὰς πύλας· ἦν δ' ὁ κτύπος
Αὐτῶν πελεκώντων ὥσπερ ἐν ναυπηγίῳ. 1150
Καὶ νῦν ἅπαντ' ἐκεῖνα πεπύλωται πύλαις,
Καὶ βεβαλάνωται καὶ φυλάττεται κύκλῳ,
Ἐφοδεύεται, κωδωνοφορεῖται, πανταχῇ
Φυλακαὶ καθεστήκασι καὶ φρυκτωρίαι
Ἐν τοῖσι πύργοις. Ἀλλ' ἐγὼ μὲν ἀποτρέχων 1155
Ἀπονίψομαι· σὺ δ' αὐτὸς ἤδη τἆλλα δρᾶ.

7*

ΧΟΡΟΣ.

Οὗτος, τί ποιεῖς ; Ἆρα θαυμάζεις ὅτι
Οὕτω τὸ τεῖχος ἐκτετείχισται ταχύ ;

ΠΕΙΣΘΕΤΑΙΡΟΣ.

Νὴ τοὺς θεοὺς ἔγωγε· καὶ γὰρ ἄξιον·
Ἴσα γὰρ ἀληθῶς φαίνεταί μοι ψεύδεσιν. 1160
Ἀλλ' ὅδε φύλαξ γὰρ τῶν ἐκεῖθεν ἄγγελος
Ἐσθεῖ πρὸς ἡμᾶς δεῦρο, πυρρίχην βλέπων.

ΑΓΓΕΛΟΣ Β.

Ἰοὺ ἰού, ἰοὺ ἰού, ἰοὺ ἰού.

ΠΕΙΣΘΕΤΑΙΡΟΣ.

Τί τὸ πρᾶγμα τουτί ;

ΑΓΓΕΛΟΣ Β.

Δεινότατα πεπόνθαμεν.
Τῶν γὰρ θεῶν τις ἄρτι τῶν παρὰ τοῦ Διὸς 1165
Διὰ τῶν πυλῶν εἰσέπτατ' εἰς τὸν ἀέρα,
Λαθὼν κολοιοὺς φύλακας ἡμεροσκόπους.

ΠΕΙΣΘΕΤΑΙΡΟΣ.

Ὦ δεινὸν ἔργον καὶ σχέτλιον εἰργασμένος.
Τίς τῶν θεῶν ;

ΑΓΓΕΛΟΣ Β.

Οὐκ ἴσμεν· ὅτι δ' εἶχε πτερά,
Τοῦτ' ἴσμεν.

ΠΕΙΣΘΕΤΑΙΡΟΣ.

Οὔκουν δῆτα περιπόλους ἐχρῆν 1170
Πέμψαι κατ' αὐτὸν εὐθύς ;

ΟΡΝΙΘΕΣ.

ΑΓΓΕΛΟΣ Β.

Ἀλλ' ἐπέμψαμεν
Τρισμυρίους ἱέρακας ἱπποτοξότας,
Χωρεῖ δὲ πᾶς τις ὄνυχας ἠγκυλωμένος,
Κερχνῄς, τριόρχης, γύψ, κύμινδις, ἀετός·
Ῥύμῃ τε καὶ πτεροῖσι καὶ ῥοιζήμασιν 1175
Αἰθὴρ δονεῖται τοῦ θεοῦ ζητουμένου·
Κᾆστ' οὐ μακρὰν ἄπωθεν, ἀλλ' ἐνταυθά που
Ἤδη 'στίν.

ΠΕΙΣΘΕΤΑΙΡΟΣ.

Οὐκοῦν σφενδόνας δεῖ λαμβάνειν
Καὶ τόξα· χώρει δεῦρο πᾶς ὑπηρέτης·
Τόξευε, παῖε, σφενδόνην τίς μοι δότω. 1180

ΧΟΡΟΣ.

Στροφή.

Πόλεμος αἴρεται, πόλεμος οὐ φατὸς
Πρὸς ἐμὲ καὶ θεούς. Ἀλλὰ φύλαττε πᾶς
Ἀέρα περινέφελον, ὃν Ἔρεβος ἐτέκετο,
Μή σε λάθῃ θεῶν τις ταύτῃ περῶν·

Ἄθρει δὲ πᾶς κύκλῳ σκοπῶν * *, 1185
Ὡς ἐγγὺς ἤδη δαίμονος πεδαρσίου
Δίνης πτερωτὸς φθόγγος ἐξακούεται.

ΠΕΙΣΘΕΤΑΙΡΟΣ.

Αὕτη σὺ ποῖ ποῖ ποῖ πέτει; Μέν' ἥσυχος,
Ἔχ' ἀτρέμας· αὐτοῦ στῆθ'· ἐπίσχες τοῦ δρόμου.
Τίς εἶ; Ποδαπή; Λέγειν ἐχρῆν ὁπόθεν ποτ' εἶ. 1190

ΙΡΙΣ.
Παρὰ τῶν θεῶν ἔγωγε τῶν Ὀλυμπίων.

ΠΕΙΣΘΕΤΑΙΡΟΣ.
Ὄνομα δέ σοι τί ἐστι; πλοῖον, ἢ κυνῆ;

ΙΡΙΣ.
Ἶρις ταχεῖα.

ΠΕΙΣΘΕΤΑΙΡΟΣ.
Πάραλος, ἢ Σαλαμινία;

ΙΡΙΣ.
Τί δὲ τοῦτο;

ΠΕΙΣΘΕΤΑΙΡΟΣ.
Ταυτηνί τις οὐ ξυλλήψεται
Ἀναπτάμενος τρίορχος;

ΙΡΙΣ.
Ἐμὲ συλλήψεται; 1195
Τί ποτ' ἐστὶ τουτὶ τὸ κακόν;

ΠΕΙΣΘΕΤΑΙΡΟΣ.
Οἰμώξει μακρά.

ΙΡΙΣ.
Ἄτοπόν γε τουτὶ πρᾶγμα.

ΠΕΙΣΘΕΤΑΙΡΟΣ.
Κατὰ ποίας πύλας
Εἰσῆλθες εἰς τὸ τεῖχος, ὦ μιαρωτάτη;

ΙΡΙΣ.
Οὐκ οἶδα μὰ Δί' ἔγωγε κατὰ ποίας πύλας.

ΠΕΙΣΘΕΤΑΙΡΟΣ.
Ἤκουσας αὐτῆς οἷον εἰρωνεύεται; 1200

Πρὸς τοὺς κολοιάρχους προσῆλθες ; Οὐ λέγεις ;
Σφραγίδ᾽ ἔχεις παρὰ τῶν πελαργῶν ;

ΙΡΙΣ.

Τί τὸ κακόν ;

ΠΕΙΣΘΕΤΑΙΡΟΣ.

Οὐκ ἔλαβες ;

ΙΡΙΣ.

Ὑγιαίνεις μέν ;

ΠΕΙΣΘΕΤΑΙΡΟΣ.

Οὐδὲ σύμβολον
Ἐπέβαλεν ὀρνίθαρχος οὐδείς σοι παρών ;

ΙΡΙΣ.

Μὰ Δί᾽ οὐκ ἔμοιγ᾽ ἐπέβαλεν οὐδείς, ὦ μέλε.   1205

ΠΕΙΣΘΕΤΑΙΡΟΣ.

Κᾆτα δῆθ᾽ οὕτω σιωπῇ διαπέτει
Διὰ τῆς πόλεως τῆς ἀλλοτρίας καὶ τοῦ χάους ;

ΙΡΙΣ.

Ποίᾳ γὰρ ἄλλῃ χρὴ πέτεσθαι τοὺς θεούς ;

ΠΕΙΣΘΕΤΑΙΡΟΣ.

Οὐκ οἶδα μὰ Δί᾽ ἔγωγε· τῇδε μὲν γὰρ οὔ.
Ἀδικεῖς δὲ καὶ νῦν. Ἆρά γ᾽ οἶσθα τοῦθ᾽, ὅτι   1210
Δικαιότατ᾽ ἂν ληφθεῖσα πασῶν Ἰρίδων
Ἀπέθανες, εἰ τῆς ἀξίας ἐτύγχανες ;

ΙΡΙΣ.

Ἀλλ᾽ ἀθάνατός εἰμ᾽.

ΠΕΙΣΘΕΤΑΙΡΟΣ.

Ἀλλ᾽ ὅμως ἂν ἀπέθανες.

Δεινότατα γάρ τοι πεισόμεσθ', ἐμοὶ δοκεῖ,
Εἰ τῶν μὲν ἄλλων ἄρχομεν, ὑμεῖς δ' οἱ θεοὶ   1215
Ἀκολαστανεῖτε, κοὐδέπω γνώσεσθ' ὅτι
Ἀκροατέον ὑμῖν ἐν μέρει τῶν κρειττόνων.
Φράσον δέ τοί μοι, τὼ πτέρυγε ποῖ ναυστολεῖς;

ΙΡΙΣ.

Ἐγώ; Πρὸς ἀνθρώπους πέτομαι παρὰ τοῦ πατρὸς
Φράσουσα θύειν τοῖς Ὀλυμπίοις θεοῖς   1220
Μηλοσφαγεῖν τε βουθύτοις ἐπ' ἐσχάραις
Κνισᾶν τ' ἀγυιάς.

ΠΕΙΣΘΕΤΑΙΡΟΣ.
            Τί σὺ λέγεις; ποίοις θεοῖς;

ΙΡΙΣ.
Ποίοισιν; Ἡμῖν, τοῖς ἐν οὐρανῷ θεοῖς.

ΠΕΙΣΘΕΤΑΙΡΟΣ.
Θεοὶ γὰρ ὑμεῖς;

ΙΡΙΣ.
            Τίς γάρ ἐστ' ἄλλος θεός;

ΠΕΙΣΘΕΤΑΙΡΟΣ.
Ὄρνιθες ἀνθρώποισι νῦν εἰσιν θεοί,   1225
Οἷς θυτέον αὐτούς, ἀλλὰ μὰ Δί' οὐ τῷ Διί.

ΙΡΙΣ.
Ὦ μῶρε μῶρε, μὴ θεῶν κίνει φρένας
Δεινάς, ὅπως μή σου γένος πανώλεθρον
Διὸς μακέλλῃ πᾶν ἀναστρέψῃ Δίκη,
Λιγνὺς δὲ σῶμα καὶ δόμων περιπτυχὰς   1230
Καταιθαλώσῃ σου Λικυμνίαις βολαῖς.

ΟΡΝΙΘΕΣ.

ΠΕΙΣΘΕΤΑΙΡΟΣ.
Ἄκουσον αὕτη· παῦε τῶν παφλασμάτων·
Ἔχ' ἀτρέμα. Φέρ' ἴδω, πότερα Λυδὸν ἢ Φρύγα
Ταυτὶ λέγουσα μορμολύττεσθαι δοκεῖς;
Ἆρ' οἶσθ' ὅτι Ζεὺς εἴ με λυπήσει πέρα, 1235
Μέλαθρα μὲν αὐτοῦ καὶ δόμους Ἀμφίονος
Καταιθαλώσω πυρφόροισιν ἀετοῖς,
Πέμψω δὲ πορφυρίωνας ἐς τὸν οὐρανὸν
Ὄρνις ἐπ' αὐτόν, παρδαλᾶς ἐνημμένους,
Πλεῖν ἑξακοσίους τὸν ἀριθμόν; Καὶ δή ποτε 1240
Εἷς Πορφυρίων αὐτῷ παρέσχε πράγματα.
Σὺ δ' εἴ με λυπήσεις τι, τῆς διακόνου
Πρώτης ἀνατείνας τὼ σκέλη διαμηριῶ
Τὴν Ἶριν αὐτήν, ὥστε θαυμάζειν ὅπως
Οὕτω γέρων ὢν στύομαι τριέμβολον. 1245

ΙΡΙΣ.
Διαρραγείης, ὦ μέλ', αὐτοῖς ῥήμασιν.

ΠΕΙΣΘΕΤΑΙΡΟΣ.
Οὐκ ἀποσοβήσεις; Οὐ ταχέως; Εὐρὰξ πατάξ.

ΙΡΙΣ.
Ἦ μήν σε παύσει τῆς ὕβρεως οὑμὸς πατήρ.

ΠΕΙΣΘΕΤΑΙΡΟΣ.
Οἴμοι τάλας. Οὔκουν ἑτέρωσε πετομένη
Καταιθαλώσεις τῶν νεωτέρων τινά; 1250

ΧΟΡΟΣ.
Ἀντιστροφή.
Ἀποκεκλήκαμεν διογενεῖς θεοὺς

Μηκέτι τὴν ἐμὴν διαπερᾶν πόλιν,
Μηδέ τιν' ἱερόθυτον ἀνὰ δάπεδον ἔτι
Τῇδε βροτὸν θεοῖσι πέμπειν καπνόν.

ΠΕΙΣΘΕΤΑΙΡΟΣ.
Δεινόν γε τὸν κήρυκα τὸν παρὰ τοὺς βροτοὺς   1255
Οἰχόμενον, εἰ μηδέποτε νοστήσει πάλιν.

ΚΗΡΥΞ.
Ὦ Πεισθέταιρ', ὦ μακάρι', ὦ σοφώτατε,
Ὦ κλεινότατ', ὦ σοφώτατ', ὦ γλαφυρώτατε,
Ὦ τρισμακάρι', ὦ κατακέλευσον.

ΠΕΙΣΘΕΤΑΙΡΟΣ.
                              Τί σὺ λέγεις;

ΚΗΡΥΞ.
Στεφάνῳ σε χρυσῷ τῷδε σοφίας οὕνεκα   1260
Στεφανοῦσι καὶ τιμῶσιν οἱ πάντες λεῴ.

ΠΕΙΣΘΕΤΑΙΡΟΣ.
Δέχομαι. Τί δ' οὕτως οἱ λεῴ τιμῶσί με;

ΚΗΡΥΞ.
Ὦ κλεινοτάτην αἰθέριον οἰκίσας πόλιν,
Οὐκ οἶσθ' ὅσην τιμὴν παρ' ἀνθρώποις φέρει,
Ὅσους τ' ἐραστὰς τῆσδε τῆς χώρας ἔχεις.   1265
Πρὶν μὲν γὰρ οἰκίσαι σε τήνδε τὴν πόλιν,
Ἐλακωνομάνουν ἅπαντες ἄνθρωποι τότε,
Ἐκόμων, ἐπείνων, ἐρρύπων, ἐσωκράτων,
Σκυτάλι' ἐφόρουν· νυνὶ δ' ὑποστρέψαντες αὖ
Ὀρνιθομανοῦσι, πάντα δ' ὑπὸ τῆς ἡδονῆς   1270
Ποιοῦσιν ἅπερ ὄρνιθες ἐκμιμούμενοι.

ΟΡΝΙΘΕΣ.

Πρῶτον μὲι εὐθὺς πάντες ἐξ εὐνῆς ἅμα
Ἐπέτονθ' ἕωθεν ὥσπερ ἡμεῖς ἐπὶ νομόν·
Κἄπειτ' ἂν ἅμα κατῆραν ἐς τὰ βιβλία·
Εἶτ' ἀπενέμοντ' ἐνταῦθα τὰ ψηφίσματα. 1275
Ὠρνιθομάνουν δ' οὕτω περιφανῶς ὥστε καὶ
Πολλοῖσιν ὀρνίθων ὀνόματ' ἦν κείμενα.
Πέρδιξ μὲν εἷς κάπηλος ὠνομάζετο
Χωλός, Μενίππῳ δ' ἦν χελιδὼν τοὔνομα,
Ὀπουντίῳ δ' ὀφθαλμὸν οὐκ ἔχων κόραξ, 1280
Κορυδὸς Φιλοκλέει, χηναλώπηξ Θεογένει,
Ἶβις Λυκούργῳ, Χαιρεφῶντι νυκτερίς,
Συρακοσίῳ δὲ κίττα· Μειδίας δ' ἐκεῖ
Ὄρτυξ ἐκαλεῖτο· καὶ γὰρ ἧκεν ὄρτυγι
Ὑπὸ στυφοκόπου τὴν κεφαλὴν πεπληγμένῳ. 1285
Ἧιδον δ' ὑπὸ φιλορνιθίας πάντες μέλη,
Ὅπου χελιδὼν ἦν τις ἐμπεποιημένη
Ἢ πηνέλοψ ἢ χήν τις ἢ περιστερὰ
Ἢ πτέρυγες, ἢ πτεροῦ τι καὶ σμικρὸν προσῆν.
Τοιαῦτα μὲν τἀκεῖθεν. Ἓν δέ σοι λέγω· 1290
Ἥξουσ' ἐκεῖθεν δεῦρο πλεῖν ἢ μύριοι
Πτερῶν δεόμενοι καὶ τρόπων γαμψωνύχων·
Ὥστε πτερῶν σοι τοῖς ἐποίκοις δεῖ ποθέν.

ΠΕΙΣΘΕΤΑΙΡΟΣ.

Οὐκ ἄρα μὰ Δί' ἡμῖν ἔτ' ἔργον ἑστάναι.
Ἀλλ' ὡς τάχιστα σὺ μὲν ἰὼν τὰς ἀρρίχους 1295
Καὶ τοὺς κοφίνους ἅπαντας ἐμπίπλη πτερῶν·
Μανῆς δὲ φερέτω μοι θύραζε τὰ πτερά·

ΑΡΙΣΤΟΦΑΝΟΥΣ

Ἐγὼ δ᾽ ἐκείνων τοὺς προσιόντας δέξομαι.

ΧΟΡΟΣ.

Στροφή.

Ταχὺ δ᾽ ἂν πολυάνορα τὰν πόλιν
Καλοῖ τις ἀνθρώπων. 1300

(ΠΕΙΣΘΕΤΑΙΡΟΣ.)

Τύχη μόνον προσείη.

ΧΟΡΟΣ.

Κατέχουσι δ᾽ ἔρωτες ἐμᾶς πόλεως.

ΠΕΙΣΘΕΤΑΙΡΟΣ.

Θᾶττον φέρειν κελεύω.

ΧΟΡΟΣ.

Τί γὰρ οὐκ ἔνι ταύτῃ
Καλὸν ἀνδρὶ μετοικεῖν; 1305
Σοφία, Πόθος, ἀμβρόσιαι Χάριτες,
Τό τε τῆς ἀγανόφρονος Ἡσυχίας
Εὐάμερον πρόσωπον.

ΠΕΙΣΘΕΤΑΙΡΟΣ.

Ὡς βλακικῶς διακονεῖς·
Οὐ θᾶττον ἐγκονήσεις; 1310

ΧΟΡΟΣ.

Ἀντιστροφή.

Φερέτω κάλαθον ταχύ τις πτερῶν,
Σὺ δ᾽ αὖθις ἐξόρμα,
Τύπτων γε τοῦτον ὡδί.
Πάνυ γὰρ βραδύς ἐστί τις ὥσπερ ὄνος.

ΠΕΙΣΘΕΤΑΙΡΟΣ.

Μανῆς γάρ ἐστι δειλός. 1315

ΟΡΝΙΘΕΣ.

ΧΟΡΟΣ.

Συ δὲ τὰ πτερὰ πρῶτον
Διίθες τάδε κόσμῳ·
Τά τε μουσίχ' ὁμοῦ τά τε μαντικὰ καὶ
Τὰ θαλάττι'. Ἔπειτα δ' ὅπως φρονίμως
Πρὸς ἄνδρ' ὁρῶν πτερώσεις. 1320

ΠΕΙΣΘΕΤΑΙΡΟΣ.
Οὔ τοι μὰ τὰς κερχνῇδας ἔτι σοῦ σχήσομαι,
Οὕτως ὁρῶν σε δειλὸν ὄντα καὶ βραδύν.

ΠΑΤΡΑΛΟΙΑΣ.
Γενοίμαν ἀετὸς ὑψιπέτας,
Ὡς ἂν ποταθείην ὑπὲρ ἀτρυγέτου γλαύ-
κᾶς ἐπ' οἶδμα λίμνας. 1325

ΠΕΙΣΘΕΤΑΙΡΟΣ.
Ἔοικεν οὐ ψευδαγγελὴς εἶν' ἄγγελος.
Ἄιδων γὰρ ὅδε τις ἀετοὺς προσέρχεται.

ΠΑΤΡΑΛΟΙΑΣ.
Αἰβοῖ·
Οὐκ ἔστιν οὐδὲν τοῦ πέτεσθαι γλυκύτερον·
Ἐρῶ δ' ἔγωγε τῶν ἐν ὄρνισιν νόμων. 1330
Ὀρνιθομανῶ γὰρ καὶ πέτομαι, καὶ βούλομαι
Οἰκεῖν μεθ' ὑμῶν, κἀπιθυμῶ τῶν νόμων.

ΠΕΙΣΘΕΤΑΙΡΟΣ.
Ποίων νόμων; Πολλοὶ γὰρ ὀρνίθων νόμοι.

ΠΑΤΡΑΛΟΙΑΣ.
Πάντων· μάλιστα δ' ὅτι καλὸν νομίζεται
Τὸν πατέρα τοῖς ὄρνισιν ἄγχειν καὶ δάκνειν. 1335

ΠΕΙΣΘΕΤΑΙΡΟΣ.
Καὶ νὴ Δί᾽ ἀνδρεῖόν γε πάνυ νομίζομεν,
Ὃς ἂν πεπλήγῃ τὸν πατέρα νεοττὸς ὤν.

ΠΑΤΡΑΛΟΙΑΣ.
Διὰ ταῦτα μέντοι δεῦρ᾽ ἀνοικισθεὶς ἐγὼ
Ἄγχειν ἐπιθυμῶ τὸν πατέρα καὶ πάντ᾽ ἔχειν.

ΠΕΙΣΘΕΤΑΙΡΟΣ.
Ἀλλ᾽ ἔστιν ἡμῖν τοῖσιν ὄρνισιν νόμος   1340
Παλαιὸς ἐν ταῖς τῶν πελαργῶν κύρβεσιν·
Ἐπὴν ὁ πατὴρ ὁ πελαργὸς ἐκπετησίμους
Πάντας ποιήσῃ τοὺς πελαργιδῆς τρέφων,
Δεῖ τοὺς νεοττοὺς τὸν πατέρα πάλιν τρέφειν.

ΠΑΤΡΑΛΟΙΑΣ.
Ἀπέλαυσά τἄρ᾽ ἂν νὴ Δί᾽ ἐλθὼν ἐνθαδί,   1345
Εἴπερ γέ μοι καὶ τὸν πατέρα βοσκητέον.

ΠΕΙΣΘΕΤΑΙΡΟΣ.
Οὐδέν γ᾽. Ἐπειδήπερ γὰρ ἦλθες, ὦ μέλε,
Εὔνους, πτερώσω σ᾽ ὥσπερ ὄρνιν ὀρφανόν.
Σοὶ δ᾽, ὦ νεανίσκ᾽, οὐ κακῶς ὑποθήσομαι,
Ἀλλ᾽ οἱάπερ αὐτὸς ἔμαθον ὅτε παῖς ἦ. Σὺ γὰρ   1350
Τὸν μὲν πατέρα μὴ τύπτε· ταυτηνδὶ λαβὼν
Τὴν πτέρυγα, καὶ τουτὶ τὸ πλῆκτρον θατέρᾳ,
Νομίσας ἀλεκτρυόνος ἔχειν τονδὶ λόφον,
Φρούρει, στρατεύου, μισθοφορῶν σαυτὸν τρέφε,
Τὸν πατέρ᾽ ἔα ζῆν· ἀλλ᾽ ἐπειδὴ μάχιμος εἶ,   1355
Εἰς τἀπὶ Θρᾴκης ἀποπέτου, κἀκεῖ μάχου.

ΟΡΝΙΘΕΣ.

ΠΑΤΡΑΛΟΙΑΣ.
Νὴ τὸν Διόνυσον, εὖ γέ μοι δοκεῖς λέγειν,
Καὶ πείσομαί σοι.

ΠΕΙΣΘΕΤΑΙΡΟΣ.
Νοῦν ἄρ᾽ ἕξεις νὴ Δία.

ΚΙΝΗΣΙΑΣ.
Ἀναπέτομαι δὴ πρὸς Ὄλυμπον πτερύγεσσι κούφαις·
Πέτομαι δ᾽ ὁδὸν ἄλλοτ᾽ ἐπ᾽ ἄλλαν μελέων   1360

ΠΕΙΣΘΕΤΑΙΡΟΣ.
Τουτὶ τὸ πρᾶγμα φορτίου δεῖται πτερῶν.

ΚΙΝΗΣΙΑΣ.
Ἀφόβῳ φρενὶ σώματί τε νέαν ἐφέπων

ΠΕΙΣΘΕΤΑΙΡΟΣ.
Ἀσπαζόμεσθα φιλύρινον Κινησίαν.
Τί δεῦρο πόδα σὺ κυλλὸν ἀνὰ κύκλον κυκλεῖς;

ΚΙΝΗΣΙΑΣ.
Ὄρνις γενέσθαι βούλομαι   1365
Λιγύφθογγος ἀηδών.

ΠΕΙΣΘΕΤΑΙΡΟΣ.
Παῦσαι μελῳδῶν, ἀλλ᾽ ὅ τι λέγεις εἰπέ μοι.

ΚΙΝΗΣΙΑΣ.
Ὑπὸ σοῦ πτερωθεὶς βούλομαι μετάρσιος
Ἀναπτόμενος ἐκ τῶν νεφελῶν καινὰς λαβεῖν
Ἀεροδονήτους καὶ νιφοβόλους ἀναβολάς.   1370

ΠΕΙΣΘΕΤΑΙΡΟΣ.
Ἐκ τῶν νεφελῶν γὰρ ἄν τις ἀναβολὰς λάβοι;

ΚΙΝΗΣΙΑΣ.
Κρέμαται μὲν οὖν ἐντεῦθεν ἡμῶν ἡ τέχνη.
Τῶν διθυράμβων γὰρ τὰ λαμπρὰ γίγνεται
Ἀέριά τινα καὶ σκότια καὶ κυαναυγέα
Καὶ πτεροδόνητα· σὺ δὲ κλύων εἴσει τάχα. 1375

ΠΕΙΣΘΕΤΑΙΡΟΣ.
Οὐ δῆτ' ἔγωγε.

ΚΙΝΗΣΙΑΣ.
Νὴ τὸν Ἡρακλέα σύ γε.
Ἅπαντα γὰρ δίειμί σοι τὸν ἀέρα
Εἴδωλα πετεινῶν
Αἰθεροδρόμων
Οἰωνῶν ταναοδείρων· 1380

ΠΕΙΣΘΕΤΑΙΡΟΣ.
Ὠόπ.

ΚΙΝΗΣΙΑΣ.
Τὸν ἁλάδρομον ἁλάμενος
Ἅμ' ἀνέμων πνοαῖσι βαίην,

ΠΕΙΣΘΕΤΑΙΡΟΣ.
Νὴ τὸν Δί' ἦ 'γώ σου καταπαύσω τὰς πνοάς.

ΚΙΝΗΣΙΑΣ.
Τοτὲ μὲν νοτίαν στείχων πρὸς ὁδόν,
Τοτὲ δ' αὖ βορέᾳ σῶμα πελάζων 1385
Ἀλίμενον αἰθέρος αὔλακα τέμνων.
Χαρίεντά γ', ὦ πρεσβῦτ', ἐσοφίσω καὶ σοφά.

ΠΕΙΣΘΕΤΑΙΡΟΣ.
Οὐ γὰρ σὺ χαίρεις πτεροδόνητος γενόμενος;

ΚΙΝΗΣΙΑΣ.

Ταυτὶ πεποίηκας τὸν κυκλιοδιδάσκαλον,
Ὃς ταῖσι φυλαῖς περιμάχητός εἰμ' ἀεί ; 1390

ΠΕΙΣΘΕΤΑΙΡΟΣ.

Βούλει διδάσκειν καὶ παρ' ἡμῖν οὖν μένων
Λεωτροφίδῃ χορὸν πετομένων ὀρνέων
Κεκροπίδα φυλήν ;

ΚΙΝΗΣΙΑΣ.

Καταγελᾷς μου, δῆλος εἶ.
Ἀλλ' οὖν ἔγωγ' οὐ παύσομαι, τοῦτ' ἴσθ' ὅτι,
Πρὶν ἂν πτερωθεὶς διαδράμω τὸν ἀέρα. 1395

ΣΥΚΟΦΑΝΤΗΣ.

Ὄρνιθές τινες οἵδ' οὐδὲν ἔχοντες πτεροποίκιλοι·
Τανυσίπτερε ποικίλα χελιδοῖ·

ΠΕΙΣΘΕΤΑΙΡΟΣ.

Τουτὶ τὸ κακὸν οὐ φαῦλον ἐξεγρήγορεν.
Ὅδ' αὖ μινυρίζων δεῦρό τις προσέρχεται.

ΣΥΚΟΦΑΝΤΗΣ.

Τανυσίπτερε ποικίλα μάλ' αὖθις. 1400

ΠΕΙΣΘΕΤΑΙΡΟΣ.

Ἐς θοἰμάτιον τὸ σκόλιον ᾄδειν μοι δοκεῖ,
Δεῖσθαι δ' ἔοικεν οὐκ ὀλίγων χελιδόνων.

ΣΥΚΟΦΑΝΤΗΣ.

Τίς ὁ πτερῶν δεῦρ' ἐστὶ τοὺς ἀφικνουμένους ;

ΠΕΙΣΘΕΤΑΙΡΟΣ.

Ὁδὶ πάρεστιν· ἀλλ' ὅτου δεῖ χρὴ λέγειν.

ΣΥΚΟΦΑΝΤΗΣ.

Πτερῶν πτερῶν δεῖ· μὴ πύθῃ τὸ δεύτερον. 1405

ΠΕΙΣΘΕΤΑΙΡΟΣ.
Μῶν εὐθὺ Πελλήνης πέτεσθαι διανοεῖ;

ΣΥΚΟΦΑΝΤΗΣ.
Μὰ Δί', ἀλλὰ κλητήρ εἰμι νησιωτικὸς
Καὶ συκοφάντης,

ΠΕΙΣΘΕΤΑΙΡΟΣ.
 Ὦ μακάριε τῆς τέχνης.

ΣΥΚΟΦΑΝΤΗΣ.
Καὶ πραγματοδίφης. Εἶτα δέομαι πτερὰ λαβὼν
Κύκλῳ περισοβεῖν τὰς πόλεις καλούμενος. 141

ΠΕΙΣΘΕΤΑΙΡΟΣ.
Ὑπὸ πτερύγων τί προσκαλεῖ σοφώτερον;

ΣΥΚΟΦΑΝΤΗΣ.
Μὰ Δί', ἀλλ' ἵν' οἱ λῃσταί γε μὴ λυπῶσί με,
Μετὰ τῶν γεράνων τ' ἐκεῖθεν ἀναχωρῶ πάλιν,
Ἀνθ' ἕρματος πολλὰς καταπεπωκὼς δίκας.

ΠΕΙΣΘΕΤΑΙΡΟΣ.
Τουτὶ γὰρ ἐργάζει σὺ τοὔργον; Εἰπέ μοι, 1415
Νεανίας ὢν συκοφαντεῖς τοὺς ξένους;

ΣΥΚΟΦΑΝΤΗΣ.
Τί γὰρ πάθω; Σκάπτειν γὰρ οὐκ ἐπίσταμαι.

ΠΕΙΣΘΕΤΑΙΡΟΣ.
Ἀλλ' ἔστιν ἕτερα νὴ Δί' ἔργα σώφρονα,
Ἀφ' ὧν διαζῆν ἄνδρα χρῆν τοσουτονὶ
Ἐκ τοῦ δικαίου μᾶλλον ἢ δικορραφεῖν. 1420

ΣΥΚΟΦΑΝΤΗΣ.
Ὦ δαιμόνιε, μὴ νουθέτει μ', ἀλλὰ πτέρου.

ΠΕΙΣΘΕΤΑΙΡΟΣ.
Νῦν τοι λέγων πτερῶ σε.

ΣΥΚΟΦΑΝΤΗΣ.
Καὶ πῶς ἂν λόγοις
Ἄνδρα πτερώσειας σύ;

ΠΕΙΣΘΕΤΑΙΡΟΣ.
Πάντες τοῖς λόγοις
Ἀναπτεροῦνται.

ΣΥΚΟΦΑΝΤΗΣ.
Πάντες;

ΠΕΙΣΘΕΤΑΙΡΟΣ.
Οὐκ ἀκήκοας,
Ὅταν λέγωσιν οἱ πατέρες ἑκάστοτε 1425
Τοῖς μειρακίοις ἐν τοῖσι κουρείοις ταδί·
Δεινῶς γέ μου τὸ μειράκιον Διιτρέφης
Λέγων ἀνεπτέρωκεν ὥσθ' ἱππηλατεῖν.
Ὁ δέ τις τὸν αὑτοῦ φησιν ἐπὶ τραγῳδίᾳ
Ἀνεπτερῶσθαι καὶ πεποτῆσθαι τὰς φρένας. 1430

ΣΥΚΟΦΑΝΤΗΣ.
Λόγοισί τἄρα καὶ πτεροῦνται;

ΠΕΙΣΘΕΤΑΙΡΟΣ.
Φήμ' ἐγώ.
Ὑπὸ γὰρ λόγων ὁ νοῦς τε μετεωρίζεται
Ἐπαίρεταί τ' ἄνθρωπος. Οὕτω καί σ' ἐγὼ
Ἀναπτερώσας βούλομαι χρηστοῖς λόγοις
Τρέψαι πρὸς ἔργον νόμιμον.

ΣΥΚΟΦΑΝΤΗΣ.
Ἀλλ' οὐ βούλομαι. 1435

ΠΕΙΣΘΕΤΑΙΡΟΣ.
Τί δαὶ ποιήσεις ;

ΣΥΚΟΦΑΝΤΗΣ.
Τὸ γένος οὐ καταισχυνῶ.
Παππῷος ὁ βίος συκοφαντεῖν ἐστί μοι.
Ἀλλὰ πτέρου με ταχέσι καὶ κούφοις πτεροῖς
Ἱέρακος, ἢ κερχνῆδος, ὡς ἂν τοὺς ξένους
Καλεσάμενος, κᾆτ' ἐγκεκληκὼς ἐνθαδί, 1440
Κᾆτ' αὖ πέτωμαι πάλιν ἐκεῖσε.

ΠΕΙΣΘΕΤΑΙΡΟΣ.
Μανθάνω.
Ὡδὶ λέγεις· ὅπως ἂν ὠφλήκῃ δίκην
Ἐνθάδε πρὶν ἥκειν ὁ ξένος.

ΣΥΚΟΦΑΝΤΗΣ.
Πάνυ μανθάνεις.

ΠΕΙΣΘΕΤΑΙΡΟΣ.
Κἄπειθ' ὁ μὲν πλεῖ δεῦρο, σὺ δ' ἐκεῖσ' αὖ πέτει
Ἁρπασόμενος τὰ χρήματ' αὐτοῦ.

ΣΥΚΟΦΑΝΤΗΣ.
Πάντ' ἔχεις. 1445
Βέμβικος οὐδὲν διαφέρειν δεῖ.

ΠΕΙΣΘΕΤΑΙΡΟΣ.
Μανθάνω
Βέμβικα· καὶ μὴν ἔστι μοι νὴ τὸν Δία
Κάλλιστα Κορκυραῖα τοιαυτὶ πτερά.

ΣΥΚΟΦΑΝΤΗΣ.
Οἴμοι τάλας· μάστιγ' ἔχεις.

ΟΡΝΙΘΕΣ.

ΠΕΙΣΘΕΤΑΙΡΟΣ.
Πτερὼ μὲν οὖν,
Οἷσί σε ποιήσω τήμερον βεμβικιᾶν. 1450

ΣΥΚΟΦΑΝΤΗΣ.
Οἴμοι τάλας.

ΠΕΙΣΘΕΤΑΙΡΟΣ.
Οὐ πτερυγιεῖς ἐντευθενί ;
Οὐκ ἀπολιβάξεις, ὦ κάκιστ᾽ ἀπολούμενος ;
Πικρὰν τάχ᾽ ὄψει στρεψοδικοπανουργίαν.
Ἀπίωμεν ἡμεῖς ξυλλαβόντες τὰ πτερά.

ΧΟΡΟΣ.

Στροφή.

Πολλὰ δὴ καὶ καινὰ καὶ θαυ- 1455
μάστ᾽ ἐπεπτόμεσθα, καὶ
Δεινὰ πράγματ᾽ εἴδομεν.
Ἔστι γὰρ δένδρον πεφυκὸς
Ἔκτοπόν τι, καρδίας ἀ-
πωτέρω, Κλεώνυμος, 1460
Χρήσιμον μὲν οὐδέν, ἄλ-
λως δὲ δειλὸν καὶ μέγα.
Τοῦτο τοῦ μὲν ἦρος ἀεὶ
Βλαστάνει καὶ συκοφαντεῖ,
Τοῦ δὲ χειμῶνος πάλιν τὰς 1465
Ἀσπίδας φυλλορροεῖ.

Ἀντιστροφή.

Ἔστι δ᾽ αὖ χώρα πρὸς αὐτῷ
Τῷ σκότῳ πόρρω τις ἐν

Τῇ λύχνων ἐρημίᾳ,
Ἔνθα τοῖς ἥρωσιν ἄνθρω- 1470
ποι ξυναριστῶσι καὶ ξύν-
εισι, πλὴν τῆς ἑσπέρας.
Τηνικαῦτα δ' οὐκέτ' ἦν
Ἀσφαλὲς ξυντυγχάνειν.
Εἰ γὰρ ἐντύχοι τις ἥρῳ 1475
Τῶν βροτῶν νύκτωρ Ὀρέστῃ,
Γυμνὸς ἦν πληγεὶς ὑπ' αὐτοῦ
Πάντα τἀπιδέξια.

ΠΡΟΜΗΘΕΥΣ.
Οἴμοι τάλας, ὁ Ζεὺς ὅπως μή μ' ὄψεται.
Ποῦ Πεισθέταιρός ἐστιν;

ΠΕΙΣΘΕΤΑΙΡΟΣ.
     Ἔα, τουτὶ τί ἦν 1480
Τίς οὑγκαλυμμός;

ΠΡΟΜΗΘΕΥΣ.
    Τῶν θεῶν ὁρᾷς τινα
Ἐμοῦ κατόπιν ἐνταῦθα;

ΠΕΙΣΘΕΤΑΙΡΟΣ.
    Μὰ Δί' ἐγὼ μὲν οὔ
Τίς δ' εἶ σύ;

ΠΡΟΜΗΘΕΥΣ.
   Πηνίκ' ἐστὶν ἄρα τῆς ἡμέρας;

ΠΕΙΣΘΕΤΑΙΡΟΣ.
Ὁπηνίκα; Σμικρόν τι μετὰ μεσημβρίαν.
Ἀλλὰ σὺ τίς εἶ;

ΠΡΟΜΗΘΕΥΣ.
Βουλυτός, ἢ περαιτέρω ; 1485

ΠΕΙΣΘΕΤΑΙΡΟΣ.
Οἴμ' ὡς βδελύττομαί σε.

ΠΡΟΜΗΘΕΥΣ.
Τί γὰρ ὁ Ζεὺς ποιεῖ ;
Ἀπαιθριάζει τὰς νεφέλας, ἢ ξυννεφεῖ ;

ΠΕΙΣΘΕΤΑΙΡΟΣ.
Οἴμωζε μεγάλ'.

ΠΡΟΜΗΘΕΥΣ.
Οὕτω μὲν ἐκκεκαλύψομαι.

ΠΕΙΣΘΕΤΑΙΡΟΣ.
Ὦ φίλε Προμηθεῦ.

ΠΡΟΜΗΘΕΥΣ.
Παῦε παῦε, μὴ βόα.

ΠΕΙΣΘΕΤΑΙΡΟΣ.
Τί γὰρ ἔστι ;

ΠΡΟΜΗΘΕΥΣ.
Σίγα, μὴ κάλει μου τοὔνομα· 1490
Ἀπὸ γὰρ ὀλεῖ μ', εἴ μ' ἐνθάδ' ὁ Ζεὺς ὄψεται,
Ἀλλ' ἵνα φράσω σοι πάντα τἄνω πράγματα,
Τουτὶ λαβών μου τὸ σκιάδειον ὑπέρεχε
Ἄνωθεν, ὡς ἂν μή μ' ὁρῶσιν οἱ θεοί.

ΠΕΙΣΘΕΤΑΙΡΟΣ.
Ἰοὺ ἰού· 1495
Εὖ γ' ἐπενόησας αὐτὸ καὶ προμηθικῶς.
Ὑπόδυθι ταχὺ δή, κᾆτα θαρρήσας λέγε.

ΑΡΙΣΤΟΦΑΝΟΥΣ

ΠΡΟΜΗΘΕΥΣ.
Ἄκουε δή νυν.

ΠΕΙΣΘΕΤΑΙΡΟΣ.
Ὡς ἀκούοντος λέγε.

ΠΡΟΜΗΘΕΥΣ.
Ἀπόλωλεν ὁ Ζεύς.

ΠΕΙΣΘΕΤΑΙΡΟΣ.
Πηνίκ' ἄττ' ἀπώλετο ;

ΠΡΟΜΗΘΕΥΣ.
Ἐξ οὗπερ ὑμεῖς ᾠκίσατε τὸν ἀέρα. 1500
Θύει γὰρ οὐδεὶς οὐδὲν ἀνθρώπων ἔτι
Θεοῖσιν, οὐδὲ κνῖσα μηρίων ἄπο
Ἀνῆλθεν ὡς ἡμᾶς ἀπ' ἐκείνου τοῦ χρόνου,
Ἀλλ' ὡσπερεὶ Θεσμοφορίοις νηστεύομεν
Ἄνευ θυηλῶν· οἱ δὲ βάρβαροι θεοὶ 1505
Πεινῶντες ὥσπερ Ἰλλυριοὶ κεκριγότες
Ἐπιστρατεύσειν φάσ' ἄνωθεν τῷ Διί,
Εἰ μὴ παρέξει τἀμπόρι' ἀνεῳγμένα,
Ἵν' εἰσάγοιτο σπλάγχνα κατατετμημένα.

ΠΕΙΣΘΕΤΑΙΡΟΣ.
Εἰσὶν γὰρ ἕτεροι βάρβαροι θεοί τινες 1510
Ἄνωθεν ὑμῶν ;

ΠΡΟΜΗΘΕΥΣ.
Οὐ γάρ εἰσι βάρβαροι,
Ὅθεν ὁ πατρῷός ἐστιν Ἐξηκεστίδῃ ;

ΠΕΙΣΘΕΤΑΙΡΟΣ.
Ὄνομα δὲ τούτοις τοῖς θεοῖς τοῖς βαρβάροις
Τί ἐστίν ;

ΠΡΟΜΗΘΕΥΣ.
"Ο τι ἐστίν ;   Τριβαλλοί.

ΠΕΙΣΘΕΤΑΙΡΟΣ.
                            Μανθάνω.
Ἐντεῦθεν ἄρα " τοὐπιτριβείης " ἐγένετο.   1515

ΠΡΟΜΗΘΕΥΣ.
Μάλιστα πάντων.   Ἓν δέ σοι λέγω σαφές·
Ἥξουσι πρέσβεις δεῦρο περὶ διαλλαγῶν
Παρὰ τοῦ Διὸς καὶ τῶν Τριβαλλῶν τῶν ἄνω·
Ὑμεῖς δὲ μὴ σπένδεσθ᾽, ἐὰν μὴ παραδιδῷ
Τὸ σκῆπτρον ὁ Ζεὺς τοῖσιν ὄρνισιν πάλιν,   1520
Καὶ τὴν Βασίλειάν σοι γυναῖκ᾽ ἔχειν διδῷ.

ΠΕΙΣΘΕΤΑΙΡΟΣ.
Τίς ἐστιν ἡ Βασίλεια ;

ΠΡΟΜΗΘΕΥΣ.
                  Καλλίστη κόρη,
Ἥπερ ταμιεύει τὸν κεραυνὸν τοῦ Διὸς
Καὶ τἄλλ᾽ ἁπαξάπαντα, τὴν εὐβουλίαν,
Τὴν εὐνομίαν, τὴν σωφροσύνην, τὰ νεώρια,   1525
Τὴν λοιδορίαν, τὸν κωλακρέτην, τὰ τριώβολα.

ΠΕΙΣΘΕΤΑΙΡΟΣ.
Ἅπαντά τἄρ᾽ αὐτῷ ταμιεύει.

ΠΡΟΜΗΘΕΥΣ.
                  Φήμ᾽ ἐγώ.
Ἥν γ᾽ ἢν σὺ παρ᾽ ἐκείνου παραλάβῃς, πάντ᾽ ἔχεις.
Τούτων ἕνεκα δεῦρ᾽ ἦλθον, ἵνα φράσαιμί σοι.
Ἀεί ποτ᾽ ἀνθρώποις γὰρ εὔνους εἴμ᾽ ἐγώ.   1530

ΠΕΙΣΘΕΤΑΙΡΟΣ.
Μόνον θεῶν γὰρ διά σ' ἀπανθρακίζομεν.

ΠΡΟΜΗΘΕΥΣ.
Μισῶ δ' ἅπαντας τοὺς θεούς, ὡς οἶσθα σύ.

ΠΕΙΣΘΕΤΑΙΡΟΣ.
Νὴ τὸν Δί' ἀεὶ δῆτα θεομισὴς ἔφυς.

ΠΡΟΜΗΘΕΥΣ.
Τίμων καθαρός. Ἀλλ' ὡς ἂν ἀποτρέχω πάλιν,
Φέρε τὸ σκιάδειον, ἵνα με κἂν ὁ Ζεὺς ἴδῃ 1535
Ἄνωθεν, ἀκολουθεῖν δοκῶ κανηφόρῳ.

ΠΕΙΣΘΕΤΑΙΡΟΣ.
Καὶ τὸν δίφρον γε διφροφόρει τονδὶ λαβών.

ΧΟΡΟΣ.
Στροφή.
Πρὸς δὲ τοῖς Σκιάποσιν λι-
 μνη τις ἔστ', ἄλουτος οὗ
Ψυχαγωγεῖ Σωκράτης· 540
Ἔνθα καὶ Πείσανδρος ἦλθε
Δεόμενος ψυχὴν ἰδεῖν, ἣ
Ζῶντ' ἐκεῖνον προὔλιπε,
Σφάγι' ἔχων κάμηλον ἀ-
 μνόν τιν', ἧς λαιμοὺς τεμών, 545
Ὥσπερ οὑδυσσεὺς ἀπῆλθε,
Κᾆτ' ἀνῆλθ' αὐτῷ κάτωθεν
Πρὸς τὸ λαῖμα τῆς καμήλου
Χαιρεφῶν ἡ νυκτερίς.

ΟΡΝΙΘΕΣ.

ΠΟΣΕΙΔΩΝ.

Τὸ μὲν πόλισμα τῆς Νεφελοκοκκυγίας
Ὁρᾶν τοδὶ πάρεστιν, οἷ πρεσβεύομεν.
Οὗτος, τί δρᾷς ; Ἐπ' ἀριστέρ' οὕτως ἀμπέχει ;
Οὐ μεταβαλεῖς θοἰμάτιον ὧδ' ἐπὶ δεξιάν ;
Τί, ᾧ κακόδαιμον ;   Λαισποδίας εἶ τὴν φύσιν.
Ὦ δημοκρατία, ποῖ προβιβᾷς ἡμᾶς ποτε,
Εἰ τουτονί γ' ἐχειροτόνησαν οἱ θεοί ;

ΤΡΙΒΑΛΛΟΣ.

Ἕξεις ἀτρέμας ;

ΠΟΣΕΙΔΩΝ.

Οἴμωζε· πολὺ γὰρ δή σ' ἐγὼ
Ἑόρακα πάντων βαρβαρώτατον θεῶν.
Ἄγε δὴ τί δρῶμεν, Ἡράκλεις ;

ΗΡΑΚΛΗΣ.

Ἀκήκοας
Ἐμοῦ γ' ὅτι τὸν ἄνθρωπον ἄγχειν βούλομαι,
Ὅστις ποτ' ἔσθ' ὁ τοὺς θεοὺς ἀποτειχίσας.

ΠΟΣΕΙΔΩΝ.

Ἀλλ', ὠγάθ', ᾐρήμεσθα περὶ διαλλαγῶν
Πρέσβεις.

ΗΡΑΚΛΗΣ.

Διπλασίως μᾶλλον ἄγχειν μοι δοκεῖ.

ΠΕΙΣΘΕΤΑΙΡΟΣ.

Τὴν τυρόκνηστίν μοι δότω· φέρε σίλφιον·
Τυρὸν φερέτω τις· πυρπόλει τοὺς ἄνθρακας.

9*

ΗΡΑΚΛΗΣ.
Τὸν ἄνδρα χαίρειν οἱ θεοὶ κελεύομεν
Τρεῖς ὄντες ἡμεῖς.

ΠΕΙΣΘΕΤΑΙΡΟΣ.
Ἀλλ' ἐπικνῶ τὸ σίλφιον.

ΗΡΑΚΛΗΣ.
Τὰ δὲ κρέα τοῦ ταῦτ' ἐστίν;

ΠΕΙΣΘΕΤΑΙΡΟΣ.
Ὀρνιθές τινες
Ἐπανιστάμενοι τοῖς δημοτικοῖσιν ὀρνέοις
Ἔδοξαν ἀδικεῖν.

ΗΡΑΚΛΗΣ.
Εἶτα δῆτα σίλφιον 1570
Ἐπικνᾷς πρότερον αὐτοῖσιν;

ΠΕΙΣΘΕΤΑΙΡΟΣ.
Ὦ χαῖρ', Ἡράκλεις.
Τί ἔστι;

ΗΡΑΚΛΗΣ.
Πρεσβεύοντες ἡμεῖς ἥκομεν
Παρὰ τῶν θεῶν περὶ πολέμου καταλλαγῆς.

ΟΙΚΕΤΗΣ.
Ἔλαιον οὐκ ἔνεστιν ἐν τῇ ληκύθῳ.

ΠΕΙΣΘΕΤΑΙΡΟΣ.
Καὶ μὴν τά γ' ὀρνίθεια λιπάρ' εἶναι πρέπει. 1575

ΗΡΑΚΛΗΣ.
Ἡμεῖς τε γὰρ πολεμοῦντες οὐ κερδαίνομεν,
Ὑμεῖς τ' ἂν ἡμῖν τοῖς θεοῖς ὄντες φίλοι

ΟΡΝΙΘΕΣ.

Ὄμβριον ὕδωρ ἂν εἴχετ' ἐν τοῖς τέλμασιν,
Ἀλκυονίδας τ' ἂν ἦγεθ' ἡμέρας ἀεί.
Τούτων περὶ πάντων αὐτοκράτορες ἥκομεν.

ΠΕΙΣΘΕΤΑΙΡΟΣ.

Ἀλλ' οὔτε πρότερον πώποθ' ἡμεῖς ἤρξαμεν
Πολέμου πρὸς ὑμᾶς, νῦν τ' ἐθέλομεν, εἰ δοκεῖ,
Ἐὰν τὸ δίκαιον ἀλλὰ νῦν ἐθέλητε δρᾶν,
Σπονδὰς ποιεῖσθαι. Τὰ δὲ δίκαι' ἐστὶν ταδί·
Τὸ σκῆπτρον ἡμῖν τοῖσιν ὄρνισιν πάλιν   1585
Τὸν Δί' ἀποδοῦναι· κἂν διαλλαττώμεθα,
Ἐπὶ τοῖσδε τοὺς πρέσβεις ἐπ' ἄριστον καλῶ.

ΗΡΑΚΛΗΣ.

Ἐμοὶ μὲν ἀπόχρη ταῦτα, καὶ ψηφίζομαι.

ΠΟΣΕΙΔΩΝ.

Τί, ὦ κακόδαιμον ; Ἠλίθιος καὶ γάστρις εἶ.
Ἀποστερεῖς τὸν πατέρα τῆς τυραννίδος ;   1590

ΠΕΙΣΘΕΤΑΙΡΟΣ.

Ἄληθες ; Οὐ γὰρ μεῖζον ὑμεῖς οἱ θεοὶ
Ἰσχύσετ', ἢν ὄρνιθες ἄρξωσιν κάτω ;
Νῦν μέν γ' ὑπὸ ταῖς νεφέλαισιν ἐγκεκρυμμένοι
Κύψαντες ἐπιορκοῦσιν ὑμᾶς οἱ βροτοί·
Ἐὰν δὲ τοὺς ὄρνις ἔχητε συμμάχους,   1595
Ὅταν ὀμνύῃ τις τὸν κόρακα καὶ τὸν Δία,
Ὁ κόραξ παρελθὼν τοὐπιορκοῦντος λάθρα
Προσπτάμενος ἐκκόψει τὸν ὀφθαλμὸν θενών.

ΠΟΣΕΙΔΩΝ.

Νὴ τὸν Ποσειδῶ, ταῦτά γέ τοι καλῶς λέγεις.

ΗΡΑΚΛΗΣ.
Κἀμοὶ δοκεῖ.

ΠΕΙΣΘΕΤΑΙΡΟΣ.
Τί δαὶ σὺ φῄς;

ΤΡΙΒΑΛΛΟΣ.
Ναβαισατρεῦ.   1600

ΠΕΙΣΘΕΤΑΙΡΟΣ.
Ὁρᾷς; Ἐπαινεῖ χοὗτος. Ἕτερον νῦν ἔτι
Ἀκούσαθ᾽ ὅσον ὑμᾶς ἀγαθὸν ποιήσομεν.
Ἐάν τις ἀνθρώπων ἱερεῖόν τῳ θεῶν
Εὐξάμενος, εἶτα διασοφίζηται λέγων
" Μενετοὶ θεοί," καὶ μἀποδιδῷ μισητίαν,   1605
Ἀναπράξομεν καὶ ταῦτα.

ΠΟΣΕΙΔΩΝ.
Φέρ᾽ ἴδω, τῷ τρόπῳ;

ΠΕΙΣΘΕΤΑΙΡΟΣ.
Ὅταν διαριθμῶν ἀργυρίδιον τύχῃ
Ἄνθρωπος οὗτος, ἢ κάθηται λούμενος,
Καταπτάμενος ἰκτῖνος, ἁρπάσας λάθρα,
Προβάτοιν δυοῖν τιμὴν ἀνοίσει τῷ θεῷ.   1610

ΗΡΑΚΛΗΣ.
Τὸ σκῆπτρον ἀποδοῦναι πάλιν ψηφίζομαι
Τούτοις ἐγώ.

ΠΟΣΕΙΔΩΝ.
Καὶ τὸν Τριβαλλὸν νῦν ἐροῦ.

ΗΡΑΚΛΗΣ.
Ὁ Τριβαλλός, οἰμώζειν δοκεῖ σοι;

ΟΡΝΙΘΕΣ.

ΤΡΙΒΑΛΛΟΣ.
Σαυνάκα
Βακταρικροῦσα.

ΗΡΑΚΛΗΣ.
Φησὶν εὖ λέγειν πάνυ.

ΠΟΣΕΙΔΩΝ.
Εἴ τοι δοκεῖ σφῷν ταῦτα, κἀμοὶ συνδοκεῖ. 1615

ΗΡΑΚΛΗΣ.
Οὗτος, δοκεῖ δρᾶν ταῦτα τοῦ σκήπτρου πέρι.

ΠΕΙΣΘΕΤΑΙΡΟΣ.
Καὶ νὴ Δί᾽ ἕτερόν γ᾽ ἐστὶν οὗ 'μνήσθην ἐγώ.
Τὴν μὲν γὰρ Ἥραν παραδίδωμι τῷ Διί,
Τὴν δὲ Βασίλειαν τὴν κόρην γυναῖκ᾽ ἐμοὶ
Ἐκδοτέον ἐστίν.

ΠΟΣΕΙΔΩΝ.
Οὐ διαλλαγῶν ἐρᾷς. 1620
Ἀπίωμεν οἴκαδ᾽ αὖθις.

ΠΕΙΣΘΕΤΑΙΡΟΣ.
Ὀλίγον μοι μέλει.
Μάγειρε, τὸ κατάχυσμα χρὴ ποιεῖν γλυκύ.

ΗΡΑΚΛΗΣ.
Ὦ δαιμόνι᾽ ἀνθρώπων Πόσειδον, ποῖ φέρει ;
Ἡμεῖς περὶ γυναικὸς μιᾶς πολεμήσομεν ;

ΠΟΣΕΙΔΩΝ.
Τί δαὶ ποιῶμεν ;

ΗΡΑΚΛΗΣ.
Ὅ τι ; Διαλλαττώμεθα. 1625

N

ΠΟΣΕΙΔΩΝ.

Τί, ᾧζύρ'; Οὐκ οἶσθ' ἐξαπατώμενος πάλαι ;
Βλάπτεις δέ τοι σὺ σαυτόν. Ἢν γὰρ ἀποθάνῃ
Ὁ Ζεύς, παραδοὺς τούτοισι τὴν τυραννίδα,
Πένης ἔσει σύ. Σοῦ γὰρ ἅπαντα γίγνεται
Τὰ χρήμαθ', ὅσ' ἂν ὁ Ζεὺς ἀποθνήσκων καταλίπῃ. 1630

ΠΕΙΣΘΕΤΑΙΡΟΣ.

Οἴμοι τάλας, οἷόν σε περισοφίζεται.
Δεῦρ' ὡς ἔμ' ἀποχώρησον, ἵνα τί σοι φράσω.
Διαβάλλεταί σ' ὁ θεῖος, ὦ πονηρὲ σύ.
Τῶν γὰρ πατρῴων οὐδ' ἀκαρῆ μέτεστί σοι
Κατὰ τοὺς νόμους· νόθος γὰρ εἶ κοὐ γνήσιος. 1635

ΗΡΑΚΛΗΣ.

Ἐγὼ νόθος ; Τί λέγεις ;

ΠΕΙΣΘΕΤΑΙΡΟΣ.

Σὺ μέντοι νὴ Δία,
Ὢν γε ξένης γυναικός. Ἢ πῶς ἄν ποτε
Ἐπίκληρον εἶναι τὴν Ἀθηναίαν δοκεῖς,
Οὖσαν θυγατέρ', ὄντων ἀδελφῶν γνησίων ;

ΗΡΑΚΛΗΣ.

Τί δ', ἢν ὁ πατὴρ ἐμοὶ διδῷ τὰ χρήματα 1640
Νόθῳ 'ξαποθνήσκων ;

ΠΕΙΣΘΕΤΑΙΡΟΣ.

Ὁ νόμος αὐτὸν οὐκ ἐᾷ.
Οὗτος ὁ Ποσειδῶν πρῶτος, ὃς ἐπαίρει σε νῦν,
Ἀνθέξεταί σου τῶν πατρῴων χρημάτων
Φάσκων ἀδελφὸς αὐτὸς εἶναι γνήσιος.

ΟΡΝΙΘΕΣ.

Ἐρῶ δὲ δὴ καὶ τὸν Σόλωνός σοι νόμον·
" Νόθῳ δὲ μὴ εἶναι ἀγχιστείαν, παίδων ὄντων
γνησίων. Ἐὰν δὲ παῖδες μὴ ὦσι γνήσιοι, τοῖς
ἐγγυτάτω γένους μετεῖναι τῶν χρημάτων."

ΗΡΑΚΛΗΣ.
Ἐμοὶ δ᾽ ἄρ᾽ οὐδὲν τῶν πατρῴων χρημάτων
Μέτεστιν;

ΠΕΙΣΘΕΤΑΙΡΟΣ.
Οὐ μέντοι μὰ Δία. Λέξον δέ μοι,
Ἤδη σ᾽ ὁ πατὴρ εἰσήγαγ᾽ ἐς τοὺς φράτορας;

ΗΡΑΚΛΗΣ.
Οὐ δῆτ᾽ ἐμέ γε. Καὶ δῆτ᾽ ἐθαύμαζον πάλαι.

ΠΕΙΣΘΕΤΑΙΡΟΣ.
Τί δῆτ᾽ ἄνω κέχηνας αἰκίαν βλέπων;
Ἀλλ᾽ ἢν μεθ᾽ ἡμῶν ᾖς, καταστήσω σ᾽ ἐγὼ
Τύραννον, ὀρνίθων παρέξω σοι γάλα.

ΗΡΑΚΛΗΣ.
Δίκαι᾽ ἔμοιγε καὶ πάλιν δοκεῖς λέγειν
Περὶ τῆς κόρης· κἄγωγε παραδίδωμί σοι.

ΠΕΙΣΘΕΤΑΙΡΟΣ.
Τί δαὶ σὺ φῄς;

ΠΟΣΕΙΔΩΝ.
Τἀναντία ψηφίζομαι.

ΠΕΙΣΘΕΤΑΙΡΟΣ.
Ἐν τῷ Τριβαλλῷ πᾶν τὸ πρᾶγμα. Τί σὺ λέγεις;

ΤΡΙΒΑΛΛΟΣ.
Καλάνι κόραυνα καὶ μεγάλα βασιλιναῦ
Ὄρνιτο παραδίδωμι.

ΗΡΑΚΛΗΣ.
Παραδοῦναι λέγει.

ΠΟΣΕΙΔΩΝ.
Μὰ τὸν Δί᾽ οὐχ οὗτός γε παραδοῦναι λέγει,
Εἰ μὴ βαδίζειν ὥσπερ αἱ χελιδόνες.

ΠΕΙΣΘΕΤΑΙΡΟΣ.
Οὐκοῦν παραδοῦναι ταῖς χελιδόσιν λέγει.

ΠΟΣΕΙΔΩΝ.
Σφὼ νῦν διαλλάττεσθε καὶ ξυμβαίνετε· 1665
Ἐγὼ δ᾽, ἐπειδὴ σφῷν δοκεῖ, σιγήσομαι.

ΗΡΑΚΛΗΣ.
Ἡμῖν ἃ λέγεις σὺ πάντα συγχωρεῖν δοκεῖ.
Ἀλλ᾽ ἴθι μεθ᾽ ἡμῶν αὐτὸς ἐς τὸν οὐρανόν,
Ἵνα τὴν Βασίλειαν καὶ τὰ πάντ᾽ ἐκεῖ λάβῃς.

ΠΕΙΣΘΕΤΑΙΡΟΣ.
Ἐς καιρὸν ἆρα κατεκόπησαν οὑτοιὶ 1670
Ἐς τοὺς γάμους.

ΗΡΑΚΛΗΣ.
Βούλεσθε δῆτ᾽ ἐγὼ τέως
Ὀπτῶ τὰ κρέα ταυτὶ μένων; Ὑμεῖς δ᾽ ἴτε.

ΠΟΣΕΙΔΩΝ.
Ὀπτᾷς τὰ κρέα; Πολλήν γε τενθείαν λέγεις.
Οὐκ εἶ μεθ᾽ ἡμῶν;

ΗΡΑΚΛΗΣ.
Εὖ γε μέν τἂν διετέθην.

ΠΕΙΣΘΕΤΑΙΡΟΣ.
Ἀλλὰ γαμικὴν χλανίδα δότω τις δεῦρό μοι. 1675

ΟΡΝΙΘΕΣ.

ΧΟΡΟΣ.

Ἀντιστροφή.

Εστι δ' ἐν Φαναῖσι πρὸς τῇ
Κλεψύδρᾳ πανοῦργον ἐγ-
γλωττογαστόρων γένος,
Οἳ θερίζουσίν τε καὶ σπεί-
ρουσι καὶ τρυγῶσι ταῖς γλώτ- 1680
ταισι συκάζουσί τε·
Βάρβαροι δ' εἰσὶν γένος,
Γοργίαι τε καὶ Φίλιπποι.
Κἀπὸ τῶν ἐγγλωττογαστό-
ρων ἐκείνων τῶν Φιλίππων 1685
Πανταχοῦ τῆς Ἀττικῆς ἡ
Γλῶττα χωρὶς τέμνεται.

ΑΓΓΕΛΟΣ.

Ὦ πάντ' ἀγαθὰ πράττοντες, ὦ μείζω λόγου,
Ὦ τρισμακάριον πτηνὸν ὀρνίθων γένος,
Δέχεσθε τὸν τύραννον ὀλβίοις δόμοις. 1690
Προσέρχεται γὰρ οἷος οὔτε παμφαὴς
Ἀστὴρ ἰδεῖν ἔλαμψε χρυσαυγεῖ δόμῳ,
Οὔθ' ἡλίου τηλαυγὲς ἀκτίνων σέλας
Τοιοῦτον ἐξέλαμψεν, οἷον ἔρχεται,
Ἔχων γυναικὸς κάλλος οὐ φατὸν λέγειν, 1695
Πάλλων κεραυνόν, πτεροφόρον Διὸς βέλος·
Ὀσμὴ δ' ἀνωνόμαστος ἐς βάθος κύκλου
Χωρεῖ, καλὸν θέαμα· θυμιαμάτων δ'
Αὖραι διαψαίρουσι πλεκτάνην καπνοῦ.

Ὁδὶ δὲ καὐτός ἐστιν. Ἀλλὰ χρὴ θεᾶς 1700
Μούσης ἀνοίγειν ἱερὸν εὔφημον στόμα.

ΧΟΡΟΣ.

Ἄναγε, δίεχε, πάραγε, πάρεχε,
Περιπέτεσθε
Μάκαρα μάκαρι σὺν τύχᾳ.
Ὦ φεῦ φεῦ τῆς ὥρας, τοῦ κάλλους. 1705
Ὦ μακαριστὸν σὺ γάμον τῇδε πόλει γήμας.
Μεγάλαι μεγάλαι κατέχουσι τύχαι
Γένος ὀρνίθων
Διὰ τόνδε τὸν ἄνδρ'. Ἀλλ' ὑμεναίοις
Καὶ νυμφιδίοισι δέχεσθ' ᾠδαῖς 1710
Αὐτὸν καὶ τὴν Βασίλειαν.
Ἥρᾳ ποτ' Ὀλυμπίᾳ
Τῶν ἠλιβάτων θρόνων
Ἄρχοντα θεοῖς μέγαν
Μοῖραι ξυνεκοίμισαν 1715
Ἐν τοιῷδ' ὑμεναίῳ.
Ὑμὴν ὤ, Ὑμέναι' ὤ.
Ὁ δ' ἀμφιθαλὴς Ἔρως
Χρυσόπτερος ἡνίας
Εὔθυνε παλιντόνους, 1720
Ζηνὸς πάροχος γάμων
Τῆς τ' εὐδαίμονος Ἥρας.
Ὑμὴν ὤ, Ὑμέναι' ὤ.

ΠΕΙΣΘΕΤΑΙΡΟΣ.

Ἐχάρην ὕμνοις, ἐχάρην ᾠδαῖς·

Ἄγαμαι δὲ λόγων. Ἄγε νῦν αὐτοῦ 1725
Καὶ τὰς χθονίας κλήσατε βροντάς,
Τάς τε πυρώδεις Διὸς ἀστεροπάς,
Δεινόν τ' ἀργῆτα κεραυνόν.

ΧΟΡΟΣ

Ὦ μέγα χρύσεον ἀστεροπῆς φάος,
Ὦ Διὸς ἄμβροτον ἔγχος πυρφόρον, 1730
Ὦ χθόνιαί βαρυαχέες
Ὀμβροφόροι θ' ἅμα βρονταί,
Αἷς ὅδε νῦν χθόνα σείει.
Διὰ σὲ τὰ πάντα κρατήσας,
Καὶ πάρεδρον Βασίλειαν ἔχει Διός. 1735
Ὑμὴν ὦ, Ὑμέναι' ὦ

ΠΕΙΣΘΕΤΑΙΡΟΣ.

Ἕπεσθε νῦν γάμοισιν, ὦ
Φῦλα πάντα συννόμων
Πτεροφόρ', ἐπὶ πέδον Διὸς
Καὶ λέχος γαμήλιον. 1740
Ὄρεξον, ὦ μάκαιρα, σὴν
Χεῖρα, καὶ πτερῶν ἐμῶν
Λαβοῦσα συγχόρευσον· αἴ-
ρων δὲ κουφιῶ σ' ἐγώ.

ΧΟΡΟΣ.

Ἀλαλαλαί, ἰὴ Παιών, 1745
Τήνελλα καλλίνικος, ὦ
Δαιμόνων ὑπέρτατε.

NOTES

10*

NOTES.

In the opening scene, two old Athenians appear, named Euelpides and Peisthetairos. Wearied with the annoyances to which they have been subjected in their native city, they leave it to search for Epops, the king of the birds, who was connected with the Attic traditions, under the mythical name of Tereus. They have taken with them, as guides of their journey, a raven and a jackdaw, which have led them up and down over a rough and rocky country, until the fugitives are jaded out by the fatigues of the way, and begin to scold about the cheating poulterer who has sold them, for an obol and a three-obol piece, a pair of birds good for nothing but to bite. At length they reach the forest and the steep rocks, which shut them from all farther progress.

Line 1. Ὀρθήν. This agrees with ὁδόν, to be constructed with ἰέναι, or some similar verb. *Dost thou bid me go straight up?* — addressed to the jackdaw. For the ellipsis of the substantive, see Kühner, § 263.

2. Διαρραγείης. G. § 82. This is addressed, as a sort of humorous imprecation, to Euelpides. The word occurs frequently in the orators, especially Demosthenes, to express a violent passion or effort of the person to whom it is applied; as, for instance, οὐδ᾽ ἂν διαρραγῇς ψευδόμενος, "not even if you split with lying." Translate here, *May you split.* — ἥδε

i. e. κορώνη, *but this* raven.— πάλιν, *back,* in the opposite direction.

3. πλανύττομεν. A Scholiast speaks of this word as Attic for πλανώμεθα; and Suidas, cited by Bothe, considers it as a comic usage; perhaps it may be rendered, *Why are we tramping?*

4. ἄλλως = μάτην, *to no purpose.*

5, 6. Τὸ . . . . περιελθεῖν. For the construction of the infinitive in sentences expressing exclamation, see G. § 104. For the force of the Aorist, see G. § 23, 1, N. 1. See also Clouds, 268, note.

10. ἂν ἐξεύροις. G. § 52, 2.

11. Οὐδ' ἂν . . . . Ἐξηκεστίδης, *Not even Exekestides could perceive the country hence.* G. § 42, 3, N. 2; § 53, N. 3. The name of this person occurs in two other places of the play, lines 766 and 1512. He was often introduced by the comic writers, and satirized as a person of barbarian origin, who had by fraudulent means got himself enrolled among the Athenian citizens. The meaning of the answer of Peisthetairos, then, is, "We are farther off than Exekestides: even he could not discern Athens from this spot." "It would puzzle Exekestides himself to make out Athens from here."

13. οὐκ τῶν ὀρνέων, *he of the birds;* i. e. the bird-seller or poulterer. The expression is like that applied to Hyperbolus in the Clouds (1065), οὐκ τῶν λύχνων, *the dealer in lamps.* There is also an allusion here, and in line 16, to the town of Orneae, in Argolis, which was destroyed by a combined force of Argives and Athenians, after a siege of one day, in 416 B. C. (two years before the exhibition of the Birds). See Thucyd., VI. 7, where the expression ἐκ τῶν Ὀρνεῶν occurs. The memory of this recent event made the allusion particularly applicable. The explanation given by the Scholiast — that the two Athenians are made to suffer

ἐκ τῶν ὀρνέων, because 'Ορνεαί is in Laconia (?), and the Athenians had recently suffered a loss at Mantinea — is impossible, from the circumstance that the people of 'Ορνεαί *assisted* the Athenians at the battle of Mantinea. See Thucyd., V. 67, and Arnold's note.

14. Ὁ .... μελαγχολῶν, *The poulterer Philocrates, being mad.* Philocrates would seem to have been well known as a dealer in birds in the Athenian market. He is again introduced by the Chorus (v. 1070), where a reward of one talent is offered for any one who will kill him; for any one who will take him alive, four talents; — his various offences against the race of birds being enumerated.

15. ἔφασκε .... φράσειν. G. § 73, 1; § 27.

16. ὃς .... ὀρνέων. This refers, of course, to the fable of the metamorphosis of Tereus into the Epops, or Hoopoo, for which see Ovid, Metam., VI. 423, seq. With regard to the Hoopoo, or Huppoo, Cary (Preface to Translation of the Birds) has the following note. " As this bird acts a principal part in the play, the reader may not be displeased to see the following description of it: 'At Penyrhiw, the farm to which this wild, uncultivated tract is a sheep-walk, was lately shot a Huppoo, a solitary bird, two being seldom seen together, and in this kingdom very uncommon; even in Egypt, where common, not very gregarious. Bewick's description of it is very correct. Upupa of Linnaeus, la Hupe of Buffon. This bird is of the order of Picae; its length twelve inches, breadth nineteen; bill above two inches long, black, slender, and somewhat curved; eyes hazel; tongue very short and triangular; head ornamented with a crest, consisting of a double row of feathers of pale orange color, tipped with black; highest about two inches long; neck pale reddish brown, breast and belly white; back, scapulars, and wings crossed with broad bars of black and white; lesser coverts of the wings light brown, rump white; the

tail consists of ten feathers, each marked with white, which, when closed, assumes the form of a crescent, the horns pointing downwards; legs short and black. Crest usually falls behind on its neck, except when surprised, and then erect, agreeing exactly with Pliny's character of it. " Crista visenda plicatili, contrahens eam subrigensque per longitudinem capitis," whose annotator, Dalecampius, mentions another curious particular of this bird: "Nidum ex stercore humano praecipue conficit." Bewick, Vol. I. 262; Plin. Variorum, 688. In Sweden, the appearance of this bird is vulgarly considered as a presage of war, and it was formerly deemed in our country a forerunner of some calamity.' — *Historical Tour through Pembrokeshire*, by Richard Fenton, Esq., p. 17. London, 4to, 1810. The particular mentioned by Dalecampius is observed by Aristotle also, who adds that the bird changes its appearance summer and winter, as most of the other wild birds do." Von der Mühle (Beiträge zur Ornithologie Griechenlands, p. 34) says of the Epops, that it is found in great numbers in Greece, in the month of September, but more seldom in spring; that it is fond of the oleanders near the coast, &c.

What is the point of the phrase ἐκ τῶν ὀρνέων, in this place, has been a question. The Scholiast explains it παρ' ὑπόνοιαν· ἔδει γὰρ ἐκ τῶν ἀνθρώπων; i. e. instead of saying he was changed from a *man* to a bird, the poet gives an unexpected turn to the words and says, *who became a bird from — the birds*. Bergler's opinion is, "Videtur voce ὄρνεα metaphorice significare homines *superbos aut leves et inconstantes;* hoc sensu: ex homine superbo, aut levi et inconstante, factus est ales superbus, aut levis et inconstans." Perhaps the explanation of the Scholiast, and that of Bergler combined with the remark of Cary, that " this is intended as a stroke of satire on the levity of the Athenians," may suggest the true meaning of the poet, especially as the general bearing of the play is to be explained by the circumstances and relations of Athenian affairs. See note to v. 13.

17. Θαρρελείδου, i. e. υἱόν, *this son of Tharreleides.* The jackdaw is called the son of Tharreleides, according to some, because of the loquacity of that individual, whose name was Asopodoros; according to others, from his small stature, or some other point in which a resemblance might be found or fancied.

18. ὀβολοῦ . . . . τριωβόλου. Genitive of price.

19. ἄρ'. For the conclusive signification of ἄρα, see the exact analysis of Hartung, "De Particulis," Vol. I. pp. 448, 449. See also Kühner, § 324, 3. In this place it implies a sort of consequence of the preceding statement; as if he intended to say that the vicious tricks of the birds were nothing more than might have been expected from the character of the man who sold them. Translate the whole line, *And they accordingly were nothing but biting.*

20. κέχηνας, addressed to the jackdaw. — κατὰ τῶν πετρῶν, *down the rocks.*

22. ἀτραπός, *a track*, or *path*; ὁδός is a *road, way*, or *street.*

28. Ἐς κόρακας ἐλθεῖν. There is a pun upon the double meaning of the phrase, which is commonly used as a jocose imprecation, *Go to the crows*, but here alludes also to the intention of the two old men to visit the city of the birds.

29. Ἔπειτα. For the use of this particle in questions of astonishment, see Kühner, § 344, 5 (e).

30. ἄνδρες . . . . λόγῳ. The expression is said to be borrowed from debates in the political assemblies; but it was as well applied to listeners to any discussion whatever, and is here familiarly transferred to the spectators of the comic representation.

31. Νόσον νοσοῦμεν. The common Greek construction

of the accusative of kindred signification. — Σακᾷ. A common name for slaves and servants of barbarian origin, particularly Thracians; here applied to a tragic poet named Akestor, on account of his being a foreigner. In the Cyropaedia it is the name of the cupbearer of King Astyages.

32. εἰσβιάζεται, *is forcing himself in;* i. e. is constantly trying to thrust himself into the number of legal citizens. For an account of the care with which the rights and privileges of citizenship were guarded at Athens, see, besides other works, Smith's Dict. of Gr. and Rom. Antiq., art. *Civitas.*

33. φυλῇ καὶ γένει. For the political meaning of these terms, see Hermann's Staatsalterthümer (Political Antiquities), § 94, and §§ 97, 98; and Grote, Vol. III. Chap. 10.

34. σοβοῦντος. This participle applies particularly to the *scaring away* of birds, though used metaphorically to express the act of frightening off, in general. ᾿Ανεπτόμεσθα, in the following line, is also used in a similar way; and ἀμφοῖν ποδοῖν is a comic inconsistency with the previous expression. He could say, using language metaphorically, *We flew away from the country,* but instead of adding *with both wings,* he was obliged to substitute *with both feet,* they having not yet been accommodated with the wings.

36. ἐκείνην, emphatically, "*that* great city."

37. μὴ οὐ. For the use of this double negative, see G. § 95, 3; § 95, 2. N. 1 (*b*).

38. Καὶ . . . . ἐναποτῖσαι, *And common to all — to pay away their money in;* i. e. to waste money in lawsuits, which is the more specific meaning of ἀποτίνειν. G. § 97, or § 93, 2. The poet ingeniously and wittily combines in the ridicule of this line one of the great boasts of the Athenians, namely, the liberality with which the city's resources for instruction and amusement were opened to all comers (for a particular detail of which see the funeral oration of

NOTES. 121

Pericles in Thucydides, II. 35-46; and the Panegyricus of Isocrates, pp. 15, 16, Felton's edition, and notes), and the notorious love of litigation for which the Athenians were so often reproached, and which Aristophanes exposed with infinite spirit and drollery in the "Wasps."

39. τέττιγες. The chirping of the cicadae or τέττιγες is a subject of frequent allusion in the Greek poets, from Homer down. See Iliad, III. 151, and note upon the passage. For a description of the insect, and the ancient, though erroneous, idea of its habits, see Aristotle, Hist. An., Lib. IV. 7. Particularly, he speaks of it as living on dew, — τῇ δρόσῳ τρέφεται, — on which compare the Anacreontic ode, No. 32 (43), — ὀλίγην δρόσον πεπωκώς, βασιλεὺς ὅπως ἀείδεις. See also the note of Strack, pp. 182 and 183 of his German translation of Aristotle. The manner in which the sound called singing by Aristotle and the poets is produced, is explained Lib. IV. c. 9. Swammerdam has the following statement: "Cicada duobus gaudet exiguis tympanis peculiaribus, nostro auris tympano similibus, quae duarum ope cartilaginum lunatarum percussa, aerem ita vibrant ut sonitus inde reddatur." Bibl. Nat., p. 504; cited by Camus, Vol. II. p. 230.

40. Ἐπὶ τῶν κραδῶν ᾄδουσι. Aristotle, Lib. V. 30, says of the cicadae, "Οὐ γίνονται δὲ τέττιγες ὅπου μὴ δένδρα ἐστίν"; he adds, "There are none in the plain of Cyrene, but there are many round the city, *and chiefly where there are olive-trees.*"

41. τῶν δικῶν. See note to line 38.

44. ἀπράγμονα, *free from trouble*, particularly vexatious lawsuits.

45. καθιδρυθέντε διαγενοίμεθα. For the participle expressing a condition, see G. § 109, 6; § 52, 1. Dawes proposed the present διαγινοίμεθα; but when we consider that the idea of the verb may be conceived either as continuous or as

momentary, there seems no necessity for any change, unless upon the authority of some good manuscript.

46, 47. τὸν . . . . τόν. The repetition of the article, before both the name and the further designation, emphasizes them, *the Tereus;* that ancient Tereus, well known to the Athenian people, who was changed into the Epops.

48. ᾖ, used adverbially, *where he has flown;* i. e. if he has ever seen such a city in all his travels.

49, 50. πάλαι . . . . φράζει. By a common idiom, the present is used with an adverb of the past to mean *has been doing and is still doing;* here, has been this long time talking up. G. § 10, 1, N. 3.

51. ὡσπερεὶ δεικνύς, as *if he were showing* (= ὥσπερ ἂν ἔχαινεν, εἰ ἐδείκνυ). G. § 109, N. 3 (*b*). Sometimes the more complete form ὥσπερ ἂν εἰ is used in such expressions; but generally we find only ὥσπερ. G. § 53, N. 3.

52. Κοὐκ . . . . οὐκ. The combination of particles intensifies the expression, *There is not how there are not;* i. e. *It must be that there are.*

53. ποιήσωμεν. G. § 50, 1. Observe the force of the aorist in the subjunctive to express a single act. The present here would imply a repetition. See G., Rem. before § 12.

54. οἶσθ' ὃ δρᾶσον; For an explanation of this idiom, see G. § 84, N. 3. It occurs frequently in the Attic writers, especially the tragic poets. See Soph. Oed. Tyr., 543; Eurip. Med., 605, &c. There seems to be a combination of two phrases in one: οἶσθ' ὃ δεῖ δρᾶσαι; δρᾶσον. The third person of the imperative is also used in the same way. See the same expression, v. 80. — σκέλει . . . . πέτραν. The Scholiast, cited by Bothe, says there was a proverbial expression among the boys, Δὸς τὸ σκέλος τῇ πέτρᾳ καὶ πεσοῦνται τὰ ὄρνεα, *Give your leg to the rock and the birds will fall*, not unlike the modern notion of catching birds by sprinkling salt on their tails.

57. Τί . . . . οὗτος; *What do you say, fellow?* — παῖ, the common form of addressing a servant, and therefore considered as disrespectful to Epops.

58. ἐχρῆν . . . . καλεῖν. *Ought you not to call him,* &c.? A protasis is implied, *if you were respectful,* or the like. See G. § 49, 2, N. 3.

61. τοῦ χασμήματος, *what a yawn!* For genitive of exclamation, see K. § 274, c. Comp. also Clouds, v. 153, and note to the passage.

63. Οὕτως . . . . λέγειν; Bothe punctuates the line without the interrogation, — Οὐδὲ κάλλιόν ἐστι λέγειν τι οὕτω δεινόν, *Aliquid tam terribile ne nominare quidem decet;* " 'T were better not even to mention so terrible a thing." But the position of the words and the natural construction of δέ in οὐδέ conflicts with the interpretation. Several other explanations are given. The Scholiast says: " Οὑτωσί τι δεινὸν οὐδὲ κάλλιον λέγειν, τουτέστιν, οὕτω δεινὸν ἔχομεν ἐκ τῆς ὄψεως, ὥστε ὀρνιθοθῆραι νομίζεσθαι. Οὐδὲ λέγειν σε τοῦτό ἐστι κάλλιον, ὅτι ἐσμὲν ὀρνιθοθῆραι"; i. e. *We have something so fearful in our look as to be thought bird-hunters; but it is not very handsome for you to say that we are bird-hunters.* Taking the present punctuation, which is upon the whole more suitable to the connection, we must refer the words to the alarm manifested and expressed by the Trochilos, and we may translate, *Is there anything so dreadful* (i. e. in our appearance), *and* (have you) *nothing handsomer to say?* i. e. Are we so frightful that you have nothing better to say to us than that?

64. ἀπολεῖσθον. Fut. Indic. See G. § 25, 1, N. 5.

65. Ὑποδεδιώς. A fictitious name for a bird; further designated as a strange fowl by the following epithet, Λιβυκόν.

66. Οὐδὲν λέγεις, *You say nothing* to the purpose. You talk nonsense. For this sense of the phrase, see Clouds,

v. 644. — ἐροῦ . . . . ποδῶν. "*Roga illa quae vides in cruribus meis*, quae testabuntur me esse avem timidam." Bergler. The Scholiast says: "Λέγει δὲ ὡς ὑπὸ τοῦ δέους ἐναφεικώς."

68. 'Επικεχοδώς. Another name, similarly formed. "Καὶ τοῦτο ὡς ὄρνιθος ἔπαιξε παρὰ τὸ φαίνεσθαι αὐτοῦ τὸ σκῶρ." Sch. "*Qui insuper etiam cacavit* prae timore, ut prior ille." Bergler.

69. σύ. Euelpides turns upon the bird. σύ is emphatic, *but you*.

70, 71. 'Ηττήθης . . . . 'Αλεκτρυόνος; It is stated by Voss, that after the Persian wars cock-fighting was introduced into Athens, and that the birds were brought, as an article of commerce, from Ionia. The conquered bird was called the δοῦλος. Voss, cited by Bothe. Becker (Charicles, p. 64, note 6, English translation) touches upon the subject, and gives the authorities. See also St. John's Manners and Customs of the Ancient Greeks, Vol. I. p. 190, and the references in the note, *ib*. The construction of the genitive is the same as after the comparative ἥσσων, which is implied by the verb. The Scholiast says: " Φυσικὸν τοῦτο ἐν ταῖς σομβολαῖς τῶν ἀλεκτρυόνων, τοὺς ἡττηθέντας ἕπεσθαι τοῖς νενικηκόσι."

73. ἵν' . . . . ἔχῃ. For the Subjunctive after a secondary tense, see G. § 44, 2.

74. γάρ. The particle implies the ellipsis of some expression intimating surprise on the part of the speaker. Here the spirit of it may be rendered by *What!* does a bird, &c.

75. γε is here an emphasizing particle, implying that, whatever may be the case with others, Epops certainly, as having once been a man, cannot do without a servant. — ὤν is an Imperfect Participle. G. § 16, 2. For ἅτε, see G. § 109, N. 3 (*a*).

76. ἀφύας. This name embraces several small species of fish, such as anchovies and sardines. For an account of them, see Aristotle, Hist. An., VI. 14, 2 and 3. According to Archestratos, in Athenaeus, those produced in the neighborhood of Athens were most highly prized. Chrysippus, cited by the same author, says that they were used as articles of food only by the poorer classes of the Athenians, though in other cities those of an inferior quality were greatly admired. Athen. VII.

79. Τροχίλος. There is here a play upon the name, in reference to τρέχω in the preceding lines, — *the running bird*.

80. Οἶσθ' οὖν ὃ δρᾶσον. See note to line 54.

84. Ὅτι .... ἐπεγερῶ. After uttering these words, the Trochilos disappears in the woods to wake up Epops, and the dialogue continues between the two friends.

85. Κακῶς .... δέει. Addressed to the Trochilos as he goes away. The *fear*, in this and in the reply of Euelpides, is caused by the tremendous opening of the beak of Trochilos. For ἀπόλοιο, see G. § 82. (Compare v. 2.)

86. μ' οἴχεται, i. e. μοι οἴχεται, unless, indeed, οἴχομαι may, like φεύγω, be constructed with an accusative of the person. The latter is the view adopted by Kühner (Jelf's Tr.). § 548, Obs. 1.

88. δείσας = ὑπὸ τοῦ δέους, v. 87. G. § 109, 4.

90. γάρ. For this particle in questions, see K. § 324, 2. Here it is equivalent to *then;* as, *Where* then *is he ?*

91. ἆρ' is to be understood as spoken in an ironical tone. — ὡς .... εἶ, *what a brave fellow you are !*

92. Ἄνοιγε .... ποτέ. The voice of Epops is heard, giving orders, in a tone of ludicrous importance, to open, not *the door*, but *the woods*, that he, the king of the birds, may come out.

95, 96. Οἱ .... σε. The usual formula of introducing

the twelve gods (by which are meant the twelve principal gods in the Attic worship) is in the invocation of blessings; but here, as the commentators remark, the tone is suddenly changed, and the ludicrous appearance of Epops, with his enormous crest and his feathers moulted, extorts from Euelpides the exclamation, that the twelve gods must have been afoul of him. Εἴξασιν = ἐοίκασιν. See Clouds, 341. For the Aorist Infinitive referring to the past, see G. § 23, 2.

97. γάρ. The particle here introduces an explanation of some idea to be mentally supplied, such as, "Don't laugh, O strangers, *for I was once a man.*"

99. Τὸ ῥάμφος. The jest consists in saying, "We are not laughing at you; *your beak seems to us ridiculous.*"

100, 101. Τοιαῦτα .... Τηρέα. The subject of the metamorphosis of Tereus and Procne appears to have been treated by the tragic poets more than once. A Scholiast says that Sophocles employed it first, and Philocles, who is alluded to in the present play (v. 280), handled it afterwards. There are remaining ten or a dozen fragments of the play of Sophocles, the largest of which contains twelve lines. See Dindorf's Poetae Scenici, Fragmenta 511 – 526. The poet, who was an ardent admirer of Aeschylus and Sophocles, yet takes occasion to make a good-humored hit at both of them.

102. ὄρνις ἢ ταῶς; The first means either *bird* in general, or specifically *cock* or *hen*. Something like the spirit of the question may be given by rendering it, *Are you a cock or a peacock?* but the reply of Epops takes the word in its general sense.

105. πάντα. "Mentitur," says Bothe, "sed coram hominibus urbanis, quibus quidvis ejusmodi videtur persuaderi posse." With regard to the plumage of Epops, the Scholiast says, "Παρ' ὅσον ἄνθρωπος ἐξελήλυθε, μὴ ἔχων πτερὰ πλὴν τῆς κεφαλῆς ἐπτερωμένης ὄρνιθος," referring to the manner in which the actor personated Epops.

108 Ὅθεν .... καλαί. The allusion is to the boast and pride of the Athenians, — their naval power. It has a special point here, because the splendid armament equipped for the Sicilian Expedition had so recently sailed from the Peiraeus.

109, 110. ἡλιαστά, Ἀπηλιαστά. The Heliastic court was the most important among the judicial institutions of Athens. For a particular account of it, see Hermann's Political Antiquities, § 134, seqq.; Meier and Schömann's Attischer Process, Book II. Chap. 1; Schömann's Griech. Alterthümer, V. pp. 477, seqq. Clouds, 863, note; Champlin's Demosthenes de Corona, Notes, pp. 109, 110; Schömann's Assemblies of the Athenians, § 92. Epops, as soon as he has heard that his visitors are Athenians, immediately thinks of the most prominent characteristic of an Athenian citizen; namely, his quality of member of a court. The word ἀπηλιαστής expresses the opposite of ἡλιαστής, and seems to have been made for the occasion, — *one who is averse to the courts.* The point of the reply cannot be given briefly in English. Something like it would be this: "Are you jurymen?" "No; but, on the other tack, anti-jurymen." — Μἀλλά = μἀ .... ἀλλά. The elliptical use of μά occurs generally with the article. Another reading here is Μὰ Δία · θατέρῳ τρόπου, &c.

110. γάρ, in the question here, though strictly used in an elliptical way, is equivalent to the expression of surprise, *what !*

111. Τὸ σπέρμ'. The language ascribed to Epops refers to his character of bird, though the word also means *race*, — as *seed* is often used in the Bible for *race* or descendants. — ζητῶν (= εἰ ζητοῖς) forms the Protasis to ἂν λάβοις. G. § 109, 6; § 52, 1.

115 – 118. ὠφέλησας, ἔχαιρες, ἐπεπέτου. Observe the change from the aorist, expressing the completed fact, to the imperfect, indicating the habit or general fact.

120. Ταῦτ'. A common construction = διὰ ταῦτα. See Clouds, 319.

121. εἴ τινα φράσειας, *in case you should have some city to tell us of.* G. § 53, N. 2.

122. ἐγκατακλινῆναι μαλθακήν, *soft to repose in.* G. § 93, 2. The idiom of the Greek here corresponds exactly with the English.

123. Κραναῶν. The epithet here applied to Athens has been variously explained: 1. As derived from the ancient mythical king, Kranaos. 2. As referring to the rocky surface of Attica. The latter is clearly its meaning in many places; here it is a jesting antithesis to μαλθακήν.

125, 126. Ἀριστοκρατεῖσθαι .... βδελύττομαι. There are two points intended to be made here. First, the imputation of aristocracy, which at Athens, as well as in republican France, was an efficient means of terror; and, second, a pun on the name of Aristocrates, the son of Skellias. This person was a man of much distinction at Athens, who passed through many vicissitudes in his life, for which his name is used as an illustration by Socrates in the Gorgias of Plato, p. 472, A. (See Woolsey's note to the passage.) He was a member of the oligarchical party, and belonged to the government of the Four Hundred. In B. C. 407 he was associated with Alcibiades as one of the commanders of the Athenian land forces. The next year, he was one of the generals who were brought to trial and put death after the battle of Arginousae. He is mentioned by Demosthenes, in Theocrin., p. 1343, 4; by Xenophon, Hellenica, I. 4, 5 – 7; and by many others. For δῆλος εἰ ζητῶν, see G. § 118, N. 1.

127. Ποίαν τιν'. The interrogative and indefinite thus combined mean, *What sort of a* city, &c.

128. ὅπου .... εἴη is a protasis, with the preceding line understood as the apodosis. G. § 61, 4.

129. πρῴ. *early.*

131. Ὅπως παρέσει. For the elliptical use of ὅπως with the future indic. in exhortations, see G. § 45, N. 7. See Clouds, v. 257. Bothe remarks: "Hac formula vel simili apud Graecos utebantur illi, qui aliquem invitabant ad convivium quo sensu Latini quoque dicere solebant *hodie apud me sis volo,* vel *una simus.*"

132. μέλλω . . . . γάμους, *to give a marriage-feast,* the construction being the cognate accusative. For an account of marriage-feasts, see St. John, Ancient Greeks, Vol. II. pp. 19, 174. For the marriage ceremonies in general, see Becker's Charicles, Scene XII., and Excursus to the same. Isaeus, De Ciron. Hered., § 9, has the expression, "Καὶ γάμους εἰ διττοὺς ὑπὲρ ταύτης εἱστίασεν ἢ μή," in speaking of the proofs of a marriage. See Schömann's notes to § 9, and to § 18.

133. μηδαμῶς ποιήσῃς. G. § 86. εἰ δὲ μή. G. § 52, 1, N. 2.

134. Μή . . . . κακῶς. The Scholiast says this line is a witty perversion of the proverb against those who do not visit their friends in time of trouble; the proverb being Μή μοι τότ' ἔλθῃς, ὅταν ἐγὼ πράττω καλῶς, "Do not come to me then, when I am doing well." G. § 61, 3.

135. ταλαιπώρων, *miserable,* ironically applied.

136. δαί. For the force of this particle, see Kühner, § 315, 7. — Τοιούτων, *such;* not referring, according to the general usage, to the preceding, but to the following, enumeration of objects to be desired. See K. § 303, R. 1.

137 – 142. The Scholiast, in speaking of the wishes of the two old Athenians, says: "Ὁ μὲν τὰς τῆς γαστρὸς τρυφὰς ἐβούλετο, ὁ δὲ τὰς αἰσχρὰς ἡδονάς." It is sufficient to say of the passage, that it is one of many in Aristophanes founded upon the unnatural vices which (unknown to Homer) marked the social morals of the historical ancients, and the increase of which, in progress of time, accelerated the downfall of

both Greece and Rome. The subject is partially illustrated in Becker's Charicles. It is also discussed in its bearings upon the population of the ancient states by Zumpt, in an able essay entitled, "Über den Stand der Bevölkerung und die Volksvermehrung im Alterthum," pp. 13–17. See also, in the Classical Studies, pp. 314–354, Frederick Jacobs on the "Moral Education of the Greeks," and note, pp. 411–413.

143. τῶν κακῶν. Genitive of exclamation.

145. Παρὰ .... θάλατταν. There is probably here some allusion to the profligate manners of the Orientals, like those of Sodom and Gomorrah. Bothe cites, in illustration of this view, Herod. III. 101, and adds: "Id quidem certe significare voluit (i. e. Aristophanes), amores istos nefandos barbaris digniores esse quam Graecis."

146, 147. Ἡμῖν .... Σαλαμινία. The Athenians had two sacred triremes, called the Paralos and the Salaminia, which were used on a variety of public occasions, and their crews were paid high wages at the public expense. (See Boeckh's Public Economy of the Athenians, Book II. Chap. 16.) They were sent on the *theoria*, and sometimes carried ambassadors to their place of destination. The Salaminia was employed, as it would appear from this passage and from the remarks of a Scholiast on it, to bring to Athens persons ordered thither for trial. The Paralos was sometimes used for the same purpose. There is also here a special allusion to the recall of Alcibiades on a charge of having mutilated the statues of Hermes, he having already departed with the armament for the Sicilian Expedition Thucyd. VI. 53 : Καὶ καταλαμβάνουσι τὴν Σαλαμινίαν ναῦν ἐκ τῶν Ἀθηνῶν ἥκουσαν ἐπί τε Ἀλκιβιάδην, ὡς κελεύσοντας ἀποπλεῖν ἐς ἀπολογίαν ὧν ἡ πόλις ἐνεκάλει, κ. τ. λ. See also Thirlwall's History of Greece, Vol. III. pp. 390, seq.; and Grote, Vol. VII. Chap. 58. — κλητῆρ'. This term was commonly applied to those who acted as witnesses to the fact, that the prosecutor had personally summoned his opponent to appear in court on a certain day. (See Meier and Schömann, Attic Process, B. IV. Cap. 2.) If, however, the defendant was out of the country, so that the plaintiff could not summon him in person, a special summons was sent by one of the public triremes, and the servants of the court who served such a summons were also called κλητῆρες. This happened in the case of Alcibiades; and it is in this sense that κλητήρ is used here. For the ordinary process of summoning (πρόσκλησις or κλῆσις), see Clouds, 495, 496, note; also Hermann's Political Antiquities, § 140.

149. Ἠλεῖον Λέπρεον. This city is mentioned in Pausanias, Eliaca, I. c. 5. Four years before this comedy was brought upon the stage, the town was occupied by the Lacedaemonians, who established some of their manumitted Helots there. The old Athenians, fleeing from the oppression of the Attic democracy, are advised to take refuge in a city inhabited by liberated slaves. The name gives an opportunity for a pun in the following lines.

150. ὃς οὐκ ἰδὼν βδελύττομαι. G. § 59, N. 2. The sentence begun with ὅτιή, *because*, is not finished.

151. τὸν Λέπρεον .... Μελανθίου. Melanthios, the tragic poet, is said by the Scholiast to have been ridiculed by the comic writers for his vices and for being afflicted with leprosy (λεπρός). He is also said to have been a native of the Elean city.

152, 153. Ὀπούντιοι, Ὀπούντιος. The name of the Locrian Opuntians appears to have been selected merely for the opportunity of a punning sarcasm upon a man bearing the name of Opountios, said by the Scholiast to have been a stupid fellow with only one eye.

154. ἐπὶ ταλάντῳ, *at the rate of a talent*. See Mtt. § 585, b. β. G. § 52, 1.

157, 158. βαλαντίου . . . . κιβδηλίαν. The idea of living without a purse, that is, without money, immediately suggests the other idea of falsification or adulteration of the coin; and so the word κιβδηλία is naturally used in a metaphorical sense for fraud or dishonesty.

159 – 161. Νεμόμεσθα . . . . βίον. For an account of the festivities and rejoicings in celebration of marriage, see St. John's work above cited, Vol. II. pp. 18, seq. Bothe quotes, in illustration, from Ovid, Fasti, IV. 869, "*Cumque sua dominae date grata Sisymbria myrto.*"

164. πιθοισθέ. Observe the particular force of the aorist, *If you listen to my advice;* not generally, but in the particular case now to be considered. The same specific limitation is to be noted in the repetitions of the word in the following line.

165. Τί πιθώμεσθ'; G. § 88. ὅ τι πίθησθε (sc. ἐρωτᾶτε); is the same question in an indirect form. G. § 71.

166. Μὴ περιπέτεσθε. G. § 86. (See v. 133.)

167. Αὐτίκα, *just for example.* "Οἷον εὐθέως," says the Scholiast.

168. Ἐκεῖ παρ' ἡμῖν, *there* (i. e. at Athens, whence we have just fled) *among us*, men, or Athenians. — τοὺς πετομένους, accusative for genitive with περί; illustrated by the Scholiast, who cites a similar construction from Homer. The phrase is used in application to *flighty* persons.

169. Τελέας. According to the Scholiast, he was a person much ridiculed for his inconstant character and his infamous vices.

170. Ἄνθρωπος ὄρνις, according to Bothe = ὀρνίθειος ἄνθρωπος, *a man-bird.*

173. Τί ἂν ποιοῖμεν; G. § 52, 2, N.

175. Ἀληθές, *Ha! sayest thou so?* See Clouds, 841.

176. Καὶ δή. For the various senses in which these two particles are used in connection, see Hartung, Vol. I. pp. 253,

254. The spirit of the expression may be rendered here by *Well then.*

178. εἰ διαστραφήσομαι, *if I shall get a twist;* either a twisted neck or a squinting eye. G. § 50, 1, N. 1.

180. πόλος. This word is used in various senses as a scientific term. Here, it has its popular meaning of *sky, heavens, vault of the heavens.* It is introduced partly for the punning alliteration between πόλος, πόλις, and πολεῖσθαι, in this and the following lines.

181. Ὥσπερ εἴποι. G. § 50, 2, N. 1.

184. G. § 50, 1.

186. παρνόπων, *locusts.* This refers to them in the character of birds, which would naturally give them dominion over the insects.

187. λιμῷ Μηλίῳ. For the particulars of the transaction here alluded to, see Thucydides, Lib. V. 84 – 116. It took place B. C. 416. See Isocrates, Panegyricus, p. 32 (Felton's edition), and note.

189. ἢν βουλώμεθα. G. § 51.

190. Βοιωτοὺς . . . . αἰτούμεθα. The principal route from Attica to the northern parts of Greece lay through Boeotia. Without the permission of the Boeotians, the Athenians could not easily consult the oracle of the Pythian Apollo.

193. τοῦ χάους. The word *chaos* is used here, as in the Clouds several times, in the sense of *the air* or *the sky;* properly, *the surrounding void;* but not in the modern sense of the term *chaos.* See Clouds, 424, 627.

196, 197. Μὰ . . . . πω. Epops, in his ludicrous delight at the proposal and its immense benefits to the race of the birds, breaks into exclamations and oaths which have a comical relation to his position as a bird. Observe the use of the negative μά, followed by a sentence which also implies a negative; for which see Kühner, § 317, 4. — νεφέλας. According to a Scholiast, a very light species of net was so called. — Μή . . . . ἤκουσα. There is something very unusual in the hypothetical negative in this place. The commentators have not generally noticed it, with the exception of Bothe, who says, " Ellipsis verbi ἐξεπλάγην vel cujusdam similis, *vereor ut unquam callidius commentum audiverim*." But the meaning, with this construction, would be the opposite to that given by Bothe and required by the sense, — *I am afraid lest I have heard* (NE *audiverim*, not UT *audiverim*) ; whereas Epops clearly wishes to say, with more or less directness, that he *never* heard a better scheme. This would seem to require μὴ οὐκ ἤκουσα. G. § 46, N. 5. The grammarians also seem generally to have overlooked the peculiarity of the construction. The editors of the new edition of Passow's Lexicon, however, refer to this and to other similar passages as examples of a rare use of μή in independent sentences containing a protestation or oath ; μή in *independent* sentences being regularly confined to prohibitions and expressions of a wish. The following examples (besides the present one) are cited in Passow, s. v. μή : —

Ἴστω νῦν Ζεὺς αὐτός, ἐρίγδουπος πόσις Ἥρης,
Μὴ μὲν τοῖς ἵπποισιν ἀνὴρ ἐποιχήσεται ἄλλος
Τρώων, ἀλλὰ σέ φημι διαμπερὲς ἀγλαιεῖσθαι. — Il. X. 330.

Ἴστω νῦν τόδε γαῖα καὶ οὐρανός, ...
Μὴ δι' ἐμὴν ἰότητα Ποσειδάων ἐνοσίχθων
Πημαίνει Τρῶάς τε καὶ Ἕκτορα. — Il. XV. 36 – 42.

Μὰ τὸν Ἀπόλλω μή σ' ἐγὼ κατακλινῶ χαμαί. Aristoph. Lysistr. 917.

Μὰ τὴν Ἀφροδίτην, ἥ μ' ἔλαχε κληρουμένη, μὴ 'γώ σ' ἀφήσω. Aristoph. Eccles. 1000.

It would be difficult to explain all these passages consistently by assuming the ellipsis of a leading verb.

199. Εἰ ξυνδοκοίη . . . . ὀρνέοις, *If the other birds should agree to it.* Note the force of ξύν in composition.

NOTES. 135

201. βαρβάρους, *barbarian;* i. e. without articulate speech. The Greeks regarded all who spoke in unknown languages as barbarians, and compared their sounds to the voices of birds. Comp. Aesch. Ag. 974, 975, where Clytaemnestra likens an unknown speech to the twittering of the swallow.

205. τὴν ἐμὴν ἀηδόνα, *my* (wife) *the nightingale.* Procne, who was metamorphosed into the nightingale, according to the poets and mythographers.

206. Καλοῦμεν, *We will call.* The number changes from the singular to the plural, by a construction sufficiently explained by Mtt., Gr. Gr., § 562, 1. The acts expressed by the participles ἐμβάς and ἀνεγείρας are those of Epops alone; but in the subject of καλοῦμεν, Epops is included, together with the nightingale.

207. G. § 50, 1. Cf. v. 189.

215. 'Ελελιζυμένη. " Exprimit sonum gementis lusciniae." B. — διεροῖς. The Scholiast explains, " Διύγροις ἐκ τῶν δακρύων;" Does it not rather express the general character of the notes of the nightingale? with μέλεσιν, *liquid notes,* like the Latin *liquidae voces.*

227. τοῦ φθέγματος. Genitive of explanation, — *What a voice!* — referring probably to the music of the flute (αὐλεῖ, i. e. τις), by which the song of the nightingale, according to the statement of the Scholiast, is represented.

229. Οὐ σιωπήσει; G. § 25, 1, N. 5 (*b*).

233. τις. Used indefinitely for *many a one,* or *every one,* who is present or within hearing. For this sense, see Mtt. § 487, 2. — ὁμοπτέρων, *birds of a feather,* of the same feather with myself; my companions or kindred.

239. ἀμφιτιττυβίζεθ', *twitter about.* It is an imitative word, expressing particularly the twittering of swallows, but also the voices of other birds; λεπτόν qualifies it.

245. 'Ανύσατε πετόμενα. The imperative and the participle of ἀνύω are often constructed with the participle and

imperative of other verbs in the adverbial sense of doing *quickly* what the other verbs signify. Here, *fly quickly.* For the opposite construction of the participle of ἀνύω with the imperative of another verb, see G. § 109, N. 8; and Liddell and Scott, s. v. ἀνύω.

247. ὀξυστόμους. This epithet of the ἐμπίδες is explained by the Scholiast = ὀξυαδούσας, *sharply singing;* but it is much more natural to refer it, with Bergler, to the sharp proboscis. The insect is found by travellers in Attica as annoying now as it was in the days of Aristophanes. The reader will remember the problem of the singing of the empis, in the Clouds, 157, seq. The bite of the empis is very troublesome and painful, in the beautiful summer nights of Athens. A pair of thick woollen stockings worn over the hands and wrists, I found a good defence. Their singing must be patiently borne. The insect is mentioned several times in Aristotle's Hist. An.

251. Ἀτταγᾶς. Aristotle, Hist. An., IX. 19, alludes to the plumage of this bird, which is probably the *moor-hen* or *hazel-hen*. St. John (Hellenes, Vol. II. p. 152) says: " Among the favorite game of the Athenian gourmands was the attagas, or francolin, a little larger than the partridge, variegated with numerous spots, and of common tile color, somewhat inclining to red. It is said to have been introduced from Lydia into Greece, and was found in extraordinary abundance in the Megaris." See also note to the place, with references to the authorities for various opinions.

257. ἥκει, as Perfect. G. § 10, 1, N. 4. — δριμύς, *sharp, crafty*. It is used in a comic sense.

267, 268. ἄρ' .... μιμούμενος. The particle is slightly inferential, — *then;* i. e. since I have been gaping up into the sky, and can see none. The charadrios is mentioned by Aristotle several times. It appears to have been a species of plover called the *gold plover.* The voice of the bird is harsh and disagreeable, and perhaps the *imitating* mentioned by Euelpides is a back-handed compliment to the singing of Epops; this is also supported by the word ἐπῷζε, which does not describe a melodious sound.

270. ἀλλὰ .... ἔρχεται. The accumulation of particles is expressive of the comic astonishment of Peisthetairos at the flaming appearance of the bird just arrived, — *Sure enough, here* IS *a bird coming now!* But the phoenicopteros excited astonishment not only by his brilliant plumage. He was a rare bird, hardly ever seen in the latitude of Greece. "Fuit inter rarissimas Athenis aves." Bothe. Von der Mühle (in his monograph, cited above, upon the birds of Greece, p. 118) states that he was unable to learn anything of the existence of the phoenicopteros in Greece, but thought it impossible the bird should be wanting there, since it was found on the Adriatic coast, in Asia Minor, on the Caspian Sea, and on the Wolga, between which regions Greece is situated. He adds, that he saw some which were brought from Smyrna. This passage in Aristophanes shows that the above-mentioned writer was correct in including the phoenicopteros among the birds of Greece. Heliodorus (Aethiopica, Lib. VI. c. 3) introduces one of the personages in the story carrying, by command of Isias, his mistress, a phoenicopteros of the Nile (ὄρνιν τινὰ τοῦτον, ὡς ὁρᾷς, Νειλῷον φοινικόπτερον).

271. Οὐ .... ταῶς; *It is not surely a peacock?* The whole tone of the dialogue shows how unusual a sight the bird was to the Athenians; and the reply of Epops is in the spirit of one who is determined to make the most of a great curiosity.

272. Οὗτος αὐτός, i. e. Epops, *this one himself;* pointing to the bird.

274. λιμναῖος. Applied to birds, this epithet signifies, not *water-fowl,* as it is incorrectly translated by Liddell

and Scott, and generally in the versions, but those birds which haunt the water's edge and are known by the generic name of *waders*.

274, 275. φοινικιοῦς .... φοινικόπτερος. The pun here may be preserved by rendering φοινικόπτερος *flamingo*, the name of the family to which he belongs: — *How handsome and flaming, — naturally, for his name is flamingo.*

276. σέ τοι. Constructed with καλῶ, or some such word, to be supplied.

277, 278. Νὴ .... ὀριβάτης; The first line is said, by the Scholiast, to be a parody on Sophocles (the beginning of the Tyro), and the second from a passage in Aeschylus. The Μῆδος is the same as the Περσικὸς ὄρνις in v. 485. — ἔξεδρον χώραν ἔχων, *a bird from foreign parts.* — μουσόμαντις. "Ὁ κομπώδης· τοιοῦτοι γὰρ οἱ μάντεις καὶ οἱ ποιηταί." Sch. The description, originally applied to a character in Aeschylus, is here transferred to the strutting cock.

280. ἄνευ καμήλου. The Scholiast says: "Ὡς τῶν Μήδων ὡς ἐπὶ τὸ πολὺ ἐπὶ καμήλων ὀχουμένων ἐπὶ τῇ τῶν πολέμων ἐξόδῳ." — εἰσέπτατο. *flew in.*

281. Ἕτερος .... οὑτοσί. The pun here turns upon the military meaning of λόφον κατειληφώς, *having occupied a hill;* and here, *having got a crest.* See note to v. 295.

283 – 285. 'Ἀλλ' .... Καλλίας. In answer to the question of Peisthetairos, whether there is another Epops, — the question being put in a tone of some surprise, — the poet takes occasion to make a hit at several persons. Philocles, the poet, who imitated Sophocles in his play of Tereus, has already been mentioned. Epops means to say that the present bird is not the genuine Epops, but only an imitation, like that in Philocles; and as he himself is, as it were, the father of the Epops in Sophocles, so he may be said to be, in the same way, the grandfather of this one. And this suggests the Athenian mode of naming children, upon which

St. John (Ancient Greeks, Vol. I. p. 131) says: "The right of imposing the name belonged, as hinted above, to the father, who likewise appears to have possessed the power afterwards to alter it, if he thought proper. They were compelled to follow no exact precedent; but the general rule resembled one apparently observed by nature, which, neglecting the likeness in the first generation, sometimes reproduces it with extraordinary fidelity in the second. Thus the grandson, inheriting often the features, inherited also very generally the name of his grandfather; and precisely the same rule applied to women, the granddaughter nearly always receiving her grandmother's name. Thus Andocides, son of Leagoras, bore the name of his grandfather; the father and son of Miltiades were named Cimon; the father and son of Hipponicos, Callias." These particular names are probably selected by the poet, not only because the family to whom they belong present a remarkable instance of this customary alternation through many generations, but because the last Callias, the individual especially alluded to, was notorious for his prodigality and profligacy, and ruined the fortunes of the family. The first Hipponicos known to Athenian history was a contemporary of Solon, about six hundred years before Christ; and the last Callias, the third of the name, flourished about two hundred years later. He held in the course of his life many high offices in the state, in spite of his folly and profligacy, which early fastened upon him the name of the ἀλιτήριος,* or evil genius of his family. His portrait is drawn by Andocides in very forbidding colors.* Plato also gives some traits of his character. See

---

* Andocides, p. 277. Ἱππόνικος ἐν τῇ οἰκίᾳ ἀλιτήριον τρέφει, ὃς αὐτοῦ τὴν τράπεζαν ἀνατρέπει·.... Οἰόμενος γὰρ Ἱππόνικος υἱὸν τρέφειν, ἀλιτήριον αὐτῷ ἔτρεφεν, ὃς ἀνατέτροφεν ἐκείνου τον πλοῦτον, τὴν σωφροσύνην, τὸν ἄλλον βίον ἅπαντα, κ. τ. λ.

the Protagoras, the scene of which is laid at the house of Callias; and the Apology (p. 20 A), where Callias is spoken of as ἀνδρί, ὃς τετέλεκε χρήματα σοφισταῖς πλείω ἢ ξύμπαντες οἱ ἄλλοι. He is said to have been reduced to great destitution, and finally to have died a beggar. The particulars of the history, and all the important facts respecting their wealth, have been carefully collected by Boeckh (Public Economy of the Athenians, Book IV. Chap. 3). See also Xenophon's Hellenica, IV. 5, 13; Aristotle's Rhet. III. 2. In many respects the family was one of the most famous, as well as one of the oldest, in Athens. — ὥσπερ εἰ. We might have had ὥσπερ ἂν εἰ. G. § 53, N. 3.

286. πτεροῤῥυεῖ. *he is moulting;* and in this respect resembles Callias, or is a Callias. The next two lines continue the allusions in the same vein.

287, 288. Ἅτε .... πτερά. The sycophants at Athens were the pest of society. No age or character or public services shielded a man of wealth from their attacks. Aristophanes holds them up to ridicule and reprobation in several of his pieces, and the other comic writers lost no opportunity of exposing their practices. They figure largely in the remains of the Attic orators. On account of his noble birth, his high rank, and his wealth, Callias was an inviting object to these miscreants, and his vices facilitated the success of their machinations. — θήλειαι. The allusion here is to the licentiousness which notoriously marked the life of Callias (see above). — For ἅτε ὤν, see G. § 109, N. 3 (*a*).

In the following passage, all the birds which constitute the chorus make their appearance. Many of them it is not possible to identify with existing species. *Catophagas*, for instance, the glutton, is said not to have been the specific name of any bird at all, though that does not seem quite probable. The Cleonymos, to whom this bird is compared, is the one mentioned in a similar way in the Clouds (see

v. 353 and note) as a *shield-dropper*, and elsewhere as a coward and sensualist. It is in reference to the former that Euelpides asks *why he did not cast off his crest* (v. 292).

292. ὧν = εἰ ἦν. G. § 109, 6; § 52, 1.

293, 294. 'Αλλὰ .... ἦλθον; Peisthetairos wonders at the crests of the birds, and immediately calls to mind the practice fashionable among the young Athenians of entering the δίαυλος, or double course, armed with crested helmets. A great variety of races were run over the δίαυλος. The armed races, of which that alluded to by Aristophanes in this place was one, formed a part of several *panegyrical* festivities. For a full account of them, see Krause, Gymnastik und Agonistik der Hellenen, pp. 777, seq. In a note to that work (p. 905), the author remarks that the armed race appears but seldom on the antique monuments of art. There is one beautiful representation of it found in the Berlin collection of vases, of which the following is in part a description. " On the inner side appears a runner, taking vigorous strides, having a large round shield in his left hand; the right is in violent motion, as are both hands of the runners in other works of art; the head is covered with a helmet. On the shield is a racer figured in the same mnaner, except that he holds the shield in his right hand," &c. See also the plate, Tab. VII. b, Fig. 14, b, c, d, of the same work.

294, 295. Ὥσπερ οἱ Κᾶρες .... οἰκοῦσιν. ("Ἡ ὅτι ἐν πέτραις ᾤκουν ὑπὲρ ἀσφαλείας, ἢ ὅτι λόφον ἔχουσιν ἐπὶ τῶν κρανῶν." Schol. The pun here, as in v. 281, turns upon the double meaning of λόφος, *a hill*, or *a crest*. The Carians are said to have been the first to use the crest; whence Alcaeus, λόφον τε σείων Καρικόν. (Strab. XIV. p. 661.) Strabo and Herodotus (I. 171) attribute to them two other inventions, that of devices on shields (σημεῖα, ἐπίσημα), and that of handles (ὄχανα) to shields. The question whether the Carians *originated* on the continent of Asia or on the islands of the

Aegaean was disputed in antiquity; the Carians maintaining the former, and the Cretans and most others the latter. (Herod. I. 171.) But the ancient authorities are hopelessly confused and inconsistent: Herodotus, who gives what he calls the Cretan version, disagrees entirely with Thucydides (I. 4); and both disagree with Strabo (XIV. p. 661), who gives what he calls the most current version (ὁ μάλισθ' ὁμολογούμενος). Diodorus Siculus and Pausanias, on the other hand, seem to have followed the Carian account: they disagree, of course, entirely with the former authorities, and they are not perfectly consistent with each other. (See Diod. V. 84 and 53; Pausan. VII. 2-4; Conon. Narrat. 47.) In the historic times, we find the Carians only on the Continent; and in their various wars with the Persians and the Greeks, they seem to have been famous for eluding their enemies by occupying the hills (λόφοι) of their mountainous country, and for harassing invaders who ventured into the interior. See Thucyd. III. 19, who says (speaking of an attempt made by Lysikles with an Athenian army to collect money in this region in 418 B. C.): Καὶ τῆς Καρίας ἐκ Μυοῦντος ἀναβὰς διὰ τοῦ Μαιάνδρου πεδίου μέχρι τοῦ Σανδίου λόφου, ἐπιθεμένων τῶν Καρῶν καὶ Ἀναιιτῶν αὐτός τε διαφθείρεται καὶ τῆς ἄλλης στρατιᾶς πολλοί. In fact, the Athenians appear to have never been masters of more than the coast of Caria, if we may judge from the mention of Καρία ἡ ἐπὶ θαλάσσῃ among their tributaries at the beginning of the Peloponnesian war. (See Thucyd. II. 9.)

296, 297. ὅσον .... ὀρνέων; Of the use of κακόν here Bothe says it is "comice dictum pro πλῆθος"; i. e. instead of saying *how great a multitude of birds*, he says *how great an evil of birds*, — equivalent to some such expression as *What a pother of birds! What a plaguy lot of birds!*

298. τὴν εἴσοδον, *the entrance;* i. e. through which the personages of the chorus entered the orchestra. See Clouds, 326, and note, pp. 136, 137.

299, seqq. Peisthetairos now points out, one after the other, the twenty-four birds who constitute the chorus proper, each of course appropriately represented by the comic masks, expressly prepared for them. On this passage, Bode (Geschichte der Hellenischen Dichtkunst, B. III. Th. II. pp. 283, 284) says : " The chorus of the birds, perhaps the most comical ever introduced by Aristophanes, comes in, after the call of the Hoopoo, in the sporadic manner. Different birds at first appear, one after another, at the arched entrance of the orchestra, and after they have passed one by one across the orchestra they disappear. They form, as it were, the van of the proper chorus. First comes running in a flamingo, with outspread purple wings ; then struts in a cock ; then trips along a hoopoo, somewhat plucked ; then waddles through the orchestra a bright-colored gullet, with grotesque mimicry. They are all four precisely designated. The proper chorus, then, of twenty-four, press through the entrance of strangers in compact groups of many colors, so that the passage is scarcely visible for their fluttering. They are likened to clouds. Even around the Thymele they seem to be gathering in groups, and, with their beaks wide open, to be peering upon the stage. By degrees they then divide themselves into Hemichoria, so that, according to the grammarians, twelve male birds of different species take their position on one side of the Thymele, and twelve females on the other. The males are the cock-partridge, the hazel-cock, the duck, the kingfisher, the tufted lark, the horned owl, the heron, the falcon, the cuckoo, the red-foot, the hawk, and the woodpecker ; the females are, the halcyon (which with the keirylos or kingfisher forms the only pair), then the night-owl, jay, turtle-dove, falcon, the pigeon, the ring-dove, the brant-goose, the purple-cap, diver, ousel, osprey. As here the gentle doves appear along with the fiercest birds of prey, so the males, mentioned above separately, enter, in the actual

144 NOTES.

Parodos of Aristophanes, mingled up with the females. In irregular haste, they run *pipping* and chattering towards the stage, so that Euelpides, full of astonishment, exclaims: —

Ἰοὺ ἰοὺ τῶν ὀρνέων,
Ἰοὺ ἰοὺ τῶν κοψίχων·
Οἷα πιππίζουσι καὶ τρέχουσι διακεκραγότες.

A manifest proof that the Parodos was sporadic."

The male birds, according to this arrangement, are περδιξ, ἀτταγᾶς, πενέλοψ, κηρύλος, κορυδός, ἐλεᾶς, νέρτος, ἱέραξ, κόκκυξ, ἐρυθρόπους, κερχνῆς, δρύοψ; the females, ἀλκυών, γλαύξ, κίττα, τρυγών, ὑποθυμίς, περιστερά, φάττα, κεβλήπυρις, πορφυρίς, κολυμβίς, ἀμπελίς, φήνη.

303. Τίς γλαῦκ' Ἀθήναζ' ἤγαγε; The Scholiast says: Παροιμία ἐπὶ τῶν μάτην ἐπισωρευόντων τινὰ ἐπὶ τοῖς προϋπάρχουσιν· οἷον εἴ τις ἐν Αἰγύπτῳ σῖτον ἐπαγάγοι, ἢ ἐν Κιλικίᾳ κρόκον. So in English, *to carry coals to Newcastle*. The poet alludes also to the owl upon the Attic coins, whence the expression γλαῦκες Λαυριωτικαί. See v. 1099, and note.

308. τῶν κοψίχων. Genitive of exclamation. This bird is singled out in the exclamation on account of its clamorous chattering.

312. Ποποποποποποῦ. The chirping of the birds is intended to be expressed by this stammering pronunciation; and so in the next line but one.

313. πάλαι πάρειμι. G. § 10, 1, N. 3.

316. λεπτὼ λογιστά, *two acute reasoners*. There is also a reference to the board of λογισταί at Athens, to whom the magistrates on leaving office must render their accounts. On the duties of the λογισταί and their relations to the similar board of εὔθυνοι, see Boeckh's Public Economy of the Athenians, Book II. Chap. 8; Hermann's Political Antiquities of Greece, § 154; Schömann's Assemblies of the Athenians, p. 279.

317. Ποῦ; The questions of the chorus, and indeed the

whole tone of the dialogue, will remind the reader of the opening scenes in the Oedipus at Colonos of Sophocles. Perhaps the poet intended a slight raillery upon the somewhat melodramatic mannerism of the tragic choruses on their first appearance in a piece, of which that of the Oedipus at Colonos was a specimen.

319. Ἥκετον .... πελωρίου. A comic imitation of tragic pomp of expression. — πρέμνον, *the bottom*, or *the root*.

320. Ὦ .... ἐξαμαρτών. Observe the construction of the participle after an exclamation, — *O thou who hast done wrong!* — ἐτράφην. Bothe says: "Dixit significanter et ridicule, quia vita avium et animantium nihil aliud esse videtur quam nutritus." The word, however, is applied in the same way where no ridicule is to be supposed.

321. φοβηθῇς. The aorist with the prohibitive negative μή limits the act to the single case. G. § 86.

322. τῆσδε .... ξυνουσίας, *this society here;* the society of the birds.

323. γ' has an emphasizing force.

326. Προδεδόμεθ' .... ἐπάθομεν. Observe the interchange of the tenses, passing in the same construction from the perfect to the aorist, according as the act or state is to be more or less precisely limited.

329. θεσμοὺς ἀρχαίους. The Scholiast says: "Ὡς τούτου νενομοθετημένου αὐτοῖς τὸ μὴ συνεῖναι ἀνθρώποις." Θεσμοί seems to have been an older expression than νόμοι, hence it is generally applied to the laws of Draco: even these, however, are sometimes called νόμοι. The chorus give a mock gravity to their charge against Epops by employing a word associated with the ancient traditions of the Athenian legislature.

334. τοῦτον, *this one;* i. e. Epops.

335. δοῦναι. The aorist infinitive here refers to the future, and not to the past; as δοκεῖ μοι means *it pleases me,*

and not *it seems to me.* See G. § 23, 2, N. 4. (Compare Clouds, v. 1141 ; and G. § 23, 2, N. 3.)

336. ἆρα, *therefore ;* expressing the logical inference from the threatening language of the birds. *We are dead men, then.*

338. ἐκεῖθεν, *thence ;* i. e. from Athens. — ἀκολουθοίης The present here implies, not the single act of following from Athens, but the permanent condition of an attendant.

339. κλάοιμι. The idiomatic use of this specific word, in a general sense, gives occasion to the joke in the next line. — ληρεῖς ἔχων. See G. § 109, N. 8.

340. τὠφθαλμὼ 'κκοπῇς. The accusative construction here is the same as in the Clouds, 24 : ἐξεκόπη τὸν ὀφθαλμόν.

342. "Επαγ', &c. Expressions borrowed from military language in drawing out an army for attack.

345, 346. οἰμώζειν, δοῦναι. Observe the change of tense in the infinitives ; the present indicating the continued or repeated act, the aorist limiting the signification to the single thing. The *groaning* is naturally continuous and repeated ; the *giving food to the beak* is viewed as a single and finished transaction.

351. Ποῦ .... κέρας. The taxiarchs, in the military system of the Athenians, were of the next grade to the στρατηγοί, being ten in number, one for each tribe. Each tribe furnished a τάξις of infantry, and the τάξεις were severally under the command of these officers ; the right wing — τὸ δεξιὸν κέρας — was the post of honor in battle (see Herod. VI. 111), and as such originally it was the right of the polemarch to hold it. For the general discussion of the subject, see Schömann, Antiquitatis Juris Publici Graecorum, pp. 251 - 256. — ποῦ φύγω ; G. § 88.

353. γάρ implies an answer to the previous question here, *yes, for how,* &c. — For ἂν ἐκφυγεῖν, see G. § 42, 2, Note ; § 41, 3 ; § 73, 1.

NOTES. 147

354. ἄν qualifies some word to be mentally supplied. — *I don't know how I can* escape.

355. λαμβάνειν .... χυτρῶν, *to take hold of the pots.* Genitive of the thing laid hold of.

356. Γλαῦξ. The owl, Peisthetairos thinks, will not attack them, because it is, like them, Athenian.

357. Τοῖς. The dative is to be constructed with an expression to be supplied, — *What shall we protect ourselves with against these crooked claws?*

358. πρὸς αὐτόν. The reading and interpretation are uncertain here. Bothe says: " Veru arrepto alites illos confige, quemadmodum πηγνύναι τι ἐπὶ κοντοῦ et similia dicuntur." And the Scholiast, cited by Bothe, gives an explanation which seems to imply the reading αὐτήν, instead of αὐτόν, viz. *Seize the spit and fix it by the pot*, to make as it were a palisade. Taking the present reading, it may be translated, *Take the spit and fix it near yourself.* This agrees substantially with the interpretation of Blaydes, who adopts the reading πρὸ σαυτοῦ: *Sibi ut hastam praetendere.* I think the explanation of Bothe and the translation of Cary — " Take a spit and have at them " — are scarcely consistent with the connection. The old men are not meditating an assault; they are taking measures of defence, and their engines consist of the pots, the spits, and a few other articles which they packed up and brought away with them from Athens. With these they prepare to make the stoutest defence they can; but they scarcely think of offensive measures. — ὀφθαλμοῖσι, *and for our eyes, what?* i. e. what shall we do for the protection of our eyes? Construction, dative of indirect object.

359. 'Οξύβαφον, *vinegar-cup.* " Among the various ways in which the Greeks and Romans made use of vinegar in their cookery and at their meals, it appears that it was customary to have upon the table a cup containing vinegar

into which the guests might dip their bread, lettuce, fish, or other viands before eating them." See Smith's Dict. of Gr. and Rom. Antiq., Art. *Acetabulum*, where there is a figure of the cup. See also Athenaeus, II. p. 67 : "Τὸ δεχόμενοι αὐτὸ (i. e. τὸ ὄξος) ἀγγεῖον ὀξύβαφον." The vinegar-cup was to be used as a sort of shield for the eyes.

360, 361. ’Ω . . . . μηχαναῖς. Aristophanes never loses an opportunity to make a jest at the expense of Nicias. According to Thucydides (Lib. III. c. 51) Nicias was sent against the island of Minoa, near Megara, to cut off the Peloponnesians from the use of this port. He accomplished the object by the skilful application of military engines. In the siege of Melos he is said also to have resorted to similar measures. He thus became famous more for this species of strategy than for boldness of conduct in the field. — Ὑπερακοντίζεις, *you overshoot, surpass;* by the same figure of speech which we constantly use in English.

362. Ἐλελελεῦ . . . . ἐχρῆν. The first word the Scholiast calls ἐπίφθεγμα πολεμικόν, a warlike shout. — κάθες, *lower* or *present beak ;* i. e. like a spear.—οὐ μένειν ἐχρῆν. G. § 49, 2, N. 3.

366. τῆς γυναικός, i. e. *Procne*, or the nightingale, daughter of the mythical Pandion, king of Athens. — φυλέτα, *tribesmen*. The division of the Athenians into tribes, phratriae, and gentes is familiar to all. It was common to designate individuals by words expressive of their relations, both for the purpose of identification, and because the rights of citizenship were legally certified to by the registers.

367. λύκων. According to Petit, there was an ancient law providing for the killing of wolves; much like modern laws in new countries, offering bounties for scalps and skins of wild beasts, and sometimes of men. St. John (Vol. I. p. 227) says: "The wolf, though a sacred animal in Attica, had by the laws a price set upon his head, at which Menage

wonders, though the Egyptians also slaughtered their sacred crocodiles when they exceeded a certain size."

370. διδάξοντες. Future expressing purpose. G. § 109, 5.

372. πάπποις, *grandfathers*. For the sake of comic effect, put for ancestors in general, as in serious discourse *fathers* is used. — φράσειαν (sc. ἄν). G. § 42, 4.

373-378. 'Αλλ'.... χρήματα. Epops, like a wise bird, quotes the maxims of the philosophers. "Fas est et ab hoste doceri," is the Latin commonplace to the same point. — γάρ introduces the general reflection, which contains the justification of the previous remark, in the abstract; and then the principle involved is shown practically by the instances. — ἐξηνάγκασεν. For the idiomatic use of the aorist, see Clouds, 520, note, in the new edition. G. § 30, 1. — Αὐτίχ', *for example*. See v. 167. — 'Εκπονεῖν. " Exempla sunt ex historia Atheniensium petita, apud quos, Xerxe fugato, Themistocles effecit, ut urbs muris cingeretur, aedificaretur Peiraeus, et quotannis viginti triremes construerentur." Bothe. — ναῦς μακράς, *naves longas;* i. e. *ships of war.* — μάθημα τοῦτο, *this lesson.*

379. ἀκοῦσαι. The aorist infinitive is properly used here on account of the action intended to be expressed being a single one, i. e. limited to the hearing in the present case.

381. χαλᾶν, *to be yielding*, the proper meaning of the present infinitive. —"Αναγ' ἐπὶ σκέλος = ἐπὶ πόδα, *retreat, fall back.*

385. καθίει, *lower ;* there being no longer any need of such defences.

386. ὀβελίσκον. In apposition with δόρυ.

388. ὅπλων ἐντός, *within the arms ;* i. e. the pot and the bowls, being placed on the ground, form as it were a camp, within the line of which Peisthetairos deems it expedient that they should still keep themselves. This he thinks will be a sufficient security, provided they still keep a sharp eye

upon the troops of the birds by watching over the edge of the pot.

390. οὐ φευκτέον νῷν. G. § 114, 2.

391. ἦν δ' ἄρ', *and if then*. ἄρα here is a slightly *inferential* particle. *If then*, i. e. in consequence of what you propose.

393. Κεραμεικός. Those who fell in battle were buried with public honors, and at the public expense, in the burying-ground called the Κεραμεικός, without the city. It was customary to appoint some distinguished citizen to pronounce a eulogy. The well-known example of the discourse pronounced by Pericles, on the Athenians who fell in the first campaign of the Peloponnesian war, will occur to the reader. See Thucydides, Lib. II. cc. 34–46, where all the ceremonies are carefully described.

395. πρὸς τοὺς στρατηγούς. For the general duties of the board of generals (ten in number), see Schömann, Griech. Alterthümer, I. 422; Hermann, Pol. Antiq., §§ 152, 153. Besides the civil and military duties there enumerated, it belonged to them to make and superintend the arrangements for the public burials. The reader will remember Xenophon's account of the trial of the generals after the battle of Arginousae, on the charge of neglecting to bury those who had perished in the engagement, and of leaving those who remained upon the wrecks to perish. See Hellenica. Lib. I. c. 7. See also Grote, Vol. VIII. Chap. 64.

397. Ὀρνεαῖς, *at Orneae*. The jest turns upon the name of an ancient town in Argolis, which had suffered in the Peloponnesian war (Bird-town). See v. 13, and note. The name is mentioned by Homer, Il. II. 571.—ἀποθανεῖν. G. § 23, 2.

398–400. Ἄναγ' .... ὁπλίτης. The language is a parody upon the terms of military command: Ἄναγ' ἐς τάξιν, *fall back in line;* τὸν θυμὸν κατάθου, *lay down your wrath*.

instead of *spear;* Παρὰ τὴν ὀργήν, *beside your anger,* instead of *shield.*

403. Ἐπὶ τίνα τ' ἐπίνοιαν, *And for what purpose,* or *on what scheme?*

405. τοῦ = τίνος.

412. Σοῦ. "*Tui ipsius,* non solum tuae, i. e. avium, vitae sub dio et in silvis campisque, quemadmodum vivunt etiam venatores, pastores, milites; sed hi senes Athenienses ipsarum avium commercium et societatem expetunt." Bothe.

416. Ἄπιστα . . . . . κλύειν, *Incredible, and more, to hear:* περὰ τῶν ἀπίστων. The infinitive depends on ἄπιστα, and not on πέρα, as the Scholiast constructs it.

417. Ὁρᾷ. Although the two have been spoken of before, the chorus here uses the singular, referring to one only of the old Athenians.

419. Κρατεῖν . . . . ἐχθρόν. Κρατεῖν with the accusative means *to conquer* by force; with the genitive, *to be master of.*—Κρατεῖν ἄν represents κρατοίη ἄν, and ἔχειν (sc. ἄν) represents ἔχοι ἄν, of the direct discourse. G. § 73, 1; § 41, 1.

421, 422. Λέγει . . . . οὔτε λεκτόν. Observe the comic exaggeration, running into something not unlike an Irish bull.

429, 430. For a similar series of words implying all kinds of craft and roguery, see Clouds, 260, and note.

433. ἀνεπτέρωμαι. The Scholiast says: "Οἰκεῖον ὄρνισι τὸ ἀνεπτέρωμαι, οἷον μετεώρισμαι."

435, 436. κρεμάσατον . . . . τοὐπιστάτου. Bothe says: "Haec ex communi Atheniensium vita sunt explicanda, qui finito bello arma suspendere solebant ad furnum vel caminum." The Scholiast describes the ἐπιστάτης as a χαλκοῦς τρίπους, χυτρόποδος ἐκτελῶν χρείαν; and he adds: "Οἱ δέ. πήλινον Ἥφαιστον πρὸς τὰς ἑστίας ἱδρυμένον, ὡς ἔφορον τοῦ πυρός, ἔνιοι δὲ καὶ ξύλον ἐπίμηκες πεπασσαλωμένον, ὅθεν ἐξαρτῶσι τὰ μαγειρικὰ σκεύη." It seems plain, from the kind of armor with which the Athenians had equipped themselves, that these allusions to the kitchen are not wholly to be explained by the usages of common life. The expressions contain rather jocose references to the pots, the bowls, and the skewers which constituted their luggage and means of defence. The ἰπνός is the chimney, but here put for the fire-place or oven, or perhaps it may be called the *chimney-place;* as the Scholiast says: "'Ιπνὸς μὲν ὁ κάμινος, καταχρηστικῶς δὲ ἡ ἐσχάρα." Of the ἐπιστάτης, Boeckh, Corpus Inscriptionum, Vol. I. p. 20, says: "Iidem Attici, eodem sensu [i. e. the same with ὑποστάτῳ and ὑποστάτῃ] ἐπίστατον sive ἐπιστάτην, dixerint. . . . . Aristophanes, Av. 436, rem conficit, licet ibi, quid sit ὁ ἐπιστάτης, sive τὸ ἐπίστατον dubitetur. Tria enim Scholiastae proponunt, *Vulcanum ex luto fictum,* qui quasi Lar familiaris sit : . . . . *trabem vel asserem ad caminum, unde ex clavis vasa culinaria suspendantur ;* . . . . *postremo basin sive tripodem, in quo ollae et lebetes igni apponantur.*" He prefers the last, remarking: "Nihil enim in illo loco hac significatione aptius : nam. Upupa jubet arma suspendi εἰς τὸν ἰπνὸν εἴσω πλησίον τοὐπιστάτου, hoc est in camino, non *prope trabem,* ex qua suspendentur vasa, sed *in ipsa trabe,* prope tripodem ibidem suspensum, ut etiam nunc mulierculae tripodes ibi suspendunt."

439, 441. *Ην . . . . ἐμέ. The person here designated as the monkey sword-maker is said to have been one Panaetius, who, according to the Scholiast, was also satirized in the piece called The Islands. The Scholiast adds: " Μικροφυὴς ἦν· διαβάλλει δὲ αὐτὸν ὡς καταλαβόντα τὴν γυναῖκα ἑαυτοῦ μοιχευομένην· ἐδυναστεύετο γὰρ ὑπ' αὐτῆς μεγάλης οὔσης μικροφυὴς αὐτὸς ὤν." " Duxerat uxorem, cum qua quum saepius rixaretur, tandem convenit, ut se invicem nec morderent, nec plagis afficerent." Bothe.

443. Τόν; The broken sentence, according to the Scholiast, is to be filled out by a gesture, — *You don't mean*

NOTES. 153

the —— *No, surely:* — striking the part of the body alluded to, πρωκτὸν δεικνύς φησιν οὖτι που. " Videtur ipse Panaetius adultero adulterorum poenam dedisse ῥαφανιδώσεως, eodemque modo ne iterum plecteretur cavisse." Bothe.

445 – 447. Ὄμνυμ᾽ . . . . μόνον. The allusion here is to the mode of deciding in competitions for the dramatic prize. In tragic representations, the number of judges appointed was ten, one for each tribe. It seems that, in the contests of the comedians, only five were called upon to judge. See Bode, Gesch. d. Hellen. Dichtkunst, III. pp. 147, 148. See also Schneider, Das Attische Theaterwesen, pp. 169 – 174. Πᾶσι τοῖς κριταῖς νικᾶν signifies, " to gain the dramatic victory by a unanimous vote of the judges," and ἑνὶ κριτῇ νικᾶν μόνον is " to gain the victory by only one vote"; giving a turn to his expression from what might naturally have been expected, namely, *to be conquered*, to a mere diminution of the number of voices, being victorious still. — Ἐπὶ τούτοις, *on these terms.* — εἰ παραβαίην. G. § 54, 2 (*a*).

448 – 450. G. § 103. The herald now, in solemn form, proclaims the truce, and orders the heavy-armed to depart to their several homes. This appears to have been the customary rite on the conclusion of a treaty of peace. It is here applied in the spirit of parody.

450. προγράφωμεν .... πινακίοις. G. § 61, 3. This refers to the mode of giving notice of the subjects to be discussed in a political assembly, namely, by exposing in public places, streets, and squares tablets fastened on columns, with the matters inscribed upon which the assembly was summoned to debate.

453. τάχα γὰρ τύχοις ἂν ἐξειπών, *for perhaps you might chance to speak of* (not, *to have spoken*). G. § 112, 2; for the Aorist Participle, § 24, N. 1.

454. μοι παρορᾷς, *you see in me,* or *in my case.*

458. ὃ γὰρ ἂν τύχῃς. G. § 61, 3. See note on v. 453.
461. ὡς οὐ μὴ παραβῶμεν. G. § 89, 1, with N. 1.
462, 463. προπεφύραται, διαμάττειν. The language is borrowed from the baker's art; both words, however, are translated in the lexicons as if they were nearly synonymous, and as if both meant *to knead*. But they probably refer to different stages in the process of bread-making. The first obviously describes the putting together of the materials, and mixing them up; the second, the careful and elaborate kneading of the dough. For a curious account of the whole matter, see St. John, Vol. III. pp. 109, seq. It may be added, that Athenian bakers had a high reputation; for, as St. John says (l. c.), "The bread sold in the marketplace of Athens was esteemed the whitest and most delicious in Greece; for the Rhodians, speaking partially of the produce of their own ovens, supposed they were bestowing on it the highest compliment when they said it was not inferior to that of Athens." It was, therefore, quite natural for the old Athenian, in announcing his excellent schemes, to borrow a figure from the bakehouse. — οὐ κωλύει. The doubts of Dindorf and the suggestion of a various reading by Bothe are unnecessary here. κωλύει is used impersonally, *hinders not*. The same usage occurs in Thucydides, Lib. I. c. 144: "Οὔτε γὰρ ἐκεῖνο κωλύει ἐν ταῖς σπονδαῖς οὔτε τόδε, — For in the truce there hinders not (there is no hindrance to) either that or this." See note on the passage in Owen's Thucydides, p. 432. For the various constructions with the Infinitive allowed after οὐ κωλύει, see G. § 95, 2, with N. 1; and § 95, 3. — στέφανον. It was customary to wear a chaplet at feasts, and before reclining at the table to have water poured over the hands. For the particulars, see Becker's Charicles, Excursus to Scene VI.

465. λαρινὸν ἔπος, *a fat word*. The epithet is suggested by the allusions to feasting.

NOTES. 155

466. ὅ τι θραύσει. G. § 65, 1.

467. βασιλῆς. The speech of Peisthetairos is here interrupted by the chorus, who, astonished to hear of their former dignity, cannot wait until the sentence is completed.

471. πολυπράγμων. This generally is used in a bad sense, — *a busy-body*, — but here only *knowing many things;* observant and experienced in many things. — πεπάτηκας. The fables of Aesop, in some form, were as familiar to the Athenians of Aristophanes's age as similar compositions are to the children of modern times. What they were precisely, and whether they were written or not, are questions among the learned; but it is certain that the current jests, drolleries, and odd stories at Athens were generally palmed upon the old fabulist. Aristophanes has several other allusions to him; Socrates versified some of his apologues, and, afterwards, Demetrius Phalereus; but none of these metrical essays are preserved. At a much later period, Babrius versified them in choliambics. Some of these are extant, and have high merit. But the collections of prose fables now in existence under the name of Aesop were proved by Bentley to be forgeries; and no person at all accustomed to discriminate between the styles of different ages in Greek literature can doubt the justness of his decision. The phrase used in the cited line, *you have not trodden*, is a comic equivalent to *you are not familiar with;* perhaps selected here in allusion to the birds, who would be obliged to use their claws in the place of hands, for holding a book. The same expression is cited by Blaydes, from Plato's Phaedo: "Ἀλλὰ μὴν τόν γε Τισίαν πεπάτηκας ἀκριβῶς."

473, 474. ἀποθνήσκειν and προκεῖσθαι are in the *Imperfect* Infinitive, representing the Imperfect Indicative of the direct discourse; as γενέσθαι (v. 472) and κατορύξαι (v. 475) represent the Aorist. G. § 15, 3; § 23, 2; § 73, 1. —

προκεῖσθαι πεμπταῖον, *was lying out for the fifth day.* In Greece, the body of the dead, after having been washed and anointed, was laid out in the vestibule of the house, with the feet towards the door, as a symbolical intimation that it was about to take its last journey.

476. Κεφαλῆσιν. A pun on Κεφαλαί, the name of one of the δῆμοι of the tribe Acamantis. Κατορύξαι. " 'Επεὶ λόφον ἔχει ἡ κορυδός." Schol.

478. 'Ωs .... ὄντων. For ὡς with a causal Participle, see G. § 109, N. 4.

480. δρυκολάπτῃ. The reason why Zeus would be slow to restore the sceptre to this bird is, that the oak is sacred to him.

481. ἦρχον, *were rulers.* G. § 19, Notes 1 and 2.

484. Darius and Megabazos are named here as representing the Persians, because their names were notorious from their connection with the first Persian invasion of Greece. See Herod., V.

487. κυρβασίαν .... ὀρθήν. " Reges Persarum gestabant, etiam serioribus temporibus, tiaram rectam, ut ceteri Persae retro flexam .... atque ea ὀρθὴ τιάρα dicebatur proprie κυρβασία." Bothe. This upright head-dress of the Persian monarchs may be seen in the mosaic of the battle of Issus, found in one of the houses of Pompeii, and engraved in most of the works upon the ruins of that city. See particularly the German work, Herculanum und Pompeii, Vol. IV. pl. 3.

489. ὁπόταν ὄρθριον ᾄσῃ, *whenever he sings his morning song.* G. § 62. With ὄρθριον understand νόμον, *song:* Porson indeed reads (by conjecture) ὁπόταν νόμον ὄρθριοι ᾄσῃ. So Meineke. For an account of the handicrafts enumerated in the following lines, and for a valuable summary of Athenian industry in general, see St. John, Vol. III. pp. 96–214.

492. ὑποδησάμενοι. This word originally described the tying on of the simple sandal, such as is seen in many ancient statues. But in the progress of luxury, a great variety of shoes and boots, some richly adorned (see Hope's Costumes), came into use, and the same word was still employed to describe the act of putting them on, though its etymological signification was partly lost sight of. See St. John, Vol. II. pp. 64, seq.

493. Φρυγίων ἐρίων. The fine wool of Phrygia is mentioned among the exports of that country. The Phrygian dyers were particularly skilful in the practice of the art of coloring wool.

494. δεκάτην. Upon this word it is worth while to read the following passage: "While the poor, as we have seen, were driven by despair to imbrue their hands in the blood of their offspring, their more wealthy neighbors celebrated the birth of a child with a succession of banquets and rejoicings. Of these, the first was held on the fifth day from the birth, when took place the ceremony called Amphidromia, confounded by some ancient authors with the festival of the tenth day. On this occasion the accoucheuse, or the nurse, to whose care the child was now definitively consigned, having purified her hands with water, ran naked with the infant in her arms, and accompanied by all the other females of the family, in the same state, round the hearth, which was regarded as the altar of Hestia, the Vesta of the Romans. By this ceremony the child was initiated in the rites of religion, and placed under the protection of the fire-goddess, probably with the same view that infants are baptized among us.

"Meanwhile the passer-by was informed that a fifth-day feast was celebrating within, by symbols suspended from the street-door, which, in case of a boy, consisted in an olive crown; and of a lock of wool, alluding to her future occu·

pations, when it was a girl. Athenaeus, apropos of cabbage, which was eaten on this occasion, as well as by ladies 'in the straw,' as conducing to create milk, quotes a comic description of the Amphidromia from a drama of Ephippos, which proves they were well acquainted with the arts of joviality.

>   How is it
> No wreathed garland decks the festive door,
> No savory odor creeps into the nostrils
> Since 't is a birth-feast? Custom, sooth, requires
> Slices of rich cheese from the Chersonese,
> Toasted and hissing; cabbage too in oil,
> Fried brown and crisp, with smothered breast of lamb.
> Chaffinches, turtle-doves, and good fat thrushes
> Should now be feathered; rows of merry guests
> Pick clean the bones of cuttle-fish together,
> Gnaw the delicious foot of polypi,
> And drink large drafts of scarcely mingled wine.'

" A sacrifice was likewise this day offered up for the life of the child, probably to the god Amphidromos, first mentioned, and therefore supposed to have been invented by Aeschylus. It has moreover been imagined that the name was now imposed, and gifts were presented by the friends and household slaves.

" But it was on the seventh day that the child generally received its name, amid the festivities of another banquet; though sometimes this was deferred till the tenth. The reason is supplied by Aristotle. They delayed the naming thus long, he says, because most children that perish in extreme infancy die before the seventh day, which being passed, they considered their lives more secure. The eighth day was chosen by other persons for bestowing the name, and this, considered the natal day, was solemnized annually as the anniversary of its birth, on which occasion it was customary for the friends of the family to assemble together, and present gifts to the child, consisting sometimes of the polypi and cuttle-fish to be eaten at the feast. However, the tenth day appears to have been very commonly observed. Thus Euripides: —

' Say, who delighting in a mother's claim
'Mid tenth-day feasts bestowed the ancestral name?

"Aristophanes, too, on the occasion of naming his Bird-city, which a hungry poet pretends to have long ago celebrated, introduces Peisthetairos saying, —

' What! have I not but now the sacrifice
Of the tenth day completed and bestowed
A name as on a child?' "

St. John, Vol. I. pp. 128 – 130.

— ὑπέπινον, *I was taking a drop.* " Simili euphemismo Latini *subbibere*, Germani dicunt *sich ein Raüschchen trinken.*" Bothe.— ἐν ἄστει, *in town.* He had come in from the country on the occasion of solemnizing the naming of a friend's child.

495. κἄρτι καθεῦδον, *and was just dropping asleep.* — πρὶν δειπνεῖν. πρὶν usually takes the Infinitive in Attic Greek when the leading verb is affirmative. G. § 67; § 106.

496. οὗτος ἄρ', *this fellow then;* the cock. — ἐχώρουν Ἁλιμοῦνταδε, *I set out for Halimus.* Observe the force of the imperfect tense. Halimus was a *deme* of the tribe of Leontis, particularly famous as being the birthplace of Thucydides, the historian, whose epitaph is said to have been, Θουκυδίδης Ὀλόρου Ἁλιμούσιος ἐνθάδε κεῖται.

499. For the Imperfects, see v. 481.

501. Προκυλινδεῖσθαι τοῖς ἰκτίνοις. The allusion is to the custom of prostrating when the kite first appeared in spring, signifying joy at the return of that season. "'Εφ' ᾧ ἡδόμενοι κυλίνδονται ὡς ἐπὶ γόνυ. Παίξας οὖν ὡς βασιλεῖ φησι τὸ κυλινδεῖσθαι ὑπὸ ἀνθρώπων." Scholiast.

502, 503. Ἐκυλινδούμην .... ἀφεῖλκον. Euelpides makes a sly allusion to the cause of his rolling over, in the oath by Dionysos, which is quite in keeping with the story of the frolic in town, related a few lines back. Then he does not say that he bowed forward, προὐκυλινδεῖτο; on the contrary, he was on his back. —Ὀβολὸν κατεβρόχθισα, *I gulped down an obolos*. The custom of carrying coins in the mouth is several times alluded to in Aristophanes, as Eccles. 817, 818:—

" Πωλῶν γὰρ βότρυς
Μεστὴν ἀπῆρα τὴν γνάθον χαλκῶν ἔχων,
Κἄπειτ' ἐχώρουν εἰς ἀγορὰν ἐπ' ἄλφιτα.
Ἔπειθ' ὑπέχοντος ἄρτι μου τὸν θύλακον," etc.

See also Vesp. 790, seq.

505. ὁπότε εἴποι. G. § 62.
506. ἐθέριζον ἄν. G. § 30, 2.
507. κόκκυ. The rite of circumcision was practised by many Oriental nations, as the Egyptians, Phoenicians, and Jews; and as the cry of the cuckoo was the signal to begin harvesting among the people of these countries, the proverb came into use,— *Cuckoo! Afield, ye circumcised!*
508. εἴ τις βασιλεύοι. G. § 51.
510. Ἐπὶ .... ὄρνις. They placed upon the head of the kingly sceptre the figure of some bird. This is often alluded to by the poets, and may be seen on coins, medals, and other works of art. See Quatremère de Quincy's Jupiter Olympien, pp. 306, seq. See also Pindar, Pyth. I. 9. — For δωροδοκοίη, see G. § 62; also for the optatives in v. 512 and 513.
512. ἐξέλθοι, here, is a word belonging to the vocabulary of the stage; *came forth*, i. e. entered the scene through the royal gate, or central entrance at the back of the stage. — ἐν τοῖσι τραγῳδοῖς, *at the tragic representations;* literally, *in the tragedians;* the person being put for the time or the occasion of their appearance. This interpretation is more

accordant with the Greek idiom than that of Bothe, — "Inter actores tragicos."

513. Λυσικράτη. Of this individual the Scholiast says: "Οὗτος στρατηγὸς ἐγένετο 'Αθηναίων κλέπτης τε καὶ πανοῦργος. Διεβάλλετο δὲ (ὡς) δωροδόκος."

515. 'Αετὸν ..... κεφαλῆς. The words here used apply to the statue of Zeus, ἕστηκεν being constantly thus used by the Attic writers. According to a Scholiast, the head is put for the sceptre; or, he adds, because they were accustomed to place on the heads of the statues of the gods the images of the birds consecrated to them.

516. θυγάτηρ, i. e. Athena, the patron goddess of the city to whom the owl was consecrated. All this passage is in ridicule of the Athenian superstition, which consecrated to each god some particular bird.

520. Ὄμνυ .... ἄν. For this use of ἄν with the indicative, see G. § 30, 2. The Scholiast cites from Socrates, the historian, the following passage: "'Ραδάμανθυς δοκεῖ διαδεξάμενος τὴν βασιλείαν δικαιότατος γεγενῆσθαι πάντων ἀνθρώπων. Λέγεται δέ, αὐτὸν πρῶτον οὐδένα ἐᾶν ὅρκους ποιεῖσθαι κατὰ τῶν θεῶν, ἀλλ' ὀμνύναι κελεῦσαι χῆνα, καὶ κύνα, καὶ κριόν, καὶ τὰ ὅμοια." Socrates, according to Plato and Xenophon, used to swear by the dog, or by the goose, and sometimes simply by " the ———." See Plato's Gorgias, cap. 22, and Woolsey's note.

521. Λάμπων. This is the same Lampon — a soothsayer, juggler, and impostor — who is often mentioned elsewhere, and who, according to the Scholiast, obtained the honor of being entertained in the Prytaneum. See Clouds, 331 – 334, and note upon the passage. It is said that he used to swear by the goose because that bird was of a prophetic character. — ὅταν ἐξαπατᾷ. G. § 51.

522. ἐνόμιζον, *used to think.*

523. Μανᾶς. "Οὕτω γὰρ ἐκάλουν τοὺς οἰκέτας πελλάκις.' Scholiast.

525. ἱεροῖς. "Nam in templis tutae debebant esse aves, tanquam diis supplices; nefas autem violare supplices. Hinc cum Aristodicus Cumaeus in templo apud Branchidas nidos avium detraxisset et pullos exemisset, ex adyto talis vox audita fertur: Ἀνοσιώτατε ἀνθρώπων, τί τάδε τολμᾷς ποιέειν; Τοὺς ἱκέτας μου ἐκ τοῦ νηοῦ κεραΐζεις. Ut est ap. Herodotum I. 159; ap. Euripidem tamen Ion aedituus Apollinis Delphici pellit aves e templo in cognomini dramate 106, etc." Bergler.

530. βλιμάζοντες. "Βλιμάζειν κυρίως τὸ τοῦ ὑπογαστρίου καὶ τοῦ στήθους ἅπτεσθαι· ὅπερ ἐποίουν οἱ τοὺς ὄρνιθας ὠνούμενοι, κ. τ. λ." Scholiast.

532. παρέθενθ'. The frequentative aorist. For a full discussion of this usage, see Clouds, v. 520, note in Felton's edition. Κατεσκέδασαν, v. 536, is another example of the same idiom. G. § 30, 1.

541. κάκην = κακίαν.

542. προγόνων παραδόντων, genitive absolute, *ancestors having handed them down.*

543. Ἐπ' ἐμοῦ, *in my case*, i. e. here, *to my harm.*

547. οἰκήσω, *I will dwell.* Upon this expression, Cary remarks: "The word *dwell*, in our language, according to the old use of it, answers precisely to οἰκήσω, 'do good, and *dwell* for evermore,' Psalm xxxvii. 27, meaning simply *to abide*, or *live.*"

549. εἰ μὴ κοιμιούμεθα. § 50, 1, N. 1.

552. Βαβυλῶνα. For a full account of Babylon, see Herod. I.

553. Ὦ .... πόλισμα. The names here are those of two of the giants. The second is also the name of a bird, which offers an occasion for a jest below (1241). They are brought in here on account of the designed hostilities against the gods, as if another giants' war should disturb the peace of Olympus.

556. Ἱερὸν πόλεμον πρωυδᾶν, *to proclaim a sacred war;* like the wars against the Phocians for violating the sacred precincts and the temple of Pythian Apollo. The following lines give a ludicrous and satirical history of the mythical amours of the gods, and show, with many other passages, the freedom with which the poet dealt with the Hellenic religion, as well as with the politics of the time.

563–570. προσνείμασθαι, *to distribute* or *assign.* The meaning of the passage is, to apportion the birds individually to the gods, according to some fanciful analogy, so that, whenever a sacrifice is offered to a god, the corresponding bird may receive also an appropriate gift. The Scholiast and commentators have taken great pains to give the reasons why the particular selections and adaptations of gods, birds, and articles of food were adopted by the poet. Thus the name φαληρίς contains an allusion to the φάλλος, and of πυροί the Scholiast says: "Ἐπεὶ οἱ ἐφθοὶ πυροὶ πρὸς συνουσίαν ἐγερτικοί." The sheep is one of the victims sacrificed to Poseidon in the Odyssey, and the duck is connected with Poseidon, because he is a water bird. The λάρος is assigned to Hercules, on account of his gluttonous propensities. The ναστοί were a large species of cake, eaten at Athens with honey. With regard to Zeus and the wren, the Scholiast says: "Ἐπεὶ κατωφερὴς ὁ Ζεὺς καὶ μοιχός, διὰ τοῦτο ὀρχίλον παρέλαβε, διὰ τοὺς ὄρχεις. Τὸ δὲ σέρφον ἔνορχιν ὡς κριὸν ἔνορχιν."

570. ἤσθην. G. § 19, N. 5.— Βροντάτω .... Ζάν. These words are probably quoted from some old lyric poet. Bothe cites from the epigrams: "Ὁ Ζεὺς πρὸς τὸν Ἔρωτα· Βέλη τὰ σὰ πάντ' ἀφελοῦμαι. Χὦ πτανός· Βρόντα, καὶ πάλι κύκνος ἔσῃ."

572–575. Several of the deities were represented with wings. Hermes, as mentioned here, thus appears. The more ancient forms of the goddess Nike, or Victory, were without wings. To her a temple was dedicated, standing, according to Pausanias, near the entrance to the Acropolis. The ruins of this temple of Νίκη Ἄπτερος were discovered in excavating, in the year 1836, on the spot indicated by Pausanias, and it has been almost entirely restored. But Nike was generally represented, in works of art, with wings, and sometimes with golden or gilded ones; a figure of this kind was held in the right hand of the Olympian Zeus. (See Quatremère de Quincy, Jupiter Olympien; also Boetticher's Schriften, B. II. pp. 173, seq.) Especially was Eros, or Cupid, so represented. In alluding to Homer, the poet's memory failed him, the comparison to the timid dove being in a description of the flight of Hera and Athena (Il. V. 778), or there has been a change in the text, i. e. the substitution of Ἴριν for Ἥραν.

577. τὸ μηδέν. The article gives emphasis to the expression, and probably refers it to the phraseology of the philosophers. The subject of the preceding verb is *men*, ἄνδρες, to be supplied. Μηδέν (not οὐδέν) is used, because the Infinitive depends on a Protasis. The Infinitive after νομίζω usually takes οὐ as its negative, since it stands in indirect discourse.

580. Κἄπειτ' . . . . μετρείτω. The importation of corn was one of the most important public interests at Athens, and was carefully superintended by the municipal authorities. At certain times, distributions of corn (σιτοδοσίαι) took place among the people, — particularly, of course, in periods of scarcity, — each citizen receiving a certain measure. For a minute examination of this subject, see Boeckh's Public Economy of Athens, Book I. cap. 15. The language of Peisthetairos, in the present passage, doubtless alludes to this practice. Connected with the administration of the market, there were public officers called Μετρόνομοι and Προμετρηταί. The poet ludicrously makes Demeter the meas-

urer, and represents her as finding excuses, in the famine, for her inability to distribute corn.

583. ἐπὶ πείρᾳ. The Scholiast says: "'Επὶ βλάβῃ, ἢ ἵνα πειραθῶσιν ἡμῶν, εἰ θεοί ἐσμεν." The latter is doubtless correct; the idea being, that the birds shall peck out the eyes of the cattle to give a proof of what they can do if their power is called in question.

584. Apollo was the god of medicine, as well as of poetry. With regard to the word μισθοφορεῖ, the Scholiast says: "Τοῦτο δὲ εἶπεν, ἐπεὶ Λαομέδοντα τῆς τειχοδομίας μισθὸν ᾔτησεν." But there is also an allusion to the support of certain physicians at the public charge, for an account of whom see Boeckh, Book I. cap. 21. Hippocrates held this position at Athens.

585. Μή. Supply ἐκκοψάντων. For πρὶν ἄν, see G. § 67.

586. σὲ δὲ Γῆν. The particle is used here to single out the clause.

589. λόχος εἷς. In the Athenian army, the λόχος was a small subdivision of soldiers, consisting of twenty-four besides the officer, or one fourth of a τάξις. The smallness of the number makes the expression more emphatic.

591. ἀγέλη. Perhaps the word here refers to the ἀγέλαι, or bands into which the youth were divided in Crete and Sparta, though it is also used in a general sense of a flock of birds. See Manso's Sparta.

592. πλουτεῖν is the object of δώσομεν. G. § 92, 1.

593. μαντευομένοις, *consulting auguries.*

595. ναυκλήρων. The ναύκληροι at Athens were the owners of ships, and their business was with the shipping interest. The word was also applied to the owners of houses. In this passage the former meaning is the true one. The ναύκληρος sometimes went himself upon the voyage, but not necessarily so. — ὥστε. G. § 65, 3.

598. This must be understood to be an *asiae* of Euelpides. Upon γαῦλος the Scholiast says: "Φοινικικὸν δὲ τοῦ ἀγγείου ὀξυτόνως. Καλλίμαχος· Κυπρόθε Σιδόνιός με κατήγαγεν ἐνθάδε γαῦλος. Ἄλλως. Γαῦλος, πλοῖόν τι φορτικὸν ὡς καὶ σκάφη (σκαφὶς) ἀπὸ τῶν σκευῶν. Ὅμηρος· Γαῦλοί τε σκαφίδες τε. Ὡς αἱρετωτέρου δὲ ὄντος καὶ ἀκινδύνου τῶν ἄλλων πάντων τοῦτό φησι." And Bothe: "Γαῦλος dicebatur navis rotundior, mercibus vehendis apta, qualem Phoenices primi construxisse leguntur." — Οὐκ ἂν μείναιμι. G. § 53, 2, N.

599–601. The Athenians were as credulous about buried treasures as the moderns, and made use of superstitious means in the search for them. The language in the last line refers to the proverb, "Οὐδείς με θεωρεῖ πλὴν ὁ παριπτάμενος ὄρνις." "Τοῦτο ἐλέγετο ἐπὶ τῶν ἀγνώστων." Sch.

602. ὑδρίας. Literally, *water-vessels*, but also any urn or vessel such as might be used to hold the coins which were to be concealed in the earth.

603. ὑγίειαν. Upon this word Bothe has the following note: — "Haec est illa πλουθυγίεια, quam infra dicit 698, item Equ. 1100, et. Vesp. 647, h. e. quasi πλούτου ὑγίεια, non opes et sanitas, ut Br. reddidit Equ. v. 1, siquidem sanitatem donare nemo potest, divitias omnisque generis opes potest, quas complectitur ἡ πλουθυγίεια, ut pulcre intelligitur e Vesparum v. 1, ὑγίεντα ὄλβον serio dixit Pindarus, Ol. V. 55." It may be remarked in addition, that *health* was more sedulously studied by the ancient Greeks than by any of the moderns. Their gymnastic system formed an important and integral part of their education, and vigorous muscular exercise was not given up at any period of life. The national games also tended to keep alive a high, perhaps an exaggerated, idea of the importance of bodily health and strength. See the Panegyricus of Isocrates.

609. Οὐκ .... κορώνη; The saying quoted by Plu-

tarch (De Orac. Def.) from Hesiod was, that the crow lives *nine* generations of man. The epithet λακέρυζα occurs in Hesiod's Works and Days, 747.

613. λιθίνους, *stone*, i. e. *marble*, that being the principal material used in Athens for temples and other public buildings.

614. θυρῶσαι . . . . θύραις, *to furnish the temples with golden doors.*

616. σεμνοῖς = τοῖς τιμίοις. Sch.

618, 619. Δελφοὺς . . . . *Ἄμμων'*, i. e. to the oracle of Apollo at Delphi, and of Zeus in Libya.

626. προβαλοῦσιν, *having thrown out to them*. A burlesque upon the popular notion that the gods were to be conciliated only by gifts. The argument is, that it will be much more economical to have the birds for gods than to worship the gods themselves.

627. 'Ω . . . . μεταπίπτων. Φίλτατ' is the masculine adjective in the vocative. It is constructed with the participle, expressing the *result* of μεταπίπτων, *changing from the most hated to the most beloved*. In this respect it resembles the construction in Aesch. Ag. 628, 'Επέκρανεν δὲ γάμου πικρὰς τελευτάς.

629. 'Επαυχήσας, *having confidence in*.

638. τεταξόμεθ', *we will take our post*.

641. μελλονικιᾶν. A pun upon the name of Nikias, the general in the Scicilian Expedition whose hesitancy of conduct was more than once ridiculed by the poet. The Scholiast says: "Μελλονικιᾶν, τὸ βραδύνειν καὶ ἀναβάλλεσθαι. Νικίας γὰρ υἱὸς Νικηράτου, ὃς ἀνεβάλλετο ἀπελθεῖν εἰς Σικελίαν· βραδὺς γὰρ ἦν περὶ τὰς ἐξόδους." See Thucyd. VI. 25.

647. Κριῶθεν. The Scholiast explains: " Κριὸς δῆμος τῆς 'Αντιοχίδος φυλῆς, ἀπὸ Κριοῦ τινος ὠνομασμένος. Γράφεται δὲ καὶ Θριῆθεν, οἷον ἀπὸ δήμου τῆς Οἰνηΐδος φυλῆς.

650. 'Ατὰρ . . . . πάλιν, *But bless my soul! here, hold*

back again. Τὸ δεῖνα, says Pape (Lexicon in verb.), is from the language of the people, used when one immediately utters a sudden thought, in order not to forget it, *atat!* — or when one cannot immediately recall something. In this passage it has suddenly occurred to Peisthetairos that there will be some practical difficulty in two men without wings holding intercourse with winged birds; and this sudden idea is intimated by τὸ δεῖνα. Ἐπανάκρουσαι is thus explained by the Scholiast: "Ἡ μεταφορὰ ἀπὸ τῶν τὰς ἡνίας ἀνακρουομένων, ἢ τὰς ναῦς. Ἄλλως. Ὑπόστρεψον, ἐπανάβηθι. Ἐπανάκρουσις δέ ἐστι κυρίως τὸ ἐπισχεῖν τὴν ἐπερχομένην ναῦν καὶ μεθορμίσαι εἰς τὸν ὅρμον, ἵνα μὴ προσελθοῦσα θραυσθῇ."

653 – 655. Αἰσώπου . . . . ποτέ. The fable here referred to is probably the same as that of which we find the first few lines in a fragment of Archilochus (No. 86, Bergk): Αἶνός τις ἀνθρώπων ὅδε, ὡς ἄρ' ἀλώπηξ καἰετὸς ξυνωνίην ἔμιξαν. It must be remembered, that the ancients were accustomed to attribute to Aesop all fables that were composed in his manner. See note to v. 471.

658, 659. Ξανθία, Μανόδωρε. Names of servants.

672. ὥσπερ παρθένος, *like a maid.* An imitation of Homer, Il. II. 872. For an account of the ornaments worn by Grecian ladies, see St. John, Vol. II. pp. 50, seq.

673. μοι δοκῶ, *I have a fancy.*

674. ῥύγχος . . . . ἔχει, *she has a beak with two points,* or literally, two spits. The actor representing this character wore a mask in imitation of the beak of a bird.

676. λέμμα, *the shell.*

686. Ἄρχου . . . . ἀναπαίστων, *lead off the anapæsts.*

687 – 689. This description of the life of man is an imitation of the noble passage in Homer, Il. VI. 146. See also Aeschyl. Prom. 549, seq.

692 – 694. Upon this passage, Bothe has the following note: " Ridet poetas, qui de rerum originibus cecinerant

(ut Hesiodus), et philosophos (ut Ionicos, Empedoclem), qui de deorum rerumque omnium ortu temere multa statuerant; etiam Sophistas, inter quos fuit Prodicus Ceus [quem laudat Chorus Nubium Nub. 360, σοφίας καὶ γνώμης οὕνεκα]. Hunc missum fieri vult. — Ut χαίρειν εἰπεῖν aliquem dicuntur, qui bono et amico animo ab eo dicedunt, sic κλαίειν εἰπεῖν est male animatorum. Vide Plut. 62, Ach. 1064, B. de Prodico v. Hindenburgium et interpp. Xenophontis Memorab. Socr. 2, 1, 21, aliosque. Sextus Empir. adv. Mathem. p. 311: Πρόδικος ὁ Κεῖος· "Ἥλιον, φησί, καὶ σελήνην, καὶ ποταμούς, καὶ κρήνας, καὶ καθ' ὅλου πάντα τὰ ὠφελοῦντα τὸν βίον ἡμῶν οἱ παλαιοὶ θεοὺς ἐνόμισαν διὰ τὴν ἀπ' αὐτῶν ὠφέλειαν, καθάπερ Αἰγύπτιοι τὸν Νεῖλον· καὶ διὰ τοῦτο τὸν μὲν ἄρτον Δήμητραν νομισθῆναι, τὸν δὲ οἶνον Διόνυσον, τὸ δὲ ὕδωρ Ποσειδῶνα, τὸ δὲ πῦρ Ἥφαιστον, καὶ ἤδη τῶν εὐχρηστούντων ἕκαστον. Quam rationem irridens Cic. de Nat. Deor. I. 42: *Prodicus Ceus*, inquit, *qui ea, quae prodessent hominum vitae, deorum in numero habita esse dixit, quam tandem religionem reliquit?*"

694. κλάειν εἴπητε. G. § 15, 2, N. 3. Εἶπον seldom takes the Infinitive, unless it has the force of a verb of *commanding*, as here. In its ordinary sense, introducing indirect quotations, it takes ὅτι or ὡς. Φημί, on the other hand, takes only the Infinitive, while λέγω, *to say*, takes either ὅτι, ὡς, or the Infinitive. Λέγω may also mean *to tell, to command*.

697. ὑπηνέμιον . . . . ᾠόν. The Scholiast says: "Ὑπηνέμια καλεῖται τὰ δίχα συνουσίας καὶ μίξεως. — τίκτει, G. § 10, 2.

698. περιτελλομέναις. This is an Homeric word, often applied to the revolutions of the seasons. See Il. II. 551; Od. XI. 295.

699. εἰκὼς . . . . δίναις. "Ταῖς τοῦ ἀνέμου ὠκείαις συστροφαῖς ἐοικώς, οἷον ταχύς." Sch. "Εἰκώς Atticis idem quod ἐοικώς. (Vide Moer. p. 148.) Δίναι proprie sunt *vortices aquarum* (Callim. in Del. 149), hinc, quaecunque in orbem

aguntur (interpp. Thomae Mag. p. 241), hoc loco *turbines.* Ovid. Am. 2, 9, 49, De Amore: *Tu levis es multoque tuis* ventosior *alis.* B. Voss.: *Der am Rücken mit zwei Goldfittigen glänzt, von Natur wie die wirbelnde Windsbraut."* Bothe. See *ante,* note to v. 574.

701. Ἐνεόττευσεν, *hatched.*

702. πρίν. G. § 67, 1.

705, 706. Ἡμεῖς ... δῆλον, *And that we are children of Eros is plain by many proofs.* They proceed to enumerate the aids they render to lovers, in a way that shows what sort of presents were considered by the Greeks the most acceptable to the objects of passion, namely, *quails, geese, poultry,* and the like.

709. δούς explains διὰ ἰσχύν. G. § 109, 2.

711. ὥρας, *the seasons,* of which mention is made here according to the earliest and simplest division of the year into three portions.

712. σπείρειν, ὅταν, κ. τ. λ., i. e. *in each year, when,* &c. G. § 62.

713. Καὶ .... καθεύδειν. The rudder was taken from the ship in winter. See Hesiod, Works and Days, 45: —

"Αἰψά κε πηδάλιον μὲν ὑπὲρ καπνοῦ καταδεῖο."

714. Ὀρέστῃ. "'Ορέστης μανίαν ὑποκρινόμενος ἐν τῷ σκότει τοὺς ἀνθρώπους ἀπέδυεν. Sch. Cf. infra 1476, et Ach. 1092. Χλαῖνα crassior vestis superior fuit, hiemi apta. Vide Hesych. h. v. ῥιγῶν, *prae frigore horrens.* Vide Thom. Mag. p. 782, et Bos. Obss. Crit. p. 48. Ἀποδύειν est *aliquem spoliare vestibus,* ut Eccl. 864, 866." Bothe.

716. χλαῖναν, ληδάριον. The former was a thick outside garment, the second a light summer garment. For a minute explanation of Grecian dress, see Becker's Charicles, Scene XI. Excursus I., and St. John, Vol. II. cap. 25; also Hope's Costumes. — ἡνίκα. G. § 59. — πεκτεῖν. G. § 92, 1, N. 2.

721. *Ὄρνιν.* Here and in the following lines, there is a play on the word ὄρνις, *bird*, which is often used for any omen whatever. The things or acts mentioned were all significant to the mind of the Greek, — a *word*, a *sneeze*, an *accidental meeting*, a *sound*, a *servant* suddenly appearing, an *ass*. Upon the last a Scholiast says : " Λέγεται γάρ τι τοιοῦτον, ὡς συμβολικὸς ἐρωτώμενος περὶ ἀρρώστου εἶδεν ὄνον ἐκ πτώματος ἀναστάντα, ἀκήκοε δὲ ἑτέρου λέγοντος · Βλέπε, πῶς ὄνος ἂν ἀνέστη: Ὁ δὲ ἔφη · Ὁ νοσῶν ἀναστήσεται."

725 – 728. The oracles of the gods could not be consulted at all seasons of the year; but substituting the birds for the gods, men will have the advantage of being able to consult them at all seasons alike.

729. σεμνυνόμενοι, *putting on haughty airs.*

736. Γάλα τ' ὀρνίθων, *and milk of birds;* a proverbial expression. "Ἐν παροιμίᾳ δὲ ἐπὶ τῶν λίαν εὐδαιμονούντων καὶ πάντα κεκτημένων." Sch.

752. Φρύνιχος. "Ὃς ἐπὶ μελοποιίαις ἐθαυμάζετο..... Ποιητὴς ἡδὺς ἐν τοῖς μέλεσι." Sch. See Darley's Grecian Drama, Ch. II. The comparison of the poet to a bee gathering sweets from every flower is a very common one.

759. εἰ .... ἐστίν. G. § 49, 1.

760, 761. ἢν εἴπῃ. G. § 50, 1. — εἰ μαχεῖ, *if you want to fight.* G. § 49, 1, N. 3 (not § 50, 1, N. 1).

761. αἶρε πλῆκτρον, *lift the spur.* The expression is borrowed from cock-fighting.

762. δραπέτης ἐστιγμένος, *a branded runaway;* in allusion to the custom of burning upon the persons of fugitive slaves a mark which designated them as στιγματίαι, a common term of abuse in the popular language of Athens.

764. Σπινθάρου. "Σπινθ. ap. Demosth. p. 1259 et 1358, ed. Reisk. Spinthari memorantur. B. — Compar Spinthari Philemon, homo obscurus: cave enim cognominem intelligas Comicum, Menandri aequalem." Bothe.

765. Φρυγίλος. "Propter similitudinem cum voce *Phryx*, *Phrygis*, significari putatur *fringilla* (*der Finke*). B. *fringillam carduelem* Linn., *le chardonneret, den Stieglitz*, intelligebat Wieland. Voss.: *Frygischer* (?) *Rothfink wird er hier sein, von Filemons Vetterschaft.*" Bothe.

766. Κάρ. "Cares, ex quibus plurimi serviebant, barbaros atque agrestes, militiaeque mercenariae, quae despecta erat, auctores, habitos fuisse, monuere Spanhem. ad Ran. 1231, Hemsterh. ad argum. Pluti, Aristoph. Beck. 3, p. 7, aliique. Cf. supra, v. 295, et de Execestide 11." Bothe.

767. Φυσάτω πάππους. According to Euphronius, as quoted by Aelian, a certain species of bird was called πάππος. There is, therefore, a pun upon the expression, besides the ludicrous inversion of the order of nature which the literal meaning implies. In the rest of the line, the terms refer to the distribution of the Athenians, according to which the φρατρία was a third part of one of the four Ionic tribes, and the members of this division were called φράτορες. These divisions had their registers, in which the names and families of the individuals composing them were required to be entered. Bothe says: "Φῦσαι πάππους est facere, ut sibi avi sint, adsciscere avos; qui enim Athenis peregrinitatis accusabantur, avos et tribules nominare debebant, ut appareret, cives ipsos esse."

768. ὁ Πισίου. "Οὐδὲν σαφὲς ἔχομεν, τίς ὁ Πισίου, οὔτε περὶ τῆς προδοσίας· ὅτι δὲ τῶν λίαν πονηρῶν ἐστι, δηλοῖ Κρατῖνος ἐν Χείροσι, Πυλαίας, Ὥραις.—Ἄλλως. Οἱ μέν, τὸν Πισίαν ἕνα τῶν ἑρμοκοπιδῶν εἶναι, οἱ δὲ τὸν υἱὸν αὐτοῦ. Ἐτηροῦντο δὲ οὗτοι, ὅπως ἂν δοῖεν τῆς περικοπῆς τιμωρίαν. Εἰ οὖν, φησίν, ὁ υἱὸς αὐτοῦ τοῦ Πισίου ὅμοιος βούλεται εἶναι τῷ πατρί, γενέσθω πέρδιξ πανοῦργος." Schol.—"Τοῖς ἀτίμοις. The force of this term is not adequately expressed by our word *dishonored* or by *disfranchised*. An Athenian citizen in full possession of all his rights (τιμαί) was called ἐπίτιμος; and so soon as he lost all of these rights

or any one or more of them, he became ἄτιμος, and was said to be under ἀτιμία. 'Ατιμία could therefore be either *partial* or *complete*. 1. Partial ἀτιμία deprived a citizen of some particular right or τιμή, and was quite common as a punishment for abusing a right or privilege. For example, any prosecutor who, in a public suit, did not receive one fifth of the votes of the judges (usually 100 out of 501), was fined a thousand drachmas and prohibited from bringing a similar public suit for the future. This prohibition was called ἀτιμία. Others were prohibited from entering temples or the market-place; others from speaking in the public assembly; others from being members of the Senate or from holding office; others again from visiting certain places in the Athenian dominions. All these were ἄτιμοι; but their ἀτιμία was partial, and their other rights were not affected. 2. Complete ἀτιμία, on the other hand, deprived a man of all the rights and privileges which he had enjoyed as a citizen of Athens, and left him in a sort of *negative* condition, in which the state simply *refused to recognize* him as a part of itself. As Lysias says, it made men ἀντὶ πολιτῶν ἀπόλιδας. Demosthenes (in Mid. p. 544, 10) speaks of it as καὶ νόμων καὶ δικῶν καὶ πάντων στέρησις. It left him like a foreigner, without civic rights, dependent entirely upon the good-will or mercy of his neighbors for protection to his life and property. He could enter no public temple, and of course could sue or be sued in no court of law. See the striking description given by Demosthenes (in Mid. p. 544, 545), who calls a man who is under ἀτιμία before the court, while he narrates his story; the man, however, must stand speechless. This kind of ἀτιμία was inflicted as a punishment by law for various offences, such as corruption, embezzlement, cowardice or desertion in war, perjury, neglect or abuse of parents, prostitution (ἑταίρησις), insult to officers of the state, abuse of confidence (as in the case of an arbitrator), and similar offences.

Public debtors of all kinds were under complete ἀτιμία until their debts were paid. 'Ατιμία *in itself* included neither confiscation of property nor a descent of the father's disgrace by inheritance to the children : either or both of these could, however, be added to ἀτιμία in special cases.· Those guilty of murder, treason, or gross sacrilege, if they left the country before actual conviction, were condemned to perpetual banishment and confiscation of property. (Demosth. in Mid. p. 528, 7; Xen. Hell. I. 7, 22.) So for the offence mentioned by Demosth. in Neaer. p. 1363, 5. See also Dem. in Lept. p. 504, 22. In other cases the ἀτιμία is to descend to posterity, as is provided in the laws quoted by Demosth. in Aristocr. p. 640, 1; in Mid. p. 551, 25 : here the confiscation of property seems always to have been included. Public debtors, although they were wholly ἄτιμοι so long as they remained debtors, could yet regain their rights by payment of the debt; on the other hand, if they died indebted to the state, their ἀτιμία descended with the debt, as a part of the inheritance, to the children. Those who suffered ἀτιμία as a punishment for a crime remained ἄτιμοι through life: they could be reinstated only by an extraordinary act of grace, which was always looked upon as exceptional and illegal. Such reinstatements occurred only when the state was in extreme danger, as, for example, after the battle of Chaeronea. (See Grote, Vol. XI. p. 694.) See Hermann, Staatsalterthümer, §§ 124 and 52 ; Privatalterth. § 70; with the authorities quoted in the notes : also Meier, De Bonis Damnatorum, *passim.* An important classical passage is found in Andocides, De Myster. §§ 73 - 76." Goodwin.

770. ἐκπερδικίσαι. This word alludes to the shy habits of the partridge, and the dexterity of the bird in avoiding pursuit. *To dodge like a partridge* would express, in a roundabout way, the meaning of the Greek. The Scholiast remarks further : " Διαβάλλει δὲ ὡς κατεγνωσμένον καὶ φυγῇ

ζημιωθέντα. Οἱ δὲ πέρδικες πανοῦργοι ὄντες εὐχερῶς διαδιδράσκουσι τοὺς θηρευτάς, πολλάκις ὕπτιοι γενόμενοι καὶ ἐπιβάλλοντες ἑαυτοῖς κάρφη. Φησὶν οὖν, ὅτι καὶ παρ' ἡμῖν γενόμενος δύναται πάλιν φεύγειν."

783. ἄνακτας, *kings,* i. e. here, according to the Homeric usage, the gods.

787. Αὐτίχ', *just for example.*

788 – 790. Εἶτα .... κατέπτατο. These lines, and the freer ones which follow, must be considered in reference to the mode of dramatic representation at Athens, for a particular account of which, see Donaldson's Theatre of the Greeks. We may say here, in general, that these representations were limited to a few successive days, several dramas being brought out, one after the other, beginning early in the morning. The long exhibitions of the tragedians could not fail to be bantered by the license of the comedians. Bothe thinks it probable that the tragedies were acted in the morning, having the precedence on account of their superior dignity, and the comedies in the afternoon; "cum paratiores ad jocos essent animi spectatorum; quo pertinere dicas, quod avolantem illum a choris tragicis post prandium redire posse ait ἐφ' ἡμᾶς, *ad nos,* comoedos, *ni fallor.*" It may be presumed that the arrangements differed at different times.

795. βουλευτικῷ. The theatre was divided, and some of the seats were set apart for the several official bodies of the state, for the ἔφηβοι, for foreign ministers, &c. The portion here alluded to was that which was occupied by the members of the Senate of Five Hundred. As the Scholiast says: "Οὗτος τόπος τοῦ θεάτρου ἀνειμένος, τοῖς βουλευταῖς, ὡς καὶ ὁ τοῖς ἐφήβοις ἐφηβικός. Παρ' ὑμῶν δὲ ἀντὶ ἀπὸ τοῦ θεάτρου."

799 – 801. The Diitrephes mentioned here is said by the Scholiast to have acquired wealth by the manufacture of

willow wicker-baskets for wine-flasks. Having accom‑
plished thus much, it seems he aspired to the high offices
of state. The φύλαρχοι were ten officers of cavalry, elected
one from each tribe, but in the general assemblies of the
people. They were subordinate to the ἵππαρχοι, who were
two in number, also chosen to exercise the general com‑
mand in the cavalry service; so that Diitrephes, in passing
from one office to the other, rose a grade in military dignity.
— ἐξ οὐδενὸς μεγάλα πράττει, *from nothing* (or *nobody*) *he is
flourishing greatly.* — ἱππαλεκτρυών. " Βουλευτής. Ὁ γὰρ
ἀλεκτρυὼν ἐν τοῖς ὄρνισι τιμιώτερος. Navis hoc insigne fuisse,
ex Ran. 883, intelligitur. Praeterea monuit B., fictae avis
nomen usurpari, quo significetur, Diitrephem istum superbe
et cum fastu quodam incedere, itaque manere Comicum in
metaphora de avibus et volatu. Posse etiam ἱππαλεκτρυόνα
esse *magnum* gallinaceum secundum Sch., quae vis est τοῦ
ἵππος in multis compositis; qua de re laudat Fischeri annott.
ad Weller. III. 1, p. 237." Bothe.

802. Ταυτὶ τοιαυτί. A colloquial expression = *Well, this
will do.* Peisthetairos and Euelpides come out of the house
of Epops, having partaken of the root which should furnish
them with a growth of wings. They cannot help laughing
at each other's ridiculous appearance.

806. Εἰς .... συγγεγραμμένῳ, *to a cheaply* (or *badly*)
painted goose. " Contrarium εἰς κάλλος. Acneas Soph.,
Epist. 25 : Μὴ ταὐτὸν πάθοιμεν, ὥσπερ ἂν εἴ τις ζωγράφος τὴν
Ἑλένην εἰς κάλλος (eleganter) γράφων τῆς κεφάλης ἐπιλάθοιτο."
Bergler.

809. Τάδ' .... πτεροῖς. This refers to a passage found
in the fragments of the Myrmidons of Aeschylus. (No. 123,
Dind.; No. 135, Nauck.) The Scholiast says: " Ἐκεῖνος γὰρ
Λιβυστικὴν αὐτὴν καλεῖ παροιμίαν·

" Ὡς δ' ἔστι μύθων τῶν Λιβυστικῶν λόγος,
Πληγέντ' ἀτράκτῳ τοξικῷ τὸν ἀετὸν

NOTES.

Εἰπεῖν ἰδόντα μηχανὴν πτερώματος·
Τάδ' οὐχ ὑπ' ἄλλων, ἀλλὰ τοῖς αὑτῶν πτεροῖς
'Αλισκόμεσθα.'

Πεποίηκε γὰρ ὁ Αἰσχύλος ἀετὸν τρωννύμενον καὶ λέγοντα ταῦτα, ἐπειδὴ εἶδε τὸ βέλος ἐπτερωμένον καὶ ἐμπεπαρμένον αὐτῷ. Καὶ ἡμεῖς οὖν, φησίν, οὐχ ὑπ' ἄλλων πάσχομεν ταῦτα, ἀλλὰ τῇ ἑαυτῶν γνώμῃ." The idea was made use of by Waller, as quoted by Porson and Wheelwright: —

> " That eagle's fate and mine are one,
> Who on the shaft that made him die
> Espied a feather of his own,
> Wherewith he wont to soar so high."

And by Byron, also, in his " English Bards and Scotch Reviewers," in the beautiful lines on Kirke White: —

> " So the struck eagle, stretched upon the plain,
> No more through rolling clouds to soar again,
> Viewed his own feather on the fatal dart,
> And winged the shaft that quivered in his heart;
> Keen were his pangs, but keener far to feel
> He nursed the pinion that impelled the steel;
> While the same plumage that had warmed his nest
> Drank the last life-drop of his bleeding breast."

815. καλῶμεν. G. § 88.

816, 817. Σπάρτην .... κειρίαν. It is not easy to give an English equivalent for the pun in this passage. Besides being the name of the city, Σπάρτη meant a *rope* made of *spartum*, or *broom*, and used for bed-cords, while κειρία was also the cord, stouter than the other, for a bedstead. The whole is, probably, an expression of the Athenian dislike of Sparta, conveyed in a joke. It is likely the words had some association, now lost, which gave a pungency to the allusion that we are unable to feel. This passage is referred to by Eustathius in the commentary on Il. I.— οὐδ' ἂν χαμεύνῃ (sc. θείμην), *I would not put one even on my bedstead.*— ἔχων = εἰ ἔχοιμι. G. § 109, 6; § 52, 1.

820. Χαῦνόν τι πάνυ, *something very grand*, or *pompous.*
— Νεφελοκοκκυγίαν, *Cloud-cuckootown.* Lucian, in his amusing work, Verae Historiae (the original of Gulliver's Travels), refers to this place.

824, 825. Θεογένους, Αἰσχίνου. Of the former of these personages, both of whom were boasters of wealth which they did not possess, the Scholiast says: "Λέγεται, ὅτι μεγαλέμπορός τις ἐβούλετο εἶναι, περαίτης ἀλαζών, ψευδόπλουτος. Ἐκαλεῖτο δὲ Καπνός, ὅτι πολλὰ ὑπισχνούμενος οὐδὲν ἐτέλει. Εὔπολις ἐν Δήμοις";— and of the latter: "Οὗτος πένης, θρυπτόμενος καὶ αὐτὸς ἐπὶ πλούτῳ."

826, 827. The bragging is imputed jestingly, and in a humorous shifting of the construction, to the gods, instead of to the giants. The plain of Phlegra was in Thrace, where the poets laid the scene of the mythical conflict between the gods and giants. According to Herodotus (VII. 123), Phlegra was the ancient name of Pallene, with which the statement of Strabo (VII. frag. 27) agrees.

829. Πολιοῦχος. *Patron deity* of the city, as Athena was at Athens. — πέπλον. This was the sacred shawl, or mantle, borne in the Panathenaic procession to the Acropolis, and placed on the statue of Athena. It was wrought by the Athenian maidens, and covered with figures representing incidents in the mythical accounts connected with the history of the goddess herself. Representations of the procession still exist in the remains of the friezes of the Parthenon, which have been often published. There is a figure of Athena in the Dresden Museum, wearing a peplus which represents the Olympic gods conquering the giants. (See Müller's Denkmäler der alten Kunst, Pl. X, No. 36.) The allusion to the peplus in such close connection with this fable makes it probable that the poet has seen this very representation of the subject.

830. πολιάδα. The epithet of Athena as the goddess of the city.

832, 833. πανοπλίαν .... Κλεισθένης. The circumstance that Athena Polias was represented with a complete suit of armor gave the poet an opportunity for a sarcasm upon the effeminacy of this noted profligate

834. Πελαργικόν. There was a portion of the ancient wall of the Acropolis, called the *Pelasgic* wall, which the Athenians believed to have been built by a wandering band of Pelasgians, who were said to have appeared in Athens about 1100 B. C. (Herod. VI. 137; Pausan. I. 28, 23.) The poet here seems to allude to a fanciful derivation of the name Πελασγοί from πελαργοί, *storks*, to which Strabo refers (V. p. 221), speaking of the compiler of the 'Ατθίς as narrating, in regard to the Pelasgian race, διὰ τὸ πλανήτας εἶναι καὶ δίκην ὀρνέων ἐπιφοιτᾶν ἐφ' οὓς ἔτυχε τόπους Πελαργοὺς ὑπὸ τῶν Ἀττικῶν κληθῆναι. See also Dion. Hal. Ant. I. 28. At any rate, he has a chance, seldom neglected, of punning upon the resemblance of the name to the word πελαργός, *stork;* a name, therefore, well suited to the walls of Birdtown.

837. Ἄρεως νεοττός, *the chicken of Ares.*

838. ἐπιτήδειος οἰκεῖν. G. § 93, 1, N. 2 (*b*). — ἐπὶ πετρῶν. The Pelasgic wall was on the precipitous side of the rocky Acropolis. The Scholiast says : " Δίδυμός φησι τὸ Πελασγικὸν τεῖχος ἐπὶ πετρῶν κεῖσθαι." Here the Persian bird, the cock, as being martial and pugnacious, was to dwell and defend the citadel.

839 – 847. Peisthetairos now bids his companion to mount the air, and help the builders. He is to carry the rubble-stone (χάλικας), to strip himself and mix the mortar (πηλὸν ἀποδὺς ὄργασον), to carry up the hod (λεκάνην), and, for the sake of a little variety, to tumble down the ladder. " Quia," says Blaydes, " aliquando id aedificantibus in ascendendo eam (i. e. scalam) et descendendo accidit." Then he is to see to having the sentries stationed ; to take care

and cover the embers, so that the workmen may always have fire within reach; to run round, with a little bell, to keep the sentinels alert. This was the duty of the officers. See Thucyd. IV. 135. Then, by way of relief, he is told to get a nap whenever he can. He is also to despatch a herald up to the gods, and another down to men; and, having attended to these various orders, he is to come back for fresh directions.

848. Οἴμωζε παρ' ἔμ'. Euelpides is vexed at these orders. He gives utterance to his vexation jocosely, by repeating the last words of Peisthetairos, παρ' ἐμέ, in a different sense; and instead of the usual form of polite leave-taking, χαῖρε, the grumbles out, Οἴμωζε, groan, = *Devil take you, παρ' ἔμ', for all I care.*

851. πέμψοντα τὴν πομπήν, *who shall conduct the procession,* i. e. the religious ceremonies connected with the organization of the commonwealth, and its consecration to the gods.

852. Παῖ .... χέρνιβα. The servants are directed to take up the basket and the ewer. Says Bothe: "Monuit B. secundum Abresch. Anim. ad Aeschylum t. 1, p. 503, seq., et Dawes. Misc. Crit., p. 235, αἴρειν κανοῦν esse *afferre canistrum,* sed αἴρεσθαι κ. *id portandum in pompa suscipere,* et παῖ, παῖ, etc., dici pro hoc ὦ παῖδες (servi), ὑμῶν ὁ μὲν αἰρέσθω τὸ κανοῦν, ὁ δὲ ἕτερος τὴν χέρ ιβα. — Sch.: τὴν χέρνιβα. Τὸ ὕδωρ. — B.: τὴν χέρνιβα ap. Hom. esse aquam ad abluendas manus, χέρνιβον autem vas, quo aqua illa continetur, docuerunt interpp. Pollucis, p. 1292, hoc tamen loco χέρνιψ pro χερνίβῳ poni videtur (per synecdochen)."

853 – 860. According to the Scholiast, these lines of the chorus are a parody upon a passage in the Peleus of Sophocles. (See Nauck. Frgm. No. 446, 447.) — Πυθιὰς βοά, *the Pythian cry;* that is, the Paean. — Χαῖρις. This was a poor Theban piper. The Scholiast says: " Ὡς αὐτομάτως

ἐπιόντος αὐτοῦ ταῖς εὐωχίαις. Ἦν δὲ ὁ Χαῖρις οὗτος κιθαρῳδός, καὶ γέγονεν αὐλητής. Μνημονεύει δὲ αὐτοῦ καὶ Φερεκράτης ἐν Ἀγρίοις· Φέρ᾿ ἴδω, κιθαρῳδὸς τίς κάκιστος ἐγένετο; —Ὁ Πεισίοι Μέλης.—Μετὰ δὲ Μέλητα τίς;—Ἔχ᾿ ἀτρέμ᾿, ἐγῷδα· Χαῖρις."

854. συμπαραινέσας ἔχω. G. § 112, N. 7.

863. κόρακ᾿ . . . . ἐμπεφορβιωμένον. The piper was a crow, i. e. the actor represented a crow by decking himself with a crow's head. He also wore a mouthpiece, like any other piper, and so astonished Peisthetairos by the oddity of the combination.

The scene that follows is a daring burlesque upon the sacrificial ceremonies of the Athenians in building the foundation of a new city. The priest lays the offerings upon the altar, and then invokes the new gods, beginning, according to custom, with Ἑστία (Bird-Vesta), and applying to the birds epithets parodied from the solemn designations of the deities. The comic poets were allowed to use great freedom in dealing with the popular religion.

869. Σουνιέρακε. This is taken from Σουνιάρατος, an epithet of Poseidon. See Aristoph. Eq. 560, and Σουνιάρατος in Liddell and Scott.

870. Πυθίῳ. "Epitheta Apollinis tribuit cycno, qui Apollini sacer est. Latona autem in Ortygia insula, quae ἀπὸ τῶν ὀρτύγων, a *coturnicibus* dicta est, Apollinem peperit et Dianam." Bergler. To which Blaydes adds: "Latona igitur, quoad mulier est, ὀρτυγομήτρα dicitur, ut quae in Ortygia insula pepererit; quoad avis est, quia coturnix ingens."

872. Κολαινίς. A name under which Artemis was worshipped by the inhabitants of Myrrhinus, an Athenian deme of the tribe Pandionis. Pausanias speaks of a wooden statue of the goddess, under this appellation, which existed in the district of Myrrhinus in his day. The joke upon the

paronomasia between Κολαινίς and 'Ακαλανθίς, *a goldfinch*, is not very pointed.

873. φρυγίλῳ Σαβαζίῳ. Sabazius was the name of the Phrygian Bacchus. Φρυγίλος, *a chaffinch*, is a punning allusion to the Phrygians.

875. Κλεοκρίτου. This individual is mentioned in the Frogs (1437) as a large, heavy person, and this is the reason why Peisthetairos makes the *ostrich* mother Cybele and mother of Cleocritus.

877. αὐτοῖσι καὶ Χίοισι. The Chians were useful allies to the Athenians at the beginning of the Peloponnesian war, and at other times. Wherefore, according to the statement of the historian Theopompus, quoted by the Scholiast, they were accustomed to pray to the gods, Χίοις τε διδόναι ἀγαθὰ καὶ σφίσιν αὐτοῖς, *to bestow blessings on the Chians and on themselves.* See Thucyd. IV. 51. Eupolis, also quoted by the Scholiast, has the following lines: —

" Αὕτη Χίος, καλὴ πόλις·
Πέμπει γὰρ ὑμῖν ναῦς μακράς, ἄνδρας δ' ὅταν δεήσῃ
Καὶ τἄλλα πειθαρχεῖ καλῶς, ἄπληκτος ὥσπερ ἵππος."

878. Χίοισιν . . . . προσκειμένοις. The manner in which Peisthetairos speaks of the custom of always adding the Chians in public prayers shows, as the commentators well remark, that their fidelity was a subject of ironical commendation. And, in point of fact, immediately after the disasters of the Sicilian expedition, the Chians, together with the Erythraeans, went over to the Lacedaemonians. See Thucyd. VIII. 4.

879 – 883. The birds joined as heroes in the invocation are: — πορφυρίωνι, *the porphyrion* (purple water-fowl).— πελεκᾶντι, *pelican,* still called in Greece πελεκάνι (the *Pelecanus crispus;* see Von der Mühle, p. 132, who says this was the only pelican known to the ancient Greeks, and that it is very common in Greece through the whole year, frequenting

especially the lakes and swamps). — πελεκίνῳ, *the spoon* or *shovel-bill* (*Platalea leucerodius*, Von der Mühle, p. 118). — φλεξίδι. This is considered an unknown bird. The name does not occur in Aristotle. From its etymology, however, it must have been bright-colored. I venture to suggest that it may be one of the bloodfinches, and probably the *Pyrrhula serinus*, of which Von der Mühle says: " It is very common in Greece, wherever there are fruit-trees. It assumes there an external *fiery* " (φλεξίς) " or intense coloring. In autumn and winter, it wanders about the solitary fields in company with linnets and greenfinches." (p. 46.) — τέτρακι, *the heathcock*. — ταῶνι, *the peacock*. — ἐλεᾷ, a bird mentioned by Aristotle, Hist. An. IX. 16. 2, as having a pleasant voice. Its habits, as described by him, correspond with those of the dipper, or water-ousel, which it probably is. — βάσκᾳ, *the teal;* probably the *Anas crecca*, described by Von der Mühle as being found pretty frequently in Greece, in the winter. — ἐλασᾷ, another unknown bird ; but from the company which he keeps here, he must have affinities with the *teal*. The name would seem to mean *the marcher*, or *driver*, from ἐλαύνω. Probably it is the bittern (*Ardea stellaris*), which, according to Von der Mühle (p. 116), is found in Greece all the year round. Its attitudes and movements are stiff, like those of a soldier on the march. — ἐρωδιῷ, *the heron*. — καταράκτῃ, a bird described by Aristotle, Hist. An. IX. 12, 1, as living on the sea, and diving and remaining long under water; commonly, but incorrectly, translated *gannet*. It is a diver, and should be called *shear-water*, or *storm-petrel*. — μελαγκορύφῳ, *the black-headed warbler, or black-cap* (*Sylvia melanocephala*), whose habits are described by Von der Mühle (p. 71), and mentioned several times by Aristotle; sometimes called *the monk*. — αἰγιθάλλῳ, *the titmouse*, of which Aristotle mentions three species (Hist. An. VIII. 5, 3), probably *Aegithallus pendulinus*. See Von der Mühle, p. 48.

884. Παῦ', παῦσαι. Observe that the active and middle forms are used apparently without distinction. — καλῶν. G. § 112, 1. — ἐς κόρακας, a ludicrous introduction of a common imprecation, suggested here by the invocation of so many birds.

885. ἱερεῖον, *the victim* which the priest is about to sacrifice; the same as the προβάτιον in v. 858.

887. τοῦτο, i. e. the victim.

890. The priest, ordered away by Peisthetairos, changes his tune, and promises to invoke only one of the gods. "Sollicitus nimirum," says Blaydes, "ne, cura sacri peragendi Pisthetaero mandata, ipse nullam extorum partem habiturus sit. Sacerdoti enim victimae reliquiae ut et pellis solebant dari."

894, 895. εἴπερ ἕξετε, *at least, if you are to have*, &c. G. § 49, 1, N. 3. (See above, v. 761, and note.)

897. Γένειον καὶ κέρατα. Like the English *skin and bone.*

899. In the entertaining scene which follows, the poet indulges in a pleasant vein of satire at the expense of the lyric and dithyrambic poets. The reader of the Clouds will remember several passages in the same spirit in that play. Before the consecrating ceremonies are fairly completed, one of these ballad-mongers arrives, with dithyrambic verses cut and dried in honor of the new city. The reader will note the amusing mockery by which the poet introduces the Doric peculiarities of style, and, in general, the lyrical movements even of Pindar himself. Peisthetairos meets him with astonishment and contempt.

904. Μουσάων θεράπων ὀτρηρός. The poet perhaps alludes to such passages in Homer as Odys. IV. 23 : —

Οτρηρὸς θεράπων Μενελάου κυδαλίμοιο.

Perhaps he had also in mind the lines preserved from the Margites : —

Ἠλθέ τις εἰς Κολοφῶνα γέρων καὶ θεῖος ἀοιδός,
Μουσάων θεράπων καὶ ἐκηβόλου Ἀπόλλωνος,
Φίλης ἔχων ἐν χερσὶν εὔφθογγον λύρην.

Compare also Archilochus, Frag. 1 (52):—

Εἰμὶ δ' ἐγὼ θεράπων μὲν Ἐνυαλίοιο ἄνακτος,
Καὶ Μουσέων ἐρατὸν δῶρον ἐπιστάμενος.

906. κόμην ἔχεις. It was the fashion among the young gentlemen at Athens to wear long hair. See Clouds, v. 348. But, of course, the slaves could not be allowed to imitate them. The poet calls himself "the busy slave of the honey-tongued Muses."

907. διδάσκαλοι, *teachers*. In dramatic affairs, the διδάσκαλος was properly the one who trained the chorus and the actors, and, as this was done mostly by the poet himself, it also meant the poet.

910. ὀτρηρὸν ληδάριον. Brunck says: "Poetae amiculum ὀτρηρόν jocose vocat, quia erat τετρημένον." Cary translates the line, "Troth, and thy jacket has seen service, too." It is as if the poet had called himself *the holy servant of the Muses*, and Peisthetairos had replied, "Thou hast a *holy* jacket, too."

911. κατὰ .... ἀνεφθάρης; A jocose perversion, instead of ἀνέπτης, equivalent to "What the devil brought you up here?" Bothe, however, shows that φθείρεσθαι is also used, though in a somewhat different sense, where no such play upon the word is intended. He cites from Demosthenes, in Mid. p. 560, 8: 'Αλλὰ δεινοί τινές εἰσιν, ὦ ἄνδρες Ἀθηναῖοι, φθείρεσθαι πρὸς τοὺς πλουσίους, i. e. *in joining themselves to the rich to their own hurt*.

912-914. Μέλη, κύκλια, παρθένεια, Σιμωνίδου. *Cyclic songs*, that is, songs sung by circular choruses round the altars of the gods, generally in honor of Dionysos; and songs sung in the same manner by choruses of maidens, in the composition of which Simonides excelled. For an excellent account of the different species of Greek lyrical composition, see Müller's History of Greek Literature, Chapters XIV., XV.

916. πάλαι κλήζω. G. § 10, 1, N. 3.

917. δεκάτην. See note to 494.

919–925. This poetical flight is in imitation of one of Pindar's Hyporchemes. See Donaldson's Pindar, pp. 356, 357. The words are also alluded to by Plato, Phaedrus, p. 236 D.

924. Τᾷ κεφαλᾷ, "*nutu tui capitis.*" Blaydes.

925. ἐμὶν τεΐν. Says Blaydes: "*Mihi tibi.* Dorice pro *emoi, soi.* Dithyrambicos irridet, et praecipue Pindarum, qui hujusmodi Dorismos ingerebant. Apud Pindarum τὸ ἐμίν frequens est in petitionibus, ut monet Scholiasta. Ridicule hic igitur τεΐν post ἐμίν infert dithyrambicus, quasi poetam donando aliquo munere sibimet benefacturus sit Pisthetaerus, propter eximia carmina, quibus eum celebrans poeta gratiam relaturus sit."

926. παρέξει .... πράγματα, *will give us trouble.*

927. Εἰ .... ἀποφευξούμεθα, *Unless we shall get rid of him by giving him something.* G. § 50, 1, N. 1.

928. Οὗτος. Addressed to an attendant.—σπολάδα. This was an outside garment made of skin.

931–940. The words of the poet are still a parody upon Pindar. See Donaldson's Pindar, p. 357.

" Νομάδεσσι γὰρ ἐν Σκύθαις ἀλᾶται Στράτων,
ʽΟς ἁμαξοφόρητον οἶκον οὐ πέπαται·
Ἀκλεὴς δ' ἔβα.

" This fragment is part of the same Hyporcheme as the preceding, and is derived from the same source (Schol. Aristoph. Av. 925). It is stated that Hiero had given the mules, with which he had won the Pythian victory in question, to his charioteer, who seems to have been one Straton, and Pindar here begs, in a roundabout way, that he will give Straton the chariot also: 'Straton is like a person wandering among the Scythians with horses only, and no chariot to live in.'" The point of the application and the parody is evident. As the Scholiast says: "Δῆλον ὅτι χιτῶνα αἰτεῖ πρὸς τῇ σπολάδι." Blaydes adds: " De Scythis, qui hiberno tempore propter frigoris inclementiam bona sua in plaustra conferentes in aliam regionem migrabant. Vid. Herodot. IV. 11-19; Aeschyl. Prom. 710; Diod. Sic. II. 43. Schol.: 'Ο μὴ ἔχων δὲ ἐκεῖσε ἅμαξαν ἄτιμος παρ' αὐτοῖς κρίνεται."

943-948. The poet, grateful for the double gift he has just received, promises to celebrate the " fearful," " chilling" city.

949, 950. ταυταγὶ τὰ κρυερὰ . . . . λαβών, But you've escaped these chills now you've got a coat.

951, 952. οὐδέποτ' ἤλπισα τοῦτον πεπύσθαι, I never dreamed of this, that this fellow had heard, &c. Here πεπύσθαι represents οὗτος πέπυσται in the oratio recta. G. § 73, 1.

953. σύ. Addressed to the priest, who is now to resume the ceremonies. But before he has had time to get fairly started again, another speculator, a dealer in oracles, appears. " Dicit haec sacerdoti, qui jam sacra denuo auspicaturus silentium imperat (εὐφημία ἔστω: vide Ran. 352, et a B. laudatum Spanh. ad Callim. h. in Apoll. 17), aquam lustralem dispergit et aram circumit; affertur hircus immolandus, cum oraculorum interpres, epularum cupidus, accurrit per medias aves, et eum mactari vetat." Bothe.

954. κατάρξῃ is a religious word, used of the preliminary ceremonies of sacrifices, particularly of plucking the hair from the head of the victim, and burning it upon the altar. Compare μὴ κατάρξῃ with μὴ φέρε in v. 956. G. § 86.

957. Βάκιδος χρησμός, an oracle of Bacis. Bacis was an ancient Boeotian prophet, supposed to have given oracles at Heleon in Boeotia, under the inspiration of the Corycian

nymphs. His oracles, some of which are preserved by Herodotus and Pausanias, were in hexameter verse. See, for example, Hdt. VIII. 20, 77. He is mentioned also in the Knights and Peace of Aristophanes. There was a collection of his oracles, like the Sibylline books at Rome. These oracles are here burlesqued, as well as the superstition of consulting soothsayers, like Lampon, for instance, before engaging in any enterprise of moment. The temper of mind which led the Athenians to find some ancient oracle applicable to any remarkable event which happened may be illustrated from Thucydides, in his account of the commencement of the Peloponnesian war. But the disposition exists everywhere among men. Scarcely a day passes without some ancient prediction appearing in the newspapers, by which present events have been foretold. But the whole race of soothsayers, and their tricks and evasions, are mercilessly dealt with more than once by Aristophanes.

959, 960. For πρὶν οἰκίσαι after a negative sentence, see G. § 106, N. 2.

962, 963. λύκοι. Referring to the λυκοφιλία, the *wolf-friendship*, and intended as a hit at the two Athenians, who are designated by the wolves, that have founded a city with the crows (see *ante*, ὀρνέαι, Bird-town, which was placed between Corinth and Sicyon), μεταξύ, &c.

966. Πανδώρᾳ, *Pandora*, i. e. *the all-giver*. The purpose of the soothsayer being to extort gifts from the founders of the new city, he significantly repeats an oracle commanding them to sacrifice to the *all-giver*. This is pleasantly brought out in the following lines.

967. ὃς δέ κε. G. § 61, 3. Notice the Epic forms κέ and δόμεν (v. 968), as well as the dactylic hexameter.

969. βιβλίον, *the book*, i. e. the book containing the oracles of Bacis.

970. σπλάγχνων, *the entrails*, i. e. of the victim about to be offered.

977. ἐξεγραψάμην, *I have had copied.* Observe the force of the middle voice.

983. Λάμπων, Διοπείθης. Both noted soothsayers. The former is mentioned in the Clouds.

987, *seq.* A new character now arrives in the city. Meton, the celebrated observer and astronomer, who devised the cycle of nineteen years. See Dict. of Antiq., under Calendar. Gr.; also, Fasti Hellenici, p. 304. Meton is also the subject of the jests of Aristophanes elsewhere. See Clouds, 615, seq., and note. The Scholiast says: "Μέτων ἄριστος ἀστρονόμος καὶ γεωμέτρης. Τούτου ἐστὶν ὁ ἐνιαυτὸς ὁ λεγόμενος Μέτωνος. Φησὶ δὲ Καλλίστρατος ἐν Κολωνῷ ἀνάθεμά τι εἶναι αὐτοῦ ἀστρολογικόν. Εὐφρόνιος δέ, ὅτι τῶν δήμων ἦν ἐκ Κολωνοῦ."

988. τί δράσων (sc. ἥκεις); G. § 109, 5.

993. Ἑλλὰς χὼ Κολωνός. Besides the explanation of the reference to Colonos, given by the Scholiast, the jest intended is much the same as if, in speaking of some famous personage, we should say of him that he was "known to America and to Hull."

996. πνιγέα. The sky is compared to a πνιγεύς, or extinguisher, in the Clouds. See Clouds, 96, and note, with the references there given. The whole passage is made purposely nonsensical.

1000. Ὁ κύκλος .... τετράγωνος, *that the circle may be squared.*

1004. Ἄνθρωπος Θαλῆς, *The fellow is a Thales.*

1007. Ξενηλατοῦνται. Strangers were sometimes driven out in a body from Sparta. The general inhospitality of Sparta is touched upon by Isocrates (Panegyricus), and contrasted with the liberality of Athens.

1009. στασιάζετε; *are you at feud?*

1010, 1011. Ὁμοθυμαδὸν .... δοκεῖ, *We are of one mind, to thrash all the rascals.*

1012, 1013. ὑπάγοιμι τἄρ' ἄν. G. § 52, 2. — Νὴ .... ἄν, *Yes, by Zeus,* you had better; *for I don't know whether you could be too quick.* — αὐταί, *they,* i. e. the blows.

1015. ἀναμετρήσεις. The word is used, of course, in allusion to Meton's offer to survey and lay out the town. He now orders him to *make tracks* (ὁδούς) in another sense.

1016. πρόξενοι. Boeckh, Public Economy of the Athenians (Book I. Chap. 9), says: "The Greeks tolerated a species of consul in the person of the Proxenus of each state, who was considered as the representative of his country, and was bound to protect the citizens who traded at the place. If, for example, an inhabitant of Heraclea died at any place, the Proxenus of Heraclea was, by virtue of his office, obliged to make inquiries concerning the property which he left behind him. On one occasion, when an inhabitant of Heraclea died at Argos, the Proxenus of Heraclea received his property." Upon the ἐπίσκοποι the same writer says: "As the Spartans had their Harmosts, so had the Athenians officers named Episcopi (ἐπίσκοποι, φύλακες), as inspectors in the tributary states; Antiphon had mentioned them in his oration concerning the tribute of the Lindians, but we are not informed whether they were in any way concerned with the collection of the tributes." He afterwards adds, that the Episcopi, who were sent to subject states, received a salary, probably at the cost of the cities over which they presided. See also Dict. of Antiq., Πρόξενος and Ἐπίσκοποι.

1017. κυάμῳ, *by the bean.* Alluding to the mode of appointing certain officers at Athens, beans being used in drawing the lots. For the various modes of election, see Hermann's Political Antiquities, § 148 (formerly § 149). The Episcopus was doubtless represented as an effeminate young fellow, like many individuals employed in diplomacy now-a-days.

NOTES. 191

1019. Φαῦλον βιβλίον. The βιβλίον is the credentials, or commission,—the certificate of his appointment, or perhaps his official instructions. Teleas, the person mentioned under that name in v. 169, is here represented as the archon, or magistrate in whose department fell the public business of the Birds. Φαῦλον is applied to the document, because it sent him away from the city, where he might have made a figure in the courts and the assembly.

1021. Μὴ πράγματ' ἔχειν, *not to get into trouble.*

1023. Φαρνάκῃ. A satirical allusion to the intrigues frequently carried on between the Greek states and the Persian court. Pharnaces was the name of a Persian satrap. The kind of intrigues here alluded to is described in Xenophon's Hellenica, and referred to in the discourses of Isocrates.

1024. οὑτοσί, *this,* giving him a blow.

1027. τὼ κάδω, *the two urns;* i. e. the urns used in the courts and assemblies for casting the votes for and against a person or a measure. The Episcopus has come provided with the apparatus necessary for organizing judicial and political proceedings on the Athenian model; but on receiving the sort of pay which Peisthetairos gives him, he makes off.

The next character who appears upon the scene is a vender of decrees and resolutions. He comes in reading one of them, dressed out in all the formalities of Athenian legislation.

1034. πωλήσων, *for the purpose of selling.* G. § 109, 5. The object of the psephism is to require the Nephelococcygians, as being an Athenian colony, founded by two Athenian citizens, to use the same weights and measures with the Athenians. But, instead of mentioning the name of Athens, he inserts the Olophyxians, an insignificant dependency of Athens in Thrace.

1038. ὠτοτύξιοι, i. e. οἱ ὀτοτύξιοι. A ludicrous name, formed from ὀτοτύζω, *to lament*, in imitation of the name of the Olophyxians. As if the decree ran, "All Californians shall use the same weights and measures *with the Greenlanders;*" and Peisthetairos replied, "But you shall speedily use the same with the *Groanlanders*."

1041. Καλοῦμαι, &c., *I summon Peisthetairos for the month Munychion, to answer for outrage.* For the forms of summoning, see Clouds, v. 495, and note. The γραφὴ ὕβρεως was an action specifically provided for in Attic law. See Meier and Schömann's Attic Process, Book III. 1, Chap. 2, § 5. The month Munychion (April) was the month in which cases between Athenians and foreigners came up for trial, that being the time when strangers, and particularly deputies from the tributary states, were present in Athens to pay the annual tax.

1045. στήλην. A στήλη was a column set up in some public place, on which were engraved laws, treaties, decrees, and other documents of public concern. *According to the column* is, then, according to law.

1047. γράφω .... δραχμάς, *I lay the damages at ten thousand drachmas.* The γραφὴ ὕβρεως was one of the actions technically called ἀγῶνες τιμητοί, i. e. cases in which the court had to decide the penalty. But, in so doing, the prosecutor was required to fix his estimate of the crime, and the other party, when found guilty, also was called upon to do the same. The question to be decided by the court was, which of the two estimates should be adopted as a legal sentence. See Notes to Kennedy's Demosthenes; Meier and Schömann, Book III., Introd. § 2.

1049. τῆς στήλης κατετίλας. "Quod nefarium erat. Sic κατατιλῶν τῶν Ἑκαταίων in Ran. 364. Videtur respicere poeta ad Alcibiadis accusationem de Hermis mutilandis, quod etiam noctu evenisse testatur Thucyd. VI. 27." Blaydes.

1050. Οὗτος. The priest, apparently out of patience with the numerous delays, is starting to go away and offer his sacrifice in some more quiet place. This is addressed to him as he turns to depart. Peisthetairos and the others follow him, leaving the Chorus alone. Bergler, however, remarks: "Excusationem hanc faciunt intus sacrificandi, ne hircus immoletur. In Pac. 1021, Trygaeus ingenue id fatetur:—

'Αλλ' εἴσω φέρων,
Θύσας τὰ μηρί' ἐξελὼν δεῦρ' ἔκφερε·
Χοὔτω τὸ πρόβατον τῷ χορηγῷ σώζεται."

Upon this, the Chorus sings a song of exultation in the pride of their new-found dignities, looking forward to the honors which their exalted position and great services are to bring them. While they are thus employed, the sacrificial rites are elsewhere performing; and at the close of the chorus, the official personages return, announcing that all the auspices are favorable.

1053. παντόπτᾳ. In this and the following lines, the birds now assume the dignity, attributes, and epithets of the gods.

1059–1061. οἱ .... ἀποβόσκεται. The construction is this: the relative οἱ refers to Θηρῶν, and has for its verb ἀποβόσκονται, to be supplied from ἀποβόσκεται; ἐφεζόμενα applies to the insects which consume the fruits of the trees, and which are devoured by the birds.

1067. Διαγόραν. Diagoras, the Melian, is often alluded to as an atheist. Lysias, in the oration against Andocides, mentions a price having been set upon his head, on account of his having thrown ridicule upon the religion of the Athenians. In the Clouds, Socrates is called *the Melian*, for the purpose of casting reproach or ridicule upon him, by connecting his name with the doctrines of the Melian unbeliever. For an excellent and candid account of this person, see the article in Smith's Dict. of Greek and Roman Biography.

1068, 1069. This is intended as a pleasant satire upon the Athenian exaggerations in expressing their hatred of tyranny, and the affectation of the orators of excessive zeal for the democracy. Here is an offer of a talent for any one who shall kill any of the *dead* tyrants. Blaydes thinks the poet alludes indirectly to the mutilators of the Hermae, the *Hermocopidae*, who were regarded by the Athenians in the light of tyrants, and for killing whom a reward was offered. (See Thucydides, VI. 61.) In imitation of these Attic proclamations, the Chorus proceeds forthwith to offer rewards for slaying certain persons who may be considered the natural enemies of the republic of the birds. Philocrates is the poulterer mentioned early in the play. Στρούθιον is formed, in imitation of gentile names, from στροῦθος, *a sparrow*.

1073. σπίνους. Probably a species of *ortolan*, a small bird sold in the market of Athens. Perhaps the *Emberoza caesia*. See Von der Mühle, p. 40.

1074. κίχλας, *thrushes*. The *Turdus musicus* probably; it is still called in Greece τζήχλα.

1075. κοψίχοισιν. See vv. 308 and 806. Usually called the blackbird, but very different from the English or American bird known under that name. It is the *Turdus merula*, still called in Greece κοτζιφός. See Von der Mühle, p. 63.

1076. εἶρξας ἔχει. G. § 112, N. 7.

1077. παλεύειν, *to decoy*. The Scholiast says: " Θηρεύειν, προκαλεῖσθαι. Εἰώθασιν ἐκτυφλοῦντές τινα τῶν ὀρνέων ἱστάναι ἐν δικτύῳ, ὅπως τῇ φωνῇ προσκαλοῖτο τὰ ὁμοιογενῆ." Decoy-birds were called by the Greeks παλεύτριαι.

In the antistrophe, other privileges of the birds are very poetically set forth.

1089. ἀχέτας, *the chirper*, is the τέττιξ, or cicada, which delights in the sunshine (ἡλιομανής, *sun-mad*).

1093, 1094. παρθένια .... κηπεύματα, *delicate, rich, white myrtle-berries, and fruits that grow in the gardens of the Graces*, i. e. the sweetest and most delicious. The Scholiast thinks the epithet παρθένια was applied to myrtle-berries because maidens were fond of eating them.

The lines that follow form a parabasis, or address to the audience, in which the poet makes the Chorus his mouthpiece, and communicates through it his opinions, wishes, or feelings to the public. The judges are those appointed to decide upon the merits of the rival pieces. See Clouds, vv. 518, seq. For the peculiarities of a parabasis, see Munk's Metres, p. 336, to which may be added the following extract from Müller's History of Greek Literature : — " It was not originally a constituent part of comedy, but improved and worked out according to rules of art. The chorus, which up to that point had kept its place between the thymele and the stage, and had stood with its face to the stage, made an evolution, and proceeded in files towards the *theatre*, in the narrower sense of the word; that is, towards the place of the spectators. This is the proper *parabasis*, which usually consisted of anapaestic tetrameters, occasionally mixed up with other long verses; it began with a short opening song (in anapaestic or trochaic verse), which was called *kommation*, and ended with a very long and protracted anapaestic system, which, from its trial of the breath, was called *pnigos* (also *makron*). In this parabasis the poet makes his chorus speak of his own poetical affairs, of the object and end of his productions, of his services to the state, of his relation to his rivals, and so forth. If the parabasis is complete, in the wider sense of the word, this is followed by a second piece, which is properly the main point, and to which the anapaests only serve as an introduction. The chorus, namely, sings a lyrical poem, generally a song of praise in honor of some god, and then recites, in trochaic verses (of which there should, regularly, be sixteen), some joking complaint, some reproach against the city, some witty sally against the people, with more or less reference to the leading subject of the play : this is called the *epirrhema*, or ' what is said in addition.' Both pieces, the lyrical strophe and the epirrhema, are repeated antistrophically. It is clear that the lyrical piece, with its antistrophe, arose from the phallic song; and the epirrhema, with its antepirrhema, from the gibes with which the chorus of revellers assailed the first persons they met. It was natural, as the parabasis came in the middle of the whole comedy, that, instead of these jests directed against individuals, a conception more significant and more interesting to the public at large should be substituted for them ; while the gibes against individuals, suitable to the original nature of comedy, though without any reference to the connection of the piece, might be put in the mouth of the chorus whenever occasion served.

" As the parabasis completely interrupts the action of the comic drama, it could only be introduced at some especial pause; we find that Aristophanes is fond of introducing it at the point where the action, after all sorts of hindrances and delays, has got so far that the crisis must ensue, and it must be determined whether the end desired will be attained or not. Such, however, is the laxity with which comedy treats all these forms, that the parabasis may even be divided into two parts, and the anapaestical introduction be separated from the choral song; there may even be a second parabasis (but without the anapaestic march), in order to mark a second transition in the action of the piece."

1096. κρίνωσιν ἡμᾶς, *adjudge us victors.* Supply νικᾶν.

1097. Ἀλεξάνδρου, *Paris ;* who, being appointed judge of beauty between the rival goddesses, received from

Aphrodite, to whom he had adjudged the palm, the gift of Helen.

1099. Γλαῦκες Λαυριωτικαί, *Laurian owls*, i. e. coins bearing the figure of an owl. See note to v. 303. Laurian, because the Attic coinage was supplied from the silver mines of Laurion, for an account of which see Boeckh's Public Economy of the Athenians, Book III. Chap. 3. See also Herodotus, VII. 144; Thucyd. III. 55. The Laurian owls are to make their nests in the purses of the judges, and hatch small change.

1103. ἐρέψομεν πρὸς ἀετόν. There is a play upon the word ἀετόν, which, besides signifying *an eagle*, is also an architectural term, like ἀέτωμα, *the pediment*.

1104. ἀρχίδιον, *a petty office*.

1106. πρηγορῶνας, *birds' crops*.

1107. ἢν δὲ μὴ κρίνητε (sc. ἡμᾶς νικᾶν). See v. 1096. — χαλκεύεσθε is Imperative middle. — Μηνίσκοι were crescent-shaped coverings, to protect the statues from being soiled by the birds. The rainbow, or glory, encircling the heads of saints in Christian statuary and painting, was borrowed from the custom of the Greek artists of placing these crescents over their statues.— φορεῖν. G. § 97. The chorus tells them that they had better make themselves bronze μηνίσκοι to wear.

1108. ὃς ἂν μὴ ἔχῃ = ἐάν τις μὴ μήν' ἔχῃ. G. § 60; § 61, 3.

Peisthetairos, having completed the sacrifices, reappears upon the scene, and at the same moment a messenger hurries in, out of breath, to announce the completion of the city wall.

1113. ὅτου πευσόμεθα. G. § 65, 1.

1114. Ἀλφειὸν πνέων, *breathing Alpheus*. The allusion is to the races at Olympia, near the banks of the Alpheus.

1116. ἄρχων = ὁ ἄρχων.

1119. Προξενίδης ὁ Κομπασεύς, *Proxenides of Bragtown.* The person here referred to as a braggart is spoken of also in the Wasps. Κομπασεύς, formed from κόμπος, as if there were a deme bearing that name. Carey translates it *of Bragland.* For Theagenes, see *ante,* v. 824. For ἄν, see G. § 42, 3.

1120 – 1122. ἅρματε .... παρελασαίτην, *might drive two chariots past each other, with horses harnessed as large as the Wooden;* alluding to the δούριος or δουράτιος ἵππος, in the capture of Troy. The allusion was the more amusing to the audience, from the circumstance that a brazen statue of the Trojan horse stood on the Acropolis, perhaps in full sight of the theatre.

1124. τοῦ μάκρους, genitive of exclamation.

1126. Αἰγύπτιος. "Πλινθοφόρος. Οἱ Αἰγύπτοι ἐκωμῳδοῦντο ὡς ἀχθοφόροι. Καὶ ἐν Βατράχοις (1332), οὓς οὐκ ἄραιντ' ἂν [ἂν ἄραιντ'] οὐδ' ἑκατὸν Αἰγύπτιοι.— Sch. notum est ex Herodoti Euterpe, ut plerique reges assidue coëgerint eos caementa portare ad exstruendas praecipue pyramides." Bergler. The labors of the Egyptians in building the Pyramids are referred to, a full account of which is given by Herodotus, Lib. II. 124, seqq. The reader will also remember the tasks imposed upon the Israelites during their enslavement in Egypt.

1130. λίθους. Perhaps the common notion, that the cranes carried in their beaks, or swallowed, stones, to steady themselves in their flight, — a notion which Aristotle remarks upon in his History of Animals, — may have arisen from observing that some birds swallow gravel as a kind of digester. It appears in several forms in the Scholiasts. One story is, that the cranes carry stones, so that, when wearied with flying, they may ascertain by dropping one whether they are over land or water. At any rate, this popular error is very happily employed by the poet in the present passage.

NOTES.   199

1131. κρέκες, *the rails.* The species here intended is the *Rallus aquaticus*, described by Von der Mühle as being very abundant in the moors of Greece, pp. 91, 92. The other birds here mentioned have already occurred.

1138. ὑποτύπτοντες, *spading;* i. e. the geese used their web-feet as spades to shovel the cement into the hods of the herons.

1141. περιεζωσμέναι. " Praecinctas eas esse facete fingit comicus, quia hujus avis plumarum dispositio albae zonae speciem refert." Blaydes. The Scholiast makes a similar remark : " Τινὲς τῶν νησσῶν ἔχουσιν ὡς ζωνὴν ἐν κύκλῳ λευκήν." Probably the *Anas boschas*. (See Von der Mühle, p. 126.) Bothe quotes from Wilmsen part of a description of this wild duck : " In front, on the under part of its neck, there is a white semicircle."

The scene described by the messenger I conceive to be this, — and the humor of it consists in the ingenious adaptation to the habits of the birds of the parts they perform in the building of the new city. The herons, geese, and ducks, not being good flyers, are the diggers and carriers. The geese, with their web-feet, remain in the mud, shovelling it upon the broad bills of the herons, which are the hods (Λεκάναι). The herons do not carry it to the city, for their haunts are in muddy places, but hand it over to the swallows, who are the best and swiftest of all upon the wing, and who carry it up to the city in their beaks, and then work it over as described in the following note. The additional fact that the swallow, when building its own nest, picks up mud only after rains, makes the division of labor natural and necessary. In this way the busy builders readily and easily accomplish their work.

1142 – 1144. ἄνω .... χελιδόνες, *and the swallows flew up with the trowel behind them, like little boys, and carrying the cement in their mouths.* The swallows are selected for this office on account of their skill in lining their nests with mud. The trowel is the swallow's tail, which bears some resemblance to the broad, flat trowel used by the ancient masons. Besides this, the poet had observed that the swallow uses its tail for the very purpose that a mason uses his trowel. It also carries the mud in its beak, as here represented; *like little boys,* "*ut pueruli,*" as explained by Blaydes, " qui gaudent aliquid a tergo trahere, et baculo ligneo equi instar insidentes cruribus divaricatis currere." Something is wanting to make the grammatical construction of the text complete; as it stands now, there is an *asyndeton*.

1156. Ἀπονίψομαι, *I'll wash myself.* He had come in great haste, and was still covered with dirt.

1157. Οὗτος. Addressed to Peisthetairos, who stands in silent amazement at what he has just heard.

1162. πυῤῥίχην βλέπων. The allusion is to a war-dance, called the *pyrrhic,* — *looking full of fight;* like φόνον βλέπων, Aesch. Sept. 478, and Ἄρη δεδορκότων, Id. 53.

The second messenger now comes running in, out of breath. Some one has passed through the gates without permission of the authorities.

1170. οὔκουν ἐχρῆν πέμψαι; *ought they not to have sent?* G. § 49, 2, N. 3. A protasis is implied, *if they had done their duty,* or something similar. περιπόλους. The young men of Athens were classed under the designation of ἔφηβοι, when they reached the age of eighteen. The two following years they were sent to the frontiers to guard the strongholds and military posts, and for the general protection of the Attic territory. During this period they were called περίπολοι, or *roamers.* The allusion and application here are obvious. See Hermann, Polit. Antiq. § 121 (formerly 123).

1171 - 1174. The περίπολοι, who are sent in pursuit, are the swiftest and strongest of the birds of prey; all with crooked talons, — the hawks, falcons, vultures, carrion-crows, ανα eagles. All the birds here mentioned are described by Von der Mühle. The tumult in the air is doubtless a parody on a passage in some play; very likely one of Aeschylus.

After a few strains of lyric verse, Iris, the messenger of the gods, is brought. She is the interloper, who, being sent on an embassy to the earth, has rashly entered the city, and now appears in the august presence of Peisthetairos.

1179, 1180. χώρει πᾶς. G. § 84, N. 2.

1190. λέγειν ἐχρῆν, *you ought to tell*. (See v. 1170.) G. § 49, 2, N. 3.

1192. πλοῖον, ἢ κυνῆ; Blaydes has the following note: "*Navis an petasus?* Navem esse eam putat, aut quia vestis ejus impetu volandi veli instar sinuosa facta erat, aut propter alas quas habebat; habent enim et naves quasi alas quasdam remos: petasum eam putat propter alas vel pinnas." But perhaps the best illustration of the text is the passage in Milton's Samson Agonistes, where the appearance of Dalilah is described: —

> " But who is this ? what thing of sea or land ?
> Female of sex it seems,
> That so bedecked, ornate, and gay,
> Comes this way sailing,
> Like a stately ship
> Of Tarsus, bound for the isles
> Of Javan or Gadire,
> With all her bravery on, and tackle trim,
> Sails filled, and streamers waving."

1193. Πάραλος, ἢ Σαλαμινία; For an account of these fast-sailing public vessels of the Athenians, see note to vv. 146, 147.

1196. οἰμώξει. G. § 25, N. 5.

1201. κολοιάρχους. "*Praefectos excubiarum.* Κολοιοῖς enim custodia novae urbis commissa erat." Blaydes. See v. 1167.

1202. Σφραγῖδ'. Lit. *the seal*, i. e. *the passport*, which, it seems, was employed in ancient times, stamped with the official seal of the proper authorities. See Becker's Charicles, Note 15 to Scene I., and the authorities there quoted.

1204. 'Επέβαλεν, *tendered.*

1210. 'Αδικεῖς δὲ καὶ νῦν, *and even now you are a trespasser.*

1211. 'Ιρίδων, genitive after δικαιότατ'.

1215, 1216. εἰ belongs to ἄρχομεν, and also to ἀκολασταινεῖτε and γνώσεσθε, as is shown by the use of μέν and δέ. G. § 54, Remark.

1217. 'Ακροατέον .... κρειττόνων, *You have got to obey your betters in turn.* G. § 114, 2. (See v. 1226.)

1218. ναυστολεῖς. The idea of the ship is still kept up.

1220. Φράσουσα θύειν, *to bid them sacrifice.* Fut. part. expressing purpose. The sacrificial forms, in the following lines, are borrowed from the religious rites of the Athenians.

1224. Θεοὶ γάρ. The use of the particle here is elliptical, and it may be rendered, *What! are you——*, and, in the next clause, *To be sure, for ——.*

1226. Θυτέον αὐτούς. The verbal in τέον is equivalent in sense to the infinitive with δεῖ; here, then, = δεῖ θύειν αὐτούς, *it is their duty to sacrifice.* The construction is *ad sensum,* since verbals usually take the dative of the agent. (See v. 1217.) G. § 114, 2.

1228, 1229. The language here is a parody upon Aeschylus, Agam. 525, 526:—

Τροίαν κατασκάψαντα τοῦ δικηφόρου
Διὸς μακέλλῃ, τῇ κατείργασται πέδον.

1231. Λικυμνίαις βολαῖς, *with Likymnian bolts.* The allusion is to a lost play of Euripides, called Likymnios, in which one of the personages was struck by a thunderbolt. The whole speech of Iris is an amusing parody on the *obligato* loftiness of the tragic style.

1233. Λυδόν, Φρύγα. Here is a parody upon some lines

in the Alcestis of Euripides, v. 675. See Woolsey's note to the passage.

1236, 1237. δόμους 'Αμφίονος .... ἀετοῖς. This passage is borrowed from the Niobe of Aeschylus. See Nauck, Frag. No. 155.

1238. πορφυρίωνας. See *ante*, vv. 553, 709.

1239. παρδαλᾶς, *panther-skins;* in allusion to the coloring of their plumage.

1241. Εἶς Πορφυρίων, one *Porphyrion;* referring to the giant of that name.

1246. διαρραγείης. See note to v. 2.

1250. νεωτέρων τινά, *some of the younger ones.* I am too old to be frightened by such stuff.

1257, seq. The herald who had been despatched to earth now returns, exulting at the brilliant success Birdtown has had among mortals.

1259. κατακέλευσον. According to the Scholiast, this means *order silence.* Cary renders it, "O, bid all here give hearing." Properly, it is used of the κελευστής, "whose business it was," says Arnold (Thucyd. II. 84, note), "to make the rowers keep time by singing to them a tune or boat-song; and also to cheer them to their work, and encourage them by speaking to them." "It was also," according to a Scholiast on the Acharnians, "the business of the κελευστής to see that the men baked their bread, and contributed their fair share to the mess, that none of the rations issued to each man might be disposed of improperly." The word is doubtless used here in allusion to these functions of the κελευστής. The fashions of Birdtown are all the rage at Athens, and multitudes are on the point of migrating thither. Under these circumstances, it will be necessary that some one should exert himself to keep order among such a miscellaneous crew, and that one must be Peisthetairos. Translate, then, *issue orders.*

1260, 1261. Στεφάνῳ χρυσῷ. One of the most noted among the honors bestowed for eminent public services was the conferring of a golden crown. Perhaps this is the best known from the fact, that the great contest of oratory between Demosthenes and Aeschines grew out of a proposition to crown the former.

1264. φέρει, 2d pers. mid., *thou receivest* for thyself.

1267, seq. Ἐλακωνομάνουν, *were Spartan-mad*. This affectation of imitating the Lacedaemonian modes of life, ways of speaking, and manners, seems at times to have been pretty extensively prevalent at Athens, and is often spoken of the ancients. See Plutarch, Life of Alcibiades, Chap. 23, τῇ διαίτῃ λακωνίζων; Demosthenes against Conon, p. 1267, 22, ἐσκυθρωπάκασι καὶ λακωνίζειν φασί; and Plato, Protag. 342 B, Gorg. 515 E. The particular modes in which the affectation manifested itself are described in the lines which follow. With respect to the whims charged upon Socrates, see the Clouds, *passim*.

1269. Σκυτάλι᾽ ἐφόρουν, *carried Spartan canes*. The allusion here is to the *scytale*, by means of which the government of Sparta corresponded with the generals or kings when absent on some foreign enterprise. Smith (Dict. of Gr. and Rom. Ant.) thus briefly describes it:— "When a king or general left Sparta, the ephors gave to him a staff of a definite length and thickness, and retained for themselves another of precisely the same size. When they had any communications to make to him, they cut the material upon which they intended to write into the shape of a narrow ribbon, wound it round their staff, and then wrote upon it the message which they had to send to him. When the strip of writing material was taken from the staff, nothing but single letters appeared, and in this state the strip was sent to the general, who, after having wound it round his staff, was able to read the communication."

1273. νομόν. There is a play upon the double meaning νομός, *pasture*, and νόμος, *law*.

1274. κατῆραν ἐς τὰ βιβλία. Here again is a play upon the word βιβλίον, which naturally suggests the βίβλος, or papyrus plant. καταίρειν is *to come ashore, to land ;* translate, *they would land,* or *alight, upon the leaves,* meaning, *they flew at once to the law cases.* For κατῆραν ἄν, see G. § 30, 2. "The whole of this," as Cary remarks : "is intended to represent the eagerness of the Athenians for legislation and law disputes ; a never-failing topic of ridicule with Aristophanes."

The reasons why the poet attaches names of birds to certain individuals cannot, in all these cases, be certainly made out. Doubtless there were personal peculiarities belonging to all these individuals, which gave the application a point highly amusing to the audience who were familiar with them.

1278. Πέρδιξ. According to the Scholiast, this was the name of a lame innkeeper; but the poet pretends it was given him on account of his craft and dishonesty.

1279. Μενίππῳ. Menippus, of whom nothing is known, was called the swallow, probably on account of some imperfection of speech ; since the Greeks compared such defects to the twittering of swallows. See Agamemnon of Aeschylus, v. 974. The Scholiast has another explanation, quite too far-fetched.

1280. κόραξ. The one-eyed Opuntius was called the crow, according to the Scholiast, because he had a large, beak-shaped nose.

1281. Κορυδός. Philocles was called the *tufted lark,* on account of the peculiar shape of his head, as the Scholiast says. He is elsewhere mentioned as deformed (see Thesm. 168), "Αἰσχρὸς ὢν αἰσχρῶς ποιεῖ." Probably there is also some allusion to the debauched character of Philocles.—

18

χηναλώπηξ. The nickname of *goose-fox* is given to Theagenes on account of his rogueries. The same person has been mentioned before.

1282. Ἴβις. Lycurgus (not the orator of that name) is said to have been called the Ibis, either on account of his having been born in Egypt, or because he had lived there. Pherecrates, as quoted by the Scholiast, called the Egyptians the countrymen of Lycurgus. It is quite as likely, however, to have been some peculiarity of his personal appearance, — as the length and small size of his legs, — which suggested the nickname. This is the view adopted by Blaydes. — νυκτερίς. Chairephon is the well-known disciple of Socrates, mentioned often by Plato and Xenophon, and ridiculed in the Clouds. He was called the *Bat*, on account of his dark color, melancholy temperament, and thin voice.

1283. κίττα. Syracusius is said to have been a prating orator, hanging about the bema, and seizing every opportunity to harangue the people. So he is compared to the pigeon, sitting and cooing upon the roof-tree.

1284. Ὄρτυξ. Meidias was called the *Ortux*, or quail, because he was like a quail struck in the head by a gamester. The allusion here is to a play called ὀρτυγοκοπία, or *quail-striking*, which is described by Pollux. The gamesters themselves were called ὀρτυγοκόποι, or στυφοκόποι. The sport consisted in throwing or striking at a quail, set up as a mark, and perhaps was not unlike the shooting-matches of our day. See Becker's Charicles, Scene V., note 6; Julius Pollux, VII. 136; Meursius, De Ludis Graecorum, ὀρτυγοκοπία. Meidias is supposed by Blaydes to have been called a quail because he was a gamester and cock-fighter. But it is more likely, I think, from the turn of the phrase here, that the point of resemblance was some singularity in the shape of the head. The Scholiast, however, quotes from Plato the Comedian, "Χρηστὸν μὴ κατὰ Μειδίαν ὀρτυγοκόπον," which confirms the interpretation of Blaydes.

1287. χελιδὼν ἐμπεποιημένη, *a swallow introduced into poetry*, as in the swallow-song of Simonides.

1294. Οὐκ .... ἑστάναι, *It is not, then, our business longer to stand*. ἔργον is used here just as ὥρα is in other places. Peisthetairos, hearing that so many emigrants are to come to his new city, orders that Manes, a servant, shall bring baskets and boxes full of all kinds of wings, with which to furnish the new-comers. A short dialogue between Peisthetairos and the Chorus sets forth the blessings that belong to the Nephelococcygians.

1301. προσείη. G. § 82.

1305. μετοικεῖν, *to live as a* μέτοικος *or resident foreigner*. The μέτοικοι at Athens formed a large class, chiefly of tradespeople, who enjoyed certain rights in return for their μετοίκιον, or annual fee to the state of twelve drachmas. According to Boeckh (Public Economy of the Athenians, Book I. Chap. VII.) the μέτοικοι with their families amounted to about 45,000, or to nearly half the number of the free Athenians.

1312. Σύ. Addressed to Peisthetairos.

1313. τοῦτον. Pointing to Manes, the slave, who forthwith brings out the wings.

1316. Σὺ δ'. Again addressed to Peisthetairos.

1317 – 1320. Διάθες .... πτερώσεις, *Arrange them* (the wings) *in order ; the singing ones by themselves, and the prophetic, and aquatic. Then, see that you wing each man, wisely looking to his character.* Blaydes says : " μουσικά, ut cycni, lusciniae, &c.; μαντικά, ut corvi, aquilae et reliquarum avium, ex quibus omina capiuntur ; θαλάττια, ut mergi, lari, ossifragae."

1321. σοῦ, *you*, i. e. Manes

The scene that follows is amusing, and closely related, as are all the scenes in Aristophanes, to the peculiarities of Hellenic society. The three personages, Parricide, Kinesias, and Sycophant, who arrive in succession, each with his characteristic purposes, and all singing in lofty dithyrambic strains, at once embody the deepest satire on the private and political vices of the times, and throw the gayest ridicule upon the empty verbosity of the popular poets.

1323. γενοίμαν. G. § 82.
1324. ὡς ἄν. G. § 44, 1, N. 3 (*b*).
1327. Ἄιδων ἀετούς, *singing of eagles.*
1329. τοῦ πέτεσθαι. G. § 95, 1.
1337. ὃς ἂν πεπλήγῃ. G. § 18, 1.

1340, seq. Peisthetairos quotes to the Parricide the law of the storks, because, says Blaydes, "inter ciconias et pullos earum summus existit amor."

1341. κύρβεσιν. The κύρβεις were columns on which laws were published, especially those which contained the laws of Solon, and which were also called ἄξονες. See Plut. Sol. 25. See Clouds, v. 448, and note.

1344. πάλιν, *in turn.*

1345, 1346. Ἀπέλαυσα .... βοσκητέον, *it would be a deal of good, by Zeus, that I got by coming here, if I must feed my father, too.*

1348. ὄρνιν ὀρφανόν, "*Tanquam avem orbam, quae non patrem alendum habeat.*" Blaydes.

1349. οὐ .... ὑποθήσομαι, *I'll suggest a good thing.* οὐ κακῶς is used exactly like the French *pas mal.*

1350 – 1356. The plan of Peisthetairos is to arm the Parricide like a fighting bird, with wing, and spur, and crest, and send him off to Thrace, bidding him to enlist in that service, to support himself by his pay, and let his father live. The sending him to Thrace is an allusion to the numerous expeditions which the Athenians sent for a series of years

NOTES.   209

into the North, to act against the Macedonians and the Lacedaemonians. See Thirlwall's History of Greece, Vols. III. and IV.; Thucyd. IV. 75, seq.; Grote, Vol. IV.

1359. The poet Kinesias, who is satirized in the Clouds also, now makes his appearance, singing appropriate strains. He was a dithyrambic poet, of no great ability, but one of the corrupters of the poetical and musical style of the time. Besides this, according to Athenaeus, he was so tall and thin, that he was obliged to wear stays made of linden-wood. To this the epithet φιλύρινον, v. 1363, refers. His life was dishonored by gross impiety and low vices.

1364. Τί . . . . κυκλεῖς; κυκλεῖν πόδα is a tragic expression, occurring in Euripides, Orest. 632. Kinesias is said to have been lame. κύκλον also refers to *his Cyclic compositions.* Translate, *Why dost thou turn thy halting foot hitherward?*

1367. Παῦσαι . . . . μοι, *Cease your singing, and tell me what you mean.* Give up poetry, and let us have prose and decency. G. § 112, 1.

1370. ἀναβολάς, *preludes.* All this is in ridicule of the frigid bombast of the dithyrambic poets.

1375. κλύων. § 109, 6; § 52, 1.

1376. Οὐ δῆτ' ἔγωγε, *Not I, in faith.* To which Kinesias replies, *Yes, you shall too, by Hercules.*

1381. Ὠόπ. The Scholiast explains this as a cry to stop the rowing of the oarsmen. But it is elsewhere used to encourage and stimulate them. — ἁλάδρομον ἁλάμενος, *having leaped the sea-course.* Blaydes very justly remarks of this and what follows: "Obscuritatem dithyrambicorum irridet poeta, qui constructionibus verborum obscuris et figuris exquisitis gaudent."

1386. Ἀλίμενον . . . . τέμνων, *cutting the harborless furrow of the air.* "Mira et audacissima metaphorarum conjunctio, more dithyrambicorum." Blaydes.

1389, 1390. Ταυτὶ . . . . ἀεί; These lines refer to the

18 *

arrangements for the poetical and musical festivities. The tribes rivalled each other in the splendor of their preparations for the dithyrambic, tragic, and comic contests. Kinesias represents himself as an object of contention to the tribes, as a trainer of the Cyclic chorus.

1392. Λεωτροφίδῃ, *for Leotrophides*, i. e. as *choregus*. The choregus was the individual whose turn it was to furnish the entertainment. He is said to have been a person of a very slight figure, for which reason the poet makes him a citizen of Nephelococcygia. He is mentioned in a fragment of the comic poet Hermippus, preserved by Athenaeus. Bothe gives a different interpretation, — *Will you stay here with us, and train a chorus of birds, light as Leotrophides.*

1393. Κεκροπίδα φυλήν. Blaydes discusses the question why the poet names the tribe Κεκροπίς. He thinks it is partly because Leotrophides belonged to that tribe, and partly in the way of a punning allusion to the bird κρέκα, as if he had said κρεκοπίδα φυλήν, and suggests that this may be the true reading. There is a question of construction which the commentators have not touched, namely, that of the accusative φυλήν. It seems to me to be in apposition with χορόν; the Chorus then is the Cecropid tribe. And why the Cecropid tribe? First, one of the tribes of Athens bore this name; and secondly, there is a play on the word, as the Athenians themselves were called Cecropians, from King Cecrops. The chorus of flying birds, then, is nothing more than a satirical description of the Athenians, who are elsewhere ridiculed for their levity and fickleness by similar comparisons to birds.

1395. πρὶν ἂν διαδράμω. G. § 67, 1.

1396. The Sycophant now makes his appearance, complaining that the winged birds have nothing. "Συκοφάντης," says Smith (Dict. of Antiq.), "in the time of Aristophanes and Demosthenes, designated a person of a peculiar class, not capable of being described by any single word in our language, but well understood and appreciated by an Athenian. He had not much in common with our sycophant, but was a happy compound of the *common barretor, informer, pettifogger, busybody, rogue, liar, and slanderer.* The Athenian law permitted any citizen (τὸν βουλόμενον) to give information against public offenders, and prosecute them in courts of justice. It was the policy of the legislature to encourage the detection of crime, and a reward (such as half the penalty) was frequently given to the successful accuser. Such a power, with such a temptation, was likely to be abused, unless checked by the force of public opinion, or the vigilance of the judicial tribunals. Unfortunately, the character of the Athenian democracy, and the temper of the judges, furnished additional incentives to the informer. Eminent statesmen, orators, generals, magistrates, and all persons of wealth and influence, were regarded with jealousy by the people. The more causes came into court, the more fees accrued to the judges, and fines and confiscation enriched the public treasury. The prosecutor, therefore, in public causes, as well as the plaintiff in civil, was looked on with a more favorable eye than the defendant, and the chances of success made the employment a lucrative one."

1397, seq. The Sycophant addresses himself especially to the swallow, perhaps in allusion to the swallow-song of Simonides; but as he repeats the salutation, Peisthetairos imagines he is singing a song to his old and worn-out robe, which stands in need of many swallows, that is, of the coming of spring; according to the proverb, " Μία χελιδὼν ἔαρ οὐ ποιεῖ," *One swallow does not make a spring.*

1405. πτερῶν πτερῶν δεῖ. Παρὰ τὸ Αἰσχύλου ἐκ Μυρμιδόνων, " ὅπλων ὅπλων δεῖ." Schol. See fragments of the *Myrmidons* of Aeschylus, No. 136 (Nauck).

1406. Πελλήνης. A city of Achaia, where cloths of peculiar excellence were manufactured. The idea of going to Pellene is suggested by the shabby garments of the informer.

1407. κλητήρ νησιωτικός, *an island summoner.* Many classes of lawsuits the inhabitants of the islands and the confederated cities were obliged to bring up for adjudication in the courts of Athens. For κλητήρ, see note on v. 146.

1409. πραγματοδίφης, *a hunter-up of lawsuits.*

1410. καλούμενος, *summoning* to court.

1411. Ὑπὸ πτερύγων .... σοφώτερον; Like the expression ὑπ' αὐλητῆρος, cited by the Scholiast from Archilochus. *Do you serve summonses any wiser on account of wings?*

1414. ἕρματος, *ballast.* This alludes to the notion, that the cranes swallow stones to steady themselves in their flight. See *ante.*—δίκας, *law cases.* He compares himself, returning from a tour among the islands and cities with a long list of cases to be tried at Athens, to the cranes laden with a ballast of stones.

1417. τί πάθω; Yes, to be sure, *for what would become of me?* G. § 88, N. 2.—σκάπτειν οὐκ ἐπίσταμαι, *I know not how to dig.* Blaydes appropriately quotes Luc. Evang. xvi. 3: "Σκάπτειν οὐκ ἰσχύω, ἐπαιτεῖν αἰσχύνομαι," *I cannot dig, to beg I am ashamed.*

1418. ἔργα σώφρονα, *honest callings.*

1419. ἄνδρα τοσουτονί, *a man of such an age.*

1422. λέγων. Participle expressing the means. G. § 109, 2.

1426. κουρείοις, *the barbers' shops,* which were the lounging-places of the idle and gossiping, called by Theophrastus "symposia without wine." See Becker's Charicles, Excursus III. to Scene XI.

1427, 1428. Δεινῶς .... ἱππηλατεῖν, *Diitrephes has dread-*

fully set my boy on the wing for horse-driving, by his talk. The person here mentioned has already been alluded to as having made a fortune. The passion for horses naturally led to extravagant expenditure among the fashionable young fellows at Athens. See Clouds, v. 74.

1429, 1430. Ὁ δέ .... φρένας, *And another says, that his son is set on the wing and is all of a flutter in his mind for tragedy.*

1436. Δαί always expresses surprise or indignation, in a question. *What the deuce will you do?* — οὐ καταισχυνῶ, *I will not dishonor my race*, as the money-changer says in the Clouds. The phrase seems to have grown so trite, that it had become slang.

1439. ὡς ἄν. G. § 44, 1, N. 2.

1440. Καλεσάμενος, ἐγκεκληκώς. The former means *having summoned to appear in court on a certain day;* the latter here means *having brought a suit against.* According to Meier and Schömann (Attic Process, Book IV. Cap. 2), ἐγκαλεῖν means strictly *to call upon one's opponent for restitution or satisfaction in the presence of witnesses,* and refers to a ceremony which usually preceded the formal *summons* (πρόσκλησις); the term seems, however, to be used also in a general sense (as here), meaning simply *to bring a suit.* See note to v. 147.

1442, 1443. ὅπως .... ξένος, *that the stranger may have lost his suit before arriving here,* i. e. by his failure to appear on the appointed day, the suit would go against him by default. Ἐρήμην δίκην ὀφλεῖν (or simply ἐρήμην ὀφλεῖν) was the phrase in Attic law, signifying *to lose a suit by default ;* while ἐρήμην δίκην ἑλεῖν (or ἐρήμην ἑλεῖν) meant *to gain a case through the absence of one's opponent.* The advantage which the Sycophant expects to gain by his wings is, that the unfortunate party against whom the suit is commenced will be unable to equal his rapid mode of doing business. —

ὅπως ἄν. See ὡς ἄν, v. 1439.—For the Perfect Subjunctive ὠφλήκῃ, see G. § 18, 1.

1446. Βέμβικος, *a whirligig*, or *top*.

1448. Κορκυραῖα πτερά. The *Corcyrean wings* are whips from Corcyra, or such as were used in Corcyra, which are mentioned in a passage of Phrynichus cited by the Scholiast. See also Thucydides, IV. 47.

1452. οὐκ ἀπολιβάξεις (from λιβάς, *a drop*), *will you not drop off?*

1453. στρεψοδικοπανουργίαν, *justice-twisting rascality*.

1455–1466. The Chorus now describe the wondrous things they have seen in flying over the earth. The poet, by ingenious turns, makes it the occasion of sly and amusing satire.— δένδρον. They describe Cleonymus, the Sycophant and Shield-dropper, as a strange tree. "Apte autem arboris mentionem faciunt aves." Blaydes. — καρδίας ἀπωτέρω. There is here a play upon the words, the phrase meaning *without heart*, i. e. *cowardly*, or, looking upon Cleonymus as a tree,—and the Scholiast says he is so called, either because he was tall or stupid as a stick,—*remote from Cardia*.— τοῦ μὲν ἦρος, *in spring it shoots forth and plays the informer;* alluding to the fact, that in the month Munychion the cases of foreigners were adjudged, as the Scholiast explains it. But Blaydes thinks *spring* is used here for the time of peace, as winter is applied (v. 1465) metaphorically to war. This tree, *the sycophant, puts forth in spring, and in winter sheds the shields;* that is, in time of peace Cleonymus busies himself as an informer, and in time of war he runs away from the enemy, and drops his shield in his flight. This is our old acquaintance, the shield-dropper of the Clouds.

1467–1478. These lines are occupied with Orestes, the robber, who is also mentioned before, and whom he classes with the heroes, on account of his name. According to the

Scholiast, some of the heroes were supposed to walk by night, and to strike with blindness or apoplexy those whom they met. The haunt of Orestes is described as *a place hard by darkness itself in the solitude of lamps.* — εἰ γὰρ ἐντύχοι. G. § 51. — Πάντα τἀπιδέξια, *all the noble parts.* The language is double-meaning, applying either to the being struck with apoplexy in the nobler parts, i. e. the head and right side, or to being stripped by Orestes of the most valuable articles of dress.

The scene that follows is one of the most humorous in the play. Prometheus, the natural friend of man, and still more the natural enemy of Zeus, comes hurrying in, to give secret information to Peisthetairos and the birds of the sad condition to which the gods have been reduced, and to advise Peisthetairos to accept no propositions that will be offered by the ambassadors already on their way, unless Zeus shall surrender the sceptre, and give Basileia, or Royalty, in marriage to Peisthetairos. The ambassadors are Poseidon, Heracles, and Triballos, a barbarian god. Heracles is gained over to assent to the demands of the birds by the prospect of a good dinner, which is to be made of certain rebellious birds who have paid the penalty of their treason, and are now cooking in the kitchen. To a Greek, accustomed to this representation of Heracles, — as, for instance, in the Alcestis of Euripides, — no small part of the amusement of the piece would flow from the manner in which the scruples of the doughty hero are overcome. A legal view of his rights of inheritance, as affected by the illegitimacy of his birth, has some weight, but not so much as the smell of the roasting birds.

1479. ὅπως μή (elliptical), I fear *that Zeus will see me.* G. § 46, N. 4.

1483. Πῆνίκ' . . . . ἡμέρας ; *What time o' day is it?*

1485. Βουλυτός, ἢ περαιτέρω; The time expressed by βουλυτός, according to its etymology, is that of unyoking the cattle; therefore, after the agricultural work of the day was over; towards evening.

1486. βδελύττομαι. Peisthetairos is out of all patience with Prometheus, whose mind, intent upon his own situation, pays no heed to what the other says: — *How I hate you.*

1488. Οὕτω μέν. Blaydes has the following note upon this expression: — " Sch.: ὡς ἐν κωμῳδίᾳ, ὡς καλόν τι ἀκούσας τὸ οἴμωζε, ἀποκαλύπτεται φανερὸν αὑτὸν δεικνύς. Festive, quasi dicat: Sic quidem, benigna tua compellatione victus, qui me in malam rem abire jubeas, omnem animo tuo dubitationem eximam et caput meum detegam." But I am inclined to think that Prometheus, still inattentive to what Peisthetairos is saying, refers in these words to his question, *Is Zeus clearing the clouds away, or gathering them?* or, *Is it fair weather or foul?* because, if it is foul, *I'll uncover.* Upon which he throws off his disguise, and stands revealed as Prometheus.

1493. σκιάδειον, *parasol.* He has come provided with this shelter, under cover of which he may safely unfold his errand.

1494. ὡς ἄν. G. § 44, 1, N. 2. (See v. 1439.)

1498. Ὡς ἀκούοντος λέγε. G. § 109, N. 4; § 110, 1, N. 1. ἀκούοντος is the ordinary *causal* Participle (G. § 109, 4), modified in its force by ὡς, and put in the genitive absolute with μοῦ understood.

1499. Πηνίκ᾽ ἄττ᾽; *about what time?* ἄττα = τινά.

1504. Θεσμοφορίοις. The ceremonies of the Thesmophoria lasted five days, one of which was spent in fasting. See Smith's Dict. of Gr. and Rom. Antiq.; also Aristophanes, Thesmophoriazusae.

1505. βάρβαροι θεοί, *the barbarian gods*, who, living farther off from men than the Olympian, are also sufferers from the stoppage of sacrificial supplies, and threaten war upon Zeus unless he will throw open the ports, so that the entrails of the victims may be imported.

1507. ἄνωθεν, *from above*, or *beyond*.

1509. ἵν' εἰσάγοιτο. G. § 44, 2, N. 2 (*b*). The Optative depends on the idea implied in the leading sentence, that the gods *threatened* war.

1512. πατρῷος. The Exekestides here mentioned is the same person who has been already satirized as an intrusive citizen. (See note to v. 11.) The constitution of Athens required a scrutiny to be made into the birth of any citizen before he could assume the functions of office. He must be able to show that Apollo was his πατρῷος, or *patrial* deity, and that he was legally under the protection of Zeus *Herkeios*; that he was an Athenian on both sides, and from the third generation. See Demosth. in Eubul. p. 1315, 15: παιδίον ὄντα με εὐθέως ἦγον εἰς τοὺς φράτορας, εἰς Ἀπόλλωνος πατρῴου ἦγον, εἰς τἆλλα ἱερά. So p. 1319, 26, the speaker alludes to the members of his γένος as Ἀπόλλωνος πατρῴου καὶ Διὸς ἑρκείου γεννῆται. Blaydes, giving the substance of Brunck's note, says : "Execestidem igitur, qui, ut peregrina origine et servili, Apollinem illum Πατρῷον Atheniensium vindicare sibi non poterat, ridicule fingit comicus habere, ut barbarum, Πατρῷον seu *Tutelarem* deum aliquem ex barbaris illis, de quibus nunc agitur."

1514. Τριβαλλοί. The Triballi were a Moesian tribe.

1515. τοὐπιτριβείης. There is a play upon the resemblance in sound between ἐπιτριβείης and Τριβαλλοί. Cary gives as an equivalent, "Trouble"; "Tribulation" would be nearer. We might, perhaps, make something like it out of the *Choctaws:* — " Ah, yes! that's where *You be choked* came from."

1526. κωλακρέτην. This was the officer who paid out the

judicial fees. See Smith's Dict. of Gr. and Rom. Antiq.; also Hermann's Political Antiquities. — τριώβολα. τριώβολον was the fee or sum paid daily to each dicast.

1531. ἀπανθρακίζομεν, *we roast,* i. e. *cook;* referring to the myth according to which Prometheus bestowed fire upon mortals, having stolen it from the gods.

1534. Τίμων καθαρός, *a pure (mere) Timon.* Timon the misanthrope is here meant. This personage was a contemporary of Alcibiades, with whom he continued his intimacy after having secluded himself from the rest of the world. He is mentioned in another place by Aristophanes (Lysistrata, 808), and Antiphanes made him the subject of a comedy. The student will remember Shakespeare's Timon of Athens, and the manner in which the great English dramatist has worked out the hints of the ancients respecting this eccentric character.

1535. ὡς ἄν. See v. 1439.

1536. κανηφόρῳ. The κανηφόροι were high-born Athenian maidens, who carried on their heads baskets containing the materials and implements of sacrifice at the great festivals, such as the Panathenaic, Dionysiac, &c. They were usually attended by persons holding sun-shades over their heads.

1538 – 1549. The Σκιάποδες, or Shade-feet, were a fabulous tribe in Lybia, mentioned by Strabo, and by Ktesias (according to Harpocration), who compares the feet to the web-feet of geese. They are described as walking τετραποδηδόν, or on all fours; or rather on all threes, using one foot, spread out like an umbrella, to protect themselves from the heat of an African sun. In this place the poet designates the philosophers, and especially, as is shown by v. 1540, the disciples of Socrates. The spirit of the passage is like that of the ludicrous scene in the Clouds, where the disciples of *the phrontistery* are represented in a variety of absurd attitudes and positions. — Ψυχαγωγεῖ signifies either *to conduct souls*, as Hermes guided the spirits of the departed; or *to evoke spirits*, as was done at Lake Avernus; or *to allure the mind*, as Socrates was accused of doing to the young men of Athens, corrupting them by his new doctrines. Here it is used ambiguously. Socrates evokes spirits at the lake of the Shade-feet. He is the necromancer of that marvellous tribe. — Πείσανδρος. This is the person mentioned in Thucydides (VIII. 65, seq.) as having been active in subverting the democracy, in the time of the Peloponnesian war. On account of his cowardice, he is represented as coming to Socrates in search of his soul, which has left him during his life. He brings with him for a victim a *camel-lamb*, either a young camel or a huge sheep. The precise meaning is uncertain. Doubtless there was some sarcastic allusion, readily taken by the audience, but now lost. At any rate, the whole scene is a parody upon the *Nekyomanteia*, in Odyssey XI. — ἀπῆλθε, *went off ;* i. e. like Odysseus in the scene above referred to, withdrew from the sacrifice that the shades of the dead might not be disturbed. — ἡ νυκτερίς, *the bat.* See *ante*, v. 1282. He is said have come up from Hades, on account of his ghostly appearance.

The gods now arrive. Poseidon is giving lessons in manners to the barbarian god, who has never before been in good society.

1552. 'Επ' .... ἀμπέχει; *Do you wear your dress so awkwardly?* Literally, *to wear it awry, upon the left;* to put it, therefore, on the wrong side. The cloak, when properly put on, was so arranged as to leave the right arm at liberty. At least, that was originally the case when the garment was worn in its simplest form. " In nothing," says Hope (Costume of the Ancients, Vol. I. p. 24), " do we see more ingenuity exerted, or more fancy displayed, than in the various modes of making the peplum form grand and contrasted draperies. Indeed, the different degrees in simplicity or of grace observable in the throw of the peplum were regarded as indicating the different degrees of rusticity or of refinement inherent in the disposition of the wearer."

1554. Λαισποδίας. Laispodias was a general, mentioned in Thucydides (VI. 105). He had a defect in the legs, which he concealed by the length of his garments.

1555. δημοκρατία. "Ludit quasi etiam apud deos sit democratia, ut Athenis." Blaydes. Other democracies besides that of the Grecian gods are open to the ridicule of sending incompetent barbarians on foreign embassies.

1559. τί δρῶμεν. G. § 88.

1563. Διπλασίως. Heracles, as Bergler remarks, is made at the outset so fierce for vengeance on the audacious mortal who has intercepted the sacrifices from the gods, whereby they live, in order to heighten the comic effect of his sudden conversion by the appetizing smell of the roasting birds. Peisthetairos, at this moment, is heard giving directions to the cook, as if unaware of the presence of Heracles.

1570. Ἔδοξαν ἀδικεῖν, *have been adjudged guilty*. A technical expression in Attic law.

1571. Ὦ .... Ἡράκλεις. Peisthetairos pretends to see Heracles now for the first time: *Ah! how do you do, Heracles?*

1574. Ἔλαιον .... ληκύθῳ. *There is no oil in the cruet.* The servant comes running in with this message from the kitchen.

1577. ὄντες φίλοι, *if you were friendly to us.* G. § 52, 1. See also § 42, 3, N. 1.

1578, 1579. Ὄμβριον .... ἀεί, *You would have rain-water always in your marshes* (instead of *tanks*, "ut ad aves"; the Greeks ordinarily used either spring-water directly from the fountains, or rain-water caught in the tanks), *and you would always pass halcyon days.* Halcyon days are the supposed seven fair days in winter in which the halcyon was accustomed to make his appearance.

1580. αὐτοκράτορες, *plenipotentiary.*

1583. ἀλλὰ νῦν is elliptical. Supply "though not before," *yet now,* i. e. if you are at last willing to do what is right.

1587. 'Επὶ .... καλῶ, *On these conditions, I will invite the ministers to dinner.*

1592. ἄρξωσιν, *gain the power.* The force of the aorist is to express the action as single and momentary, not frequent or continuous. Therefore, here, not *rule,* but *get power.* G. § 19, Notes 1 and 2.

1596. ὅταν ὀμνύῃ. G. § 61, 3.

1597. παρελθών, *coming up,* or *passing along.* The advantage promised to the gods is, that, if any mortal swear falsely by them, the crow will pounce upon him and pluck out his eyes.

1600. The barbarian god, unable to speak Greek, utters some unintelligible sounds, which Peisthetairos interprets into giving his consent.

1605. Μενετοὶ .... μισητίαν, *saying, " The gods can wait,"* and shall not repay in full. μἀποδιδῷ = μὴ ἀποδιδῷ. μισητία is *luxury, lust,* &c.; also *abundance, wastefulness;* here, perhaps, used adverbially by synecdoche.

1606. 'Αναπράξομεν, *we will exact.*

1610. τιμήν, *the value.*

1613. οἰμώζειν δοκεῖ σοι; *have you a fancy for a beating?* Intimating that, unless he is willing to yield the point, he must expect a beating. "Hercules," says Cary, "trusting that Triballus will not understand, says this for the sake of raising a laugh at the barbarian god." He translates: " Triballus, what think you — of being cursed?"

1614. Φησὶν . . . . πάνυ, *He says that I talk quite right.* The subject of λέγειν must be gathered from the context; otherwise it would be the same as that of the finite verb. Again he construes the unintelligible sounds of the barbarian god into an assent to the demand.

1618. παραδίδωμι, *I offer to give up.* G. § 10, 1, N. 2.

1620. ἐκδοτέον (sc. τῷ Διί). G. § 114, 2. — Οὐ . . . . ἐρᾷς, *So you don't want a reconciliation;* your demands are so extravagant, that there is no hope of coming to terms with you.

1621, 1622. Ὀλίγον . . . . γλυκύ, *I care but little. Cook, you must make the sauce sweet.* Peisthetairos puts on an indifferent look, but counts with certainty upon the effect of the order to the cook upon Heracles.

1623. δαιμόνι᾽ ἀνθρώπων, *my dearest fellow.* The comic force of the phrase is heightened by addressing a familiar form of speech among men to a god.

1624. Ἡμεῖς . . . . πολεμήσομεν; There is an allusion to Helen and the war of Troy: *Shall we wage a war for one woman?*

1626. ἐξαπατώμενος πάλαι. G. § 10, 1, N. 3; § 73, 2.

1631. οἷόν σε περισοφίζεται, *how he is tricking you.* Peisthetairos now expounds the Athenian law of inheritance, according to which Heracles, being the son of Zeus by a foreign woman (ὤν γε ξένης), cannot become his heir.

1634. οὐδ᾽ ἀκαρῆ, *not a penny.*

1638. ἐπίκληρον. "A technical term, signifying *a daughter who, having no brother, succeeds as heiress to her father's estate.* The Attic law made all the legitimate *sons* equally heirs to their father's estate, not allowing a man with such sons to dispose of his property by will. The daughters in this case had a right only to their dowry (προίξ), and were called on that account ἐπίπροικοι. Where there were no sons at the time of the father's death, the whole estate (κλῆρος) descended to the daughters, if there were any, — each of whom was called an ἐπίκληρος. The law, however, looked upon such an ἐπίκληρος rather as a means of transmitting the property to the proper male heir, than as an actual *heiress* in her own right. The father was allowed, if he left no sons, to dispose of his property by will; but he was obliged to adopt as sons those whom he made his heirs, and the latter assumed with their inheritance all the rights which would have belonged to them if they had been born in the testator's family. If now the testator left a daughter (ἐπίκληρος), he could leave his property to such an adopted heir only on condition of his marrying the daughter, and thus assuming the property. If he left several daughters, he could dispose of each, with her portion of his estate, in the same way. If the father of an ἐπίκληρος died without a will, the nearest male relative had a *right* to claim her in marriage with her property; and if she was poor, he was *obliged* by law either to marry her himself or to give her a dowry bearing a certain proportion to his own estate. (See the law relating to poor ἐπίκληροι, quoted in Demosth. in Macart. p. 1067, 27.) The father could dispose of an ἐπίκληρος in marriage before his death, by adopting her husband as his son. If a daughter had married while her brothers were still living, and afterwards by the death of her brothers found herself an ἐπίκληρος at the time of her father's death, the person who could have claimed her in marriage, had she been still single, could even then oblige her to desert her husband and to marry him; and even if he had a wife himself, he could divorce her for that purpose. This illustrates the position which women held in the political system of Athens. The speaker in Demosth. in Eubulid. (p. 1311, 17) describes a pleasant little family scene from his mother's history: Ὁ Πρωτόμαχος πένης ἦν· ἐπικλήρου δὲ κληρονομήσας εὐπόρου, τὴν μητέρα βουληθεὶς ἐκδοῦναι πείθει λαβεῖν αὐτὴν

Θούκριτον τὸν πατέρα τὸν ἐμόν, ὄντα ἑαυτοῦ γνώριμον, i. e. *Protomachos* (the speaker's mother's husband) *was a poor man; and on inheriting a rich* ἐπίκληρος, *wishing to dispose of my mother, he induces Thucritos, my father, who was an acquaintance of his, to take her in marriage.* (See the law quoted in Demosth. in Macart. p. 1067, 27.) See Meier and Schömann, Attic Process, Book III. 2, Chap. 2, § 2 (pp. 468 – 470); Hermann, Staatsalterth. §§ 119, 120; Privatalterth. § 63; with the passages quoted in the notes. Peisthetairos here asks Heracles how Athena could be an heiress of Zeus in her own right (as everybody knew her to be), if Zeus had any legitimate children. He seems to imply that the independent position of Athena, as protecting goddess of Athens, entitles her to the rank of ἐπίκληρος of Zeus." — Goodwin.

1639. ὄντων .... γνησίων, *if there were legitimate brothers.* G. § 52, 1.

1641. ὁ νόμος οὐκ ἐᾷ. Heracles asks why Zeus could not bequeath his estate to him. He is reminded of the law which prohibited νόθοι from succeeding to an inheritance. A νόθος at Athens was the child of an Athenian father and a foreign mother: such a child was *illegitimate* in the eye of the law, that is, he was excluded from the rights of an Athenian citizen. Heracles is jestingly called a νόθος, or illegitimate God, being the son of Zeus and a mortal woman, Alcmene, who stands in the relation of a ξένη to the Gods. A νόθος, not being a citizen, could not be adopted as a son, and therefore could not inherit property by will. (See note to v. 1638.) He must be content with the share of his father's property which the law allowed him; this was called νοθεῖα, and could not exceed 1000 drachmas. See Harpocration, s. v. νοθεῖα; and Hermann, Polit. Antiq. § 118, with the notes.

1643. ἀνθέξεταί σου .... χρημάτων, *will take precedence*

of you as an heir to the paternal property. Whereupon he proceeds to quote to Heracles a law of Solon, showing that, even if Athena were not in his way, his uncles, and especially Poseidon, would have the next claim. This law of Solon was renewed in the archonship of Eucleides (403 B. C.), and is quoted by Isaeus, de Hered. Philoct. § 47. The whole law which regulated the succession to property where there were no sons is quoted (at least in substance) in Demosth. in Macart. p. 1067, 1 : it contains a clause at the end similar to the one quoted by Peisthetairos.

1646. ἀγχιστείαν, *rights by nearness of relationship.* — εἶναι. G. § 103.

1651. Ἤδη .... φράτορας; *Did your father ever introduce you to your kith and kin?* It was required by law that all legitimate sons should be enrolled in the registers of the tribe, deme, and phratria; those of the same φρατρία were called φράτορες. See notes on v. 767 and 1512. See also Hermann's Political Antiquities, §§ 98, 99.

1653. αἰκίαν βλέπων, *looking assault,* like Shakespeare's *speaking daggers.*

1659. Ἐν .... πρᾶγμα, *The whole thing now depends on Triballos.* He has the casting vote.

1660, 1661. Καλάνι .... παραδίδωμι. Triballos tries to give his decision in Greek. The effect of his barbarous pronunciation is conveyed by Cary thus: —

      " De beautiful gran damsel Basilau
  Me give up to de fool."

1661. παραδοῦναι λέγει. G. § 23, 2, N. 4. λέγει here means *he commands, he tells us;* otherwise the sentence would mean, *he says that he once gave up.* (G. § 23, 2.)

1663. Εἰ .... χελιδόνες, *unless to go as the swallows do;* i. e. unless he means to bid her become a bird. Swallows are singled out for birds in general, because the Greeks always compared the speech of barbarians to that of swallows.

1670, 1671. 'Ες .... γάμους, *In good time, then, these fellows* (the rebel birds) *have been put to death for the nuptials.* — τέως, *in the mean time.*

1672. βούλεσθε ὀπτῶ, *do you wish that I should roast*, &c. G. § 88.

1673. τενθείαν. The expression is in reference to the tasters, προτενθαί, and means *ravenousness.*

1674. εὖ ἂν διετέθην, *I should be well disposed of, indeed!* G. § 49, 2, N. 5.

1676 – 1687. In this antistrophe the tribe of sycophants (see above) is again satirized. — Φαναῖσι, *at Phanae.* There was a promontory of that name in Chios; but here it is the pretended residence of the sycophants, or informers, in allusion to the legal action called φάσις. The Κλεψύδρα was the water-clock used to measure time in the courts; also the name of a hidden spring at the Acropolis. The poet makes it a stream in Phanae. — τέμνεται. In allusion to the custom of cutting out the tongue of the victim. Here Attica is the victim of this race of *belly-tongued,* — the Philippoi and Gorgiai, — who by the arts of speech obtained a subsistence.

1688. Ὦ πάντ', &c. A messenger comes in to herald the arrival of Peisthetairos, who is on his way, in regal state accompanied by his bride Basileia, whom he has received from the hand of Zeus. He makes his proclamation in the lofty style of sublime lyric and tragic poetry.

1692. παμφαὴς ἀστὴρ ἰδεῖν. G. § 93, 2. — ἔλαμψε .... δόμῳ, *shone upon the golden-beaming house.*

1695. οὐ .... λέγειν, *unutterable to describe.* G. § 93, 2.

1699. πλεκτάνην καπνοῦ, *a wreath of smoke.*

1702. A parody on Euripides, Troades, 308, seqq., translated by Cary: —

"Above, below, beside, around,
Let your veering flight be wound."

1704. Μάκαρι, *the happy one*, Peisthetairos.

1705. Ὦ .... κάλλους, *O the grace, and the beauty!* Genitive of exclamation.

1712. Ἥρᾳ. The Chorus, in enthusiastic strains, compares the marriage of Peisthetairos with that of Zeus and Hera.

1718. ἀμφιθαλὴς Ἔρως, *blooming Eros.*

1720. παλιντόνους, *drawn back*, or *tightened.*

1721. πάροχος, *companion* in the chariot, groomsman; — not to be confounded with πάροχος (*parochus*), from παρέχω.

1725. Ἄγε. Peisthetairos, assuming the attributes of Zeus, calls upon them now to celebrate the thunder, the lightning, and the blazing bolt.

1735. πάρεδρον, *side judge, assessor.* One who shares with another the judicial seat.

1741. ὦ μάκαιρα, *O blessed one.* Addressed to Basileia.

1742, 1743. πτερῶν .... Λαβοῦσα, *having taken hold of my wings.*

1745, seq. These lines, according to the Scholiast, are a parody upon Archilochus, — a strain of victory, with which this gayest and most entertaining of the comedies of Aristophanes ends.

TABLE OF RHYTHMS AND METRES.

[In the following Table, the letter M. stanas for Munk's Metres, American edition, translated from the German by Beck and Felton.]

PROLOGUS, vv. 1 - 264.

Verses 1 – 210. Iambic trimeter acatalectic, with comic license. See Munk, pp. 76, 162, 171, seq.

211 – 225. Anapaests.
211 – 215. Anapaestic dimeter acatalectic. M. 100.
216. Anapaestic monometer. M. 99.
217 – 221. Anapaestic dimeter acatalectic.
222. Anapaestic monometer.
223. Anapaestic dimeter acatalectic.
224. Anapaestic monometer.
225. Anap. dimeter catal., paroemiac close. M. 100.
226 – 230. Iambic trimeter acatalectic.

231, 241, 246, 262 – 264, are not intended to be rhythmical, as they are only imitations of the notes of birds.

232, 233. Iambic trimeter acatalectic.
234. Dochmiac dim. M. 11, 225, ⏑ ⏒ ⏒ ⏑ —, ⏑ ⏒ ⏒ ⏑ —.
234. Iambic tripody, anapaestic monometer. M. 78 (3).
236. Dactylic.
237. Trochaic trimeter acatalectic. Longs of the first metre resolved.
238. Dochmiac monometer, ⏑ ⏒ ⏒ ⏑ ⏒.
239. Trochaic trimeter acatalectic.
240. Choriambic dimeter catalectic. M. 141 (2).

230   TABLE OF RHYTHMS AND METRES.

242. Ionici a minore, trimeter acat., ⏑ ⏑ — —, ⏑ ⏑ — —, ⏑ ⏑ — —. M. 151 (3).

243. Dochmiac monometer, ⏑ ⌒ ⌒ ⏑ —.

244. Proceleusmatici.

245. Iambic hexameter catalectic. M. 80 (6).

247. Cretic tetrameter. M. 114 (4).

248. "   "   with the last long of second foot resolved, — ⏑ ⌒.

249. Cretic tetram. cat., ⌒ ⏑ —, — ⏑ ⌒, — ⏑ ⌣, - ⌣.

250. Dactylic.

251. Cretic dimeter acatalectic. M. 111 (2).

252 – 255. Dactylic tetrameter.

256. This verse is marked by Dindorf as a paroemiac, — — — —, ⏑ ⏑ — —. But the first syllable of ταναοδείρων is never long. The proper notation, perhaps, is — —, — ⏑ ⏑ ⏑, — —, spondee, paeon primus spondee.

257 – 259. Spondaic anapaests.

260, 261. Trochaic dimeter.

265 – 268. Iambic trimeter.

270 – 306. Trochaic tetrameter catalectic. M. 68 (J).

307, 308. Iambic dimeter.

309 – 324. Trochaic tetrameter catalectic, except 312 and 314, which may be read as dochmiac dimeters.

CHORUS.

Strophe, 325 – 333 = Antistrophe, 341 – 349.

326 – 330. Anapaests, with spondees and proceleusmatici.

331 – 333. Cretics, with longs resolved.

334 – 340. Trochaic tetrameter catalectic.

350 – 384. Trochaic tetrameter catalectic.

385 – 397. Trochaic dimeter.

398 – 403. Anapaestic.

404 – 407. Iambic dimeter.

408 – 413. Cretics, with anacrusis in 408 and 411.

414 – 425. Iambic systems.

TABLE OF RHYTHMS AND METRES. 231

426 – 429. Trochaic, dactylic, ⌒ ⌣, ⏓ ⏑ ⏑ ⏓.
431 – 433. Iambic.
434 – 450. Iambic trimeter.

CHORUS.

Strophe, 451 – 459 = Antistrophe, 539 – 547.

451. Logaoedic anapaests, ⏑ ⏑ ⏓ ⏑ ⏑ ⏓ ⏑ ⏑ ⏓ ⏑ ⏓ ⏑ ⏓.
452. Iamb. anap. or iambelegus, ⏑ ⏓ ⏑ – –, ⏓ ⏑ ⏑ ⏓ ⏑ ⏑ –.
453. Anapaestic, iambic, penthemim, ⏑ ⏑ ⏓ ⏑ ⏓ –.
454. Trochaic monometer, dactylic trimeter.
455. Anapaestic.
456. Anapaestic.
457. Anapaestic, iambic, antispast. In the antistrophe, the corresponding verse consists of an anapaestic dimeter and antispast.
458. Anapaestic.
459. Anap., trochaic dipody, ⏑ ⏑ ⏓ ⏑ ⏑ –, ⏓ ⏑ –, ⏑ – ⏓. But the verse is defective. The corresponding line in the strophe is an anapaest and antispast, ⏑ ⏑ ⏓ ⏑ ⏑ – –, ⏑ ⏓ – –.
460 – 522. Anapaestic tetrameter catalectic. M. 101.
523 – 538. Anapaestic system.
548 – 610. Anapaestic tetrameter catalectic.
611 – 626. Anapaestic system.
627, 628. Anapaestic tetrameter catalectic.
629, 630. Basis, iambic dimeter, ⏓ –, – ⏓ ⏑ – ⏑ ⏓ ⏑ –.
631. Dochmiac, – ⌒ ⌒ ⏑ ⌒ ⏓.
632. Trochaic, ⌒ ⏑ – ⏑, ⏓ ⏑ – –.
633. Anapaestic.
634. Dochmiac, ⏑ ⌒ ⏓ ⏑ –.
635, 636. Iambic.
637. Ithyphallic, ⏓ ⏑ – ⏑ – ⏓.
638, 639. Anapaestic tetrameter catalectic.
640 – 659. Iambic trimeter.
660 – 662. Anapaestic tetrameter.
663 – 667. Iambic trimeter.

TABLE OF RHYTHMS AND METRES.

678. Choriambic, $\perp \smile \smile -, - \cdot$
679. Glyconic, $\perp, \perp \smile \smile -, \smile -\cdot$
680. " $\overset{x}{\perp} -, \perp \smile \smile -, \smile -\cdot$
681. " $\overset{x}{\perp} -, - \smile \smile -, -\cdot$
682. Ithyphallic, $\perp \smile - \smile - \smile \cdot$
683 – 685. Glyconic, $\overset{x}{\perp} -, \perp \smile \smile -, \smile -\cdot$
686. Glyconic, $\perp -, \perp \smile \smile -, -\cdot$
687 – 724. Anapaestic tetrameter catalectic.
725 – 739. Anapaestic systems.

CHORUS.

Strophe, 740 – 754 = Antistrophe, 771 – 782.
740. Dactylic.
741. Not metrical. Imitation of the notes of birds.
742. Trochaic.
743. Amphibrach, dactylic, $\smile \perp \smile, \perp \smile \smile - \smile \smile - -\cdot$
744. Birds' notes.
745. Dactylic.
746. Birds' notes.
747. Anapaestic dimeter.
748. Dactylic.
749. Dactylic.
750. Birds' notes.
751. Trochaic.
752. Dactylic heptameter catalectic in dissyllabum.
753. Ithyphallic.
750 – 770. Trochaic tetrameter catalectic.
786 – 801. Trochaic tetrameter catalectic.
802 – 852. Iambic trimeter.

CHORUS.

Strophe, 853 – 860 = Antistrophe, 890 – 897.
853. Anacrusis, cretics, $\smile, \perp \smile -, \perp \smile -\cdot$
854. Trochaic.
855. Dochmiac, $\smile \frown \frown \smile =\cdot$
856, 857. Trochaic dimeter catalectic, longs resolved.

TABLE OF RHYTHMS AND METRES. 233

859. Iambic trimeter.
860. Iambic.
861 – 889. Iambic trimeter acatalectic, excepting the formulae uttered by the priest, which are not rhythmical.
898. Iambic trimeter acatalectic.
899. Basis, dochmiacs, ⏑ ⏑, ⏑ — — ⏑ —, — — — ⏑ ≃·
900. Cretic, trochaic, — ⏑ —, — ⏑·
901. Iambic, two Bacchii, ⏑ —, ⏑ — —, ⏑ — —·
902. Iambic trimeter.
903. Anacrusis, chor., iam., ⏑ — ⏑ ⏑ — — ⏑   —, ⏑ — ⏑ — —·
904. Dactylic, trochaic, — — — ⏑ ⏑ — ⏑ — —·
905. Iambic, ⏑ ⌢ ⏑ — —·
906, 907. Iambic trimeter.
908. Dactylic.
909. Iambic.
910 – 918. Iambic trimeter.
919. Dactylic, trochaic, — ⏑ ⏑ —, — ⏑ — —, — ⏑ ≃·
920. Choriambic, — ⏑ ⏑ —, — ⏑ ⏑ —·
921. Cretic, ⌢ ⏑ —, — ⏑ — —·
922. Anapaestic, iambic.
923. Trochaic, longs resolved.
924. Iambic, anapaestic, Iambic.
925. Iambic, trochaic, ⏑ —, ⌢ ⏑ — — ⏑ —·
926 – 930. Iambic trimeter.
931. Trochaic, dactylic, ⌢ ⏑ — ⏑ ⏑ — ⏑ ⏑ —·
932. Troch., anap., choriambic, — ⏑, ⏑ ⏑ — — ⏑ ⏑ —·
933. Fourth paeon, ⏑ ⏑ ⏑ — ⏑ ⏑ ⏑ —·
934. Trochaic, dactylic, — ⏑, — ⏑ ⏑ —·
935. Iambic trimeter.
936. Anapaestic, iambic, ⏑ ⏑ — ⏑ ⏑ — ⏑ —·
937. Iambic.
938. Anapaestic, iambic, ⏑ ⏑ — ⏑ ⏑ — ⏑ — ⏑ — — —'
939. Iambic, trochaic, ⏑ ⏑ — ⏑ —, — ⏑ ⏑ — — .. ⏑·
940. Trochaic penthemim, ⌢ ⏑ — — — —·

941 – 944. Iambic trimeter.
945. Trochaic, dactylic, $\_\cup\_\_, \_\cup\cup\_$
946. Anapaestic.
947. Procel., dactylic; probably $\_\cup\cup\cup\_\cup\cup\cup\_\cup\_$
948. Dactylic, anapaestic.
949 – 961. Iambic trimeter.
962, 963. Dactylic hexameter.
964, 965. Iambic trimeter.
966 – 968. Dactylic hexameter.
969. Iambic trimeter.
970. Dactylic hexameter.
971. Iambic trimeter.
972 – 974. Dactylic hexameter.
975 – 977. Iambic trimeter.
978 – 980. Dactylic hexameter.
981. Iambic trimeter.
982, 983. Dactylic hexameter.
984 – 1052. Iambic trimeter, excepting 1030, 1031, 1035-1037, 1041, 1042, 1044, and 1045, which, being imitations of legislative and legal procedures, are not rhythmical.

CHORUS.

Strophe, 1053 – 1081 = Antistrophe, 1082 – 1110.
1053 – 1059. Spondaic, anapaestic.
1060. Two paeones primi, and two paeones quarti, $\_\cup\cup\cup, \_\cup\cup\cup, \cup\cup\cup\_, \cup\cup\cup\_.$
1061. Paeons, $\_\cup\cup\cup\_\cup\cup\cup\_\cup\cup\cup\_\cup\cup.$
1062, 1063. Spondaic, anapaestic.
1064. Paeons, $\_\cup\cup\cup\_\cup\cup\cup\_\cup\cup\cup.$
1065. Paeons, cretics, $\_\cup\cup\cup\_\cup\cup\cup\_\cup\_\cup\cup\_.$
1066 – 1081. Trochaic tetrameter catalectic.
1111 – 1180. Iambic trimeter.

CHORUS.

Strophe, 1181 – 1184 = Antistrophe, 1251 – 1254.
1181 – 1184. Dochmiac dimeter with longs resolved.

TABLE OF RHYTHMS AND METRES. 235

1185 – 1250. Iambic trimeter.
1255 – 1298. Iambic trimeter.

CHORUS.

Strophe, 1299 – 1308 = Antistrophe, 1311 – 1320.
1299. Anapaestic, iambic.
1300. Iambic, antispast, ⏑ – ⏑ – – – .
1301. Iambic.
1302. Anapaestic.
1303. Iambic.
1304 – 1307. Anapaestic.
1308. Iambic.
1309, 1310. Iambic.
1321, 1322. Iambic trimeter.
1323. Iambic, dactylic, ⏑ – –, – ⏑ ⏑ – ⏑ ⏑ – .
1324. Anacrusis, troch., dact., –, – ⏑ – ⏑ – ⏑ ⏑ – ⏑ ⏑ – .
1325. – ⏑ – – – .
1326 – 1358. Iambic trimeter
1359. Choriambic, ⏜ ⏑ ⏑ –, – ⏑ ⏑ –, – ⏑ ⏑ – – .
1360. Anap., choriamb., ⏑ ⏑ – ⏑ ⏑ – ⏑ ⏑ – – ⏑ ⏑ – .
1361. Iambic trimeter.
1362. Basis, two dactyls, two anap., ⏑ ⏑ – ⏑ ⏑ – ⏑ ⏑ ,
⏑ ⏑ – ⏑ ⏑ – .
1363, 1364. Iambic trimeter.
1365. Iambic.
1366. Glyconic, ⏑ –, – ⏑ ⏑ – – .
1367 – 1377. Iambic trimeter.
1378. Dactylic, –, – ⏑ ⏑ – – .
1379. Iambic, – ⏜ ⏑ – .
1380. Spondee paeon primus, spondee, – – – ⏑ ⏑ ⏑ – –
1381. Iambic.
1382. Trochaic, ⏜ – ⏑ – ⏑ – – .
1383. Iambic trimeter.
1384 – 1386. Anapaests, with proceleusmatici.
1387 – 1454. Iambic trimeter.

1396. Basis, choriambic, $\overset{\text{x}}{-} -, \perp \smile \smile -, \perp \smile \smile -, \perp \smile \smile -.$
1397. Anapaestic, iambic, $\smile \smile \perp \smile \smile \perp \smile \perp \smile - -.$

CHORUS.

Strophe, 1455 – 1466 = Antistrophe, 1467 – 1478
Trochaic system.
1479 – 1537. Iambic trimeter.

CHORUS

Strophe, 1538 – 1549 = Antistrophe, 1676 – 1687.
Trochaic systems.
1550 – 1675. Iambic trimeter.
1688 – 1701. Iambic trimeter.
1702 – 1704. Trochaic, with longs resolved.
1705. Molossus trimeter, $- \perp -, - \perp -, - \perp -.$
1706. Choriambic.
1707 – 1711. Anapaestic system.
1717 – 1722. Glyconic system. M. 258 and 263.
 The forms are

$$\overset{\text{x}}{\smile} \smile, - \smile \smile - \smile -,$$
 and
$$\smile, \perp \smile \smile -,$$

1724 – 1728. Anapaests.
1729 – 1735. Dactylic.
1736. Glyconic.
1737. Iambic.
1738 – 1740. Trochaic.
1741. Iambic.
1742. Trochaic.
1743. Iambic.
1744. Trochaic.
1745, 1746. Iambic.
1747. Trochaic.

THE END.

www.ingramcontent.com/pod-product-compliance
Lightning Source LLC
Chambersburg PA
CBHW020758230426
43666CB00007B/753